Lumbini Tourism

Lumbini Tourism

Prof. Dr. Gitu Giri
Tribhuwan University Nepāl

Adroit Publishers
New Delhi

Published by

ADROIT PUBLISHERS

4675/21, Ganpati Bhawan, Ansari Road,

Daryaganj, New Delhi-110 002

Phone : 011-23266030

email: adroitpublishers@gmail.com

Distributors

AKHIL BOOK DISTRIBUTORS

email: akhilbooks@yahoo.com

akhilbks@gmail.com

ISBN : 978-81-87393-04-7

Printed in India on behalf of M/s Adroit Publishers by

Akhil Sharma, E-mail: adroitpublishers@gmail.com

CONTENT

PREFACE

This book on "Lumbinī Tourism" is a basic component of Lumbinī Master Plan. The study is useful in understanding the cultural role of the tradition, tourism development and modernization the complexity of Buddhist civilization. The researcher has brought to light certain facts of senario of tourism development, pilgrimage, for example, deserved to be studied carefully from different angles and in all its ramifications. The use of the places of pilgrimage have concentrated as trade and manufacturing centres and use of the network of pilgrimage organizations. Methodologically, the study of the sacred complex provides the first basic structure for such an appraisal of civilization; the present study provides the complete superstructure. This study is based on Buddhist literature, foreign accounts and personal field observation. Field observation has concentrated on traditions of various kinds of facts with the help of five types of questionnaires in the random sample technique. Lumbinī being a mini Buddhist World and the Fountain of World Peace scenario of tourism has been studied in course of this research. This study involves the geographical, historical, sociological, archaeological, anthropological and observational methods. In the present study geography, history, condition of tourism, pilgrims and pilgrimage, modes of transport, tourist accommodation, tourism promotion and changes have been studied to throw light on tourism industry and promotional components. This is a cultural-cum-tourism study.

—Gitu Giri

Acknowledgement

I would like to thank sincerely the University Grants Commission, Research Council Evaluation Committee, Research Division and Cluster Committee members of Nepāl who kindly made the present higher education project available. I am very grateful to the members of Cluster Committee for their valuable comments and suggestions in course of evaluation the report submitted at UGC. I am obliged to Prof. Dr. Tulsi Ram Vaidya, Expert of Cluster Committee, Prof. Dr. Triratna Manandhar, Vice-Chancellar of Lumbinī Buddhist University, Prof. Dr. Prem Kumar Khatry, Prof. Dr. Peshal Dahal, Prof. Dr. Bina Paudel of Tribhuwan University and Dr. Christoph Cuppers, Director of Lumbinī International Research Institute for their valuable suggestions to complete this work. I would like to express my sincere thanks to the team members Mrs. Susila Shrestha, Associate Professor of Butwal Campus; Mr. Chandra Prasad Regmi, Lecturer of Bhairahawa Multiple Campus; Mr. Krishna Chandra Giri and Mrs. Gita Sharma Research Scholars for their help they rendered to me in various ways. In my endeavour attention and care were taken by all the members of my family, particularly my wife Basundhara and son Ramesh. Thanks are also due to the people of Lumbinī area, monks, nuns and devotees who provided me great help in the collection of materials and to the writers whose writings have been utilized in this work.

Finally, I thanks to Krishna Chandra Giri of Lumbinī Research and Information Centre, who collected data from the study area and for the care he has taken in faultless computer of this research work. I would like to express my sincere thanks to Mr. D.K Sharma, Mr. Akhil Sharma and Adroit Publishers team members for their support in course of this publication.

—Gitu Giri

LIST OF ILLUSTRATIONS

LIST OF TABLE

ABBREVIATIONS USED

ADB	Asian Development Bank
CBO	Community Based Organization.
CBS	Central Bureau of Statistics
CMC	Chairman Managers' Committee.
CO	Community Organization.
DDC	District Development Committee.
DEVA	Development Associates for Rural and Regional Development
DFID	The United Kingdom's Department for International Development.
DNPWC	Department of National Parks and Wildlife Conservation.
DOA	Department of Archaeology.
DPP	District Participatory Programme.
EMP	Environmental Management Plan
FG	Functional Group.
IBS	International Buddhist Society.
IMP	Integrated Management Plan
IUOTO	International Union of Official Travel Organization
JBF	Jāpānese Buddhist Federation.
JOVC	Jāpānese Overseas Voluntary Co-operation.
LDT	Lumbinī Development Trust.
LGP	Local Governance Programme.

CHAPTER ONE

INTRODUCTION OF RESEARCH

Introduction of Research

Tourism is a very important source for foreign currency earning. It is an unrisky procedure for transfer of real resources from industrially capital surplus developed countries to developing countries. Tourism is a labour intensive industry offering employment to skilled, semi-skilled and unskilled manpower. The problems of unemployment and underemployment are more acute in the developing countries. It employs large number of people and provides a wide range of jobs. Apart from this area, a large number of specialist personnel's are required to work as accountants, housekeepers, cooks, waiters, and entertainers; semi-skilled workers, viz. porters, kitchen-staff, gardeners, chambermaids etc. Furnishing and equipment industries, farming and food supply as well as souvenir industries provide indirect employment to the local people. The basic infrastructure of tourism, i.e. roads, public awareness, sanitation, communication, transportation, water supply, airport, public utilities and accommodation units provide jobs for thousands of workers. The promotion of tourism can be a great encouragement to economic development. Cultural motivation has always stood as a unique vehicle for the cultural propagation through the process of tourism. It has always been an essential medium for broadening the limits of human knowledge. Mass of people travels to foreign countries to entertainment through usages, custom, fair, festivals, art, architecture, food and drinks of the host country. Tourism is an important medium of social and cultural development and is also of promoting lasting goodwill and friendship among the nations of the world.

Lumbinī, being the birth place of Lord Buddha, thousands of Buddhists as well as other religious people is visited every year. It is called as a paradise for the tourists. The area is 770 hectares of land as mentioned in the master plan. In this complex forty-two plots of lands are set a side. Different nations, Institutions and organizations can erect shrines in various sectors and in different styles under the permission of the project. In the complex the monasteries of Jāpān, South-Koreā, France, Vietnam, Nepāl, Austria, Thāīland, Srilanka and Indiān are under construction. In this process, International Research Institute and Museum have been operating and providing facilities for meeting, seminar and study. The circular sacred garden contains the Aśokan pillar, Māyādevi temple, sacred pond, ruined structures of stūpas and vihars and other objects within barbed area. In the complex ornamental flower and hedge plantation has been done by Jāpānese Overseas Co-opertion Volunteers (JOCV) to create a reverent atmosphere conducive to remembering and exercising Lord Buddha's Universal message of peace and harmony. The east and west monastic zones set aside for the two major sects of Buddhism. Theravada (Hinayān) and Mahāyan have witnessed a number of developments by friendly states and institutions.

These stūpas, vihārs and monasteries have been developing the Lumbinī as "A Mini World of Buddhism". Each of them has constructed their building with own their national architectural design, tradition, techniques and religious trends. Pollution, deforestation, lack of drainage system, dustbins, and pure drinking water, under ground water system, cement-work in the Master Plan area, smoky vehicles, old buses, truck and micro-buses are disturbing for tourism. The ratio of tourists was 10135, 39792 and 99508 in 2001, 2005 and 2010 respectively in Lumbinī except Indiān and Nepālese visitors. The number was 128259 and 136001 in 2011 and 2012 respectively. Among them pilgrims of Taiwan, Thāīland, Myānmār, Koreā, China and SrīLanka are in majority. They usually visit in mass. It is not sufficient as proposed in Master Plan. It has to promote in course of generating income of this region. Tourism industry provides direct and indirect benefit to the people of this region. Pilgrimage, cultural, nature, mass, sustainable, endemic and domestic tourism can promote the life style of the people in Lumbinī and its outskirt. Lumbinī Development Trust, the authority, has co-ordinated many physical, cultural, natural and architectural perspectives to promote foreign participants and to increase the rate of the tourists. Systematic and scientific study is not done of this site. So, this topic is chosen to complete proper needs of the site.

Statement of Problem

Lumbinī, the birth place of Lord Buddha, is potential for pilgrimage, nature and cultural tourism. Its physical as well as socio-economic development was the main aim of the Master Plan. Natural beautification, cultural heritages, proper management of transportation, information centre, accommodation and hospitality are basic needs for tourism development. But, these requirements are not available here. There are some challenges to promote tourism. Some of them are pollution, unmanaged industries, population growth, and encroachment of the restricted-zone as well as (buffer) agriculture zone, rapid construction of concrete bullocks for private use, old smoky buses and lack of proper hospitality. In this critical situation tourism industry will not promote in proper way. Thus, the researcher is confronted with these problems- how to promote tourism in Lumbinī? What are the promotional elements of tourism and socio-economic change of the people of Gandakī region? Viable answer will be out after this research work.

Objectives of the study

I. General objectives of this work are-
   (a) To promote tourism industry in Lumbinī area and
   b) To alleviate poverty through it in Gandaka region.

II. The specific objectives of this study are:
   (a) To find out the position of tourism and basic elements of pilgrimage tourism in the sacred complex of Lumbinī;
   (b) To point out the promotional elements of tourism and socio-economic life style of the people in the region.

Significance of the Study

Lumbinī is the centre of peace, compassion, toleration, Buddhist religion, art, architecture and cultural combination of the Buddhist world. Lord Buddha had advised to Anand that monks, nuns and his followers should visit to four sites viz. Lumbinī, Bodhagayā, Saranath and Kusinagar related to His life. Aśoka had visited Lumbinī in the third century BC. Chinese pilgrims Fahien and Hiuen-Tsing had also visited in Lumbinī in the fifth and seventh century AD respectively.

Ripu Malla had also come in the beginning of the fourteenth century. From ancient to modern period kings, nobles and other renowned persons had visited Lumbinī in course of their pilgrimage. The tradition has been continuing in an unbroken chain. Māyādevi temple, Aśoka pillar, Puskarini tank, various ancient stūpas, vihar structures, Lumbinī International Research Institute (LIRI), museum, images of Buddha, monastic zone and finding relics are attraction of pilgrims and other visitors at this sacred complex. On special occasion a large number of devotees visit from the various parts of Nepāl and foreign countries. Lumbinī represents not only monuments, but also the requisites, viz. unique life-style of the Hindu, Buddhist and Muslim people, local art, craft and indigenous religious activities. To find out the basic components and problems of tourism development is the main target of this study. This industry will support to alleviate poverty and for regional development in the twenty-one century. Due to the profit through tourism the local stock-holders will support to keep neat and clean Lumbinī. Non-polluted sacred zone will attract national and international visitors. Not only this but also future planners will take care of its main challenges to keep peace, compassion and tolerable Lumbinī. This study will help to manage Integrated Management Plan and Environmental Management Plan to secure its serenity, peace and compassion.

Review of literature

The earliest Palī text *Suttanipata* has mentioned that, "The wisdom – child that Jewel so precious, that can not be matched, has been born at Lumbinī, in the Śākya land for well being and joy in the world of men. A Muslim historian of Indiā named Abul Fazal has called Mokta (Cunningham, 1990:351). It is also known as Paderiya (Parariya) where the Aśokan pillar is located in the Nepālese Terai. The name of the site is spelt Lumbinīgrāmā and Lumbinī*vana* in the Aśokan Pillar Edict still standing at the same place (Fuhrer, 1972:31-33). The location of Lumbinī is pointed out in the Buddhist literature as well as, in the Chinese pilgrims who visited India and Nepāl in the 5th, 6th 7th and 8th centuries AD. According to *Jataka* story this *sal* garden was in joint possession of the Śākyas and Koliyas during the life time of Buddha. It was linked through popular *Uttara path* to Kapilvastu, Ramāgrāmā and other important cities during the Buddhist period. The present location of Lumbinī , the exact birth place of Lord Buddha, is absolutely clear (UNESCO, 2006:7-16). The Buddhist texts *Lalitavistara, Jatak Nidankatha,*

Divyā vadānā and *Mahāvansa* have mentioned Lumbinī as the birth place of Lord Buddha. When Buddha was lying down on the death bed at the age of eighty in Kusīnagar his disciples, monks and nuns surrounded him. On that occasion, he advised with feeling of holy reverence and awe, viz. the place where the *Tathagata* was born (Lumbinī grove), the place where he had reached perfect enlighten (Buddha-Gaya), the place where the first time he had proclaimed the law (Deer park near Varanasi), and the place of his final extinction (Kusinagar) (Bidari, 2002:110).

Thus, Lumbinī was declared as the sacred spot to the pilgrims and was visited by the scholars, nobles, Royalties and devotees from all over the world. According to *Kundala vadana* of *Divyavadana* having led king Aśoka into the Lumbinī jungle, venerable Upagupta indicated with his and said" *Asmin Maharaja Pradase bhagavan jatah* ", meaning ' Oh great king ! Here the Blessed one was born! ". King Aśoka made an offer of one hundred thousand gold coins and established the first cetiya or pagoda. In the Aśokan pillar of Lumbinī it is inscribed that, " Here *Bhagvan Śākyamuni* was born at the Lumbinī village "(Fuhrer, 1972: 33). King Aśoka installed the stone column with a clear legend inscribed on it that it is the spot of Lumbinī where the Blessed one was born. After the visit of Emperor, many monks and nuns had started visiting at the place. A large number of monasteries and Vihars had built for their stay in this sacred complex. A large number of the artifacts of the Mauryan, Sunga, Kushana and Gupta periods were recovered in course of various excavations. It is thus clear that it continued to birth place of pilgrimage since the third century BC till to date (Mitra, 1972:196-205).

Chinese pilgrims have given a more accurate and authentic description of Lumbinī. Shuī–Ching-Chu describes that at Lumbinī the Aśokan tree which was gripped by Māyādevī at the time of Siddhartha's birth was still in a living condition and an image of Māyādevī was placed there where devotees used to offer *puja* articles. The spot where Siddhartha's feet touched the earth first, Aśoka got the Siddhartha's foot prints shielded with stones. His description has been ratified by the noticeable findings discovered during the joint excavation of the DoA, LDT and JBF from 1993 to 1997. It is clearly seen that Aśoka had shielded the Siddhartha's footprints with stone in order to secure it. This significant news of the findings of the excavation was publicly declared by the then Honorable Prime Minister Sher Bahadur

Deuba on February 4, 1996. According to Fa-hien in Lumbinī the queen (Māyādevī) having entered the pool to bathe, came out on the north side, and after walking twenty paces, raised her hands and grasped the branch of a tree. He has stated that tank was used to take both of Siddhartha by two dragon kings. In this context, Hiuen-Tsiang had stated that there was the bathing tank of the Śākyas, the water of which was clear as a mirror and the surface to which was covered with a mixture of flowers. He had seen fallen Aśokan tree, stupa and water tank. He has mentioned the detail of the site (Giles, 1981:38). After Hiuen-Tsiang many other pilgrims had visited this place from time to time. One of them was Wu-kung who came in 764 AD at the 4th time. Due to the absence of records very little is known about the condition of the area.

The monumental and habitation structures, stone sculptures, terracotta human and animal figurines, fragments of pottery belonging from Mauryan to Pālā-Sena periods, found here reveal that Lumbinī was well-populated till the early-medieval period and was frequently visited by the monks, nuns and other devotees from time to time. Khasa Malla kings of Karnali Pradesh named Jitari Malla and Ripu Malla had also visited at this sacred complex in the fourteenth century in course of their pilgrimage. After their visit at Lumbinī, its existence was unknown until nineteenth century. Bhuwan Lal Pradhan has claimed that Sikandar Lodi (1489-1517AD) and Aurangzeb (1668-1707AD) were mainly responsible for the destruction of cultural heritage and property of the Lumbinī , Kapilvastu and Devadaha region (Pradhan, 1979:30). According to Prof. Dr.Tulsi Ram Vaidya temples, images and other structural remains of the region had destroyed due to the devastating earthquake in early medieval period in Nepāl.

In search of Aśokan pillar A. Führer found two broken pieces of an inscribed Aśokan pillar on the bank of Niglisagar at Taulihawa in 1895. At the end of November 1896, Führer had gone to Niglihawa to supervise the contemplated excavations there. In course of his visit Führer saw the Aśokan pillar at Lumbinī on the Ist December, 1896, which was dug by Khadaga Shamsher J.B. Rana. The importance of the Rummindei pillar inscription for understanding the history of ancient Śakya of Kapilvastu in general and the sacred history of the Buddhism in particular were published on 23rd December 1896. When the sensational news of the discovery of the Lumbinī pillar was published,

British Government of Indiā sent Mukherjī to fix the exact location of Kapilvastu. He published the structural plan of Lumbinī for the first time in his monumental archaeological report in 1901. Kesher Shamsher J.B. Rana had conducted excavation work during the years 1933-39. Debala Mitra had also excavated a small trench at the base of the Aśokan pillar to identify the nature of brick enclosure described by Mukherji and to know the nature of the pillar foundation. Nil Ratna Banerjee (1966-72), Babu Krishna Rijal (1975-83) Tara Nanda Mishra (1984-85), Jāpānese Buddhist Federation, Lumbinī Development Trust and Department of Archaeology had conducted archaeological activities at Lumbinī (Giri, 2003:3-4).

After the visit to Lumbinī in 1967 U – Thant, the then Secretary General of the UNO, had suggested to King Mahendra of Nepāl that Lumbinī should be developed as a place of pilgrimage and a tourist centre equipped with accommodations. A three-member team of UNO Mission had specific instructions to advise the Government on the infrastructural requirements, viz, .transportation facilities, drinking water, energy and appropriate accommodation for the visitors from the 10th December to 9th January 1967-68 (Tange, 1978:7-9). In 1970 International Lumbinī Development Committee was formed consisting the representatives of Pakistan, SrīLanka, Indiā, Myānmār, Afganistan, Thāīland, Cambodia, Indonesia, Lāos, Malaysiā, Jāpān, Singapore, and Nepāl. Bhutān and South Koreā later joined the committee. The Master Plan of Lumbinī Development was prepared by Prof. Kenzo Tange and URTEC. An area of Lumbinī about three-square miles divided into Sacred Garden, Monastic Enclave and New Lumbinī village have been restored. In order to monitor the Development Committee was constituted in 1971.

Late King Mahendra Bir Bikraṃ Shah had shown keen interest in developing Lumbinī as a sacred complex for all the human beings. Then His Royal Highness Prince Gyanendra Bir Bikram Shah, chairman of Lumbinī Development Committee, paid a visit to the United Nations and addressed the International Committee for the Development of Lumbinī in 1986. Javier Perez De Cuellar, then Secretary General to the UNO, has also formally addressed that world wide attention is focused on Lumbinī not only because the pilgrims and tourists come from all over the world, but because for all mankind Lumbinī has special meaning as a place of mediation spiritual renewal a centre of cultural exchange and symbol of peace. (LDT, 2067:113). At that time king Gyanendra had visited Jāpān and Koreā to promote awareness and develop friendly relationship with each other. Then king Gyanendra lit a torch of eternal peace in Lumbinī in commemoration of the International year of peace in 1986. The eternal peace flame in Lumbinī is still burning as a symbol of world peace.

According to Master Plan New Lumbinī Village area is developing as a community centre providing facilities of comfortable lodges, restaurants, and other facilities. International Monastery Zone is developing as a sacred complex to the pilgrims and devotees. In this complex forty-two plots of land are at a side. In the complex the monasteries of Jāpān, South-Koreā, Myānmār, France, Vietnam, Thāīland, China, Indiā and Nepāl have been operating regular worship to the general public. In the process, Lumbinī International Research Institute (LIRI) and Museum have been operating and providing facilities for meetings, seminars and study. The circular Sacred Garden contains the Aśokan pillar, Māyādevī temple, sacred pond, ruined structures of stupas and vihārs and other objects within barbed area (Master Plan, 1972). In the complex ornamental flower and hedge plantation have been done by Japānese Overseas Co-operative Volunteers (JOCV) to create a reverent atmosphere conducive to remembering and exercising Lord Buddha's, universal message of peace and harmony (Giri, 2003:71).

In the 19th century, the people had started to move in large numbers to places away from their usual places of residence. Railways, steamships, motorcars and aeroplane linked inter relation among the people of developed, developing and under developing countries. Rapid development in the means of transport and communication has changed the whole world as one neighborhood and has made travel an easy affair. Leisure, pleasure pilgrimage and recreation are the motivating factors of mass movement of people. Thomas Cook, the pioneer of mass tourism in England, had said that the earth in all its fullness and beauty is for the people (Pudney, 1953). Now a days a large number of people move from one country to another due to the cultural and natural attractions. Master Plan of Lumbinī has proposed to develop pilgrimage tourism in order to promote the life styles of the people of Gandaki region (Lumbinī , Dhaulagiri, Gandaki and Rapti zones) (Tange, 1978:1-8). According to Jina (1994) hydrospher, lithosphere and anthrosphere are the main attractions of the tourists.

Ruins, monuments, human activities, i.e. folklore, handicrafts, festivals, music and customs are concerned with anthrosphere (Kunwar, 1997:13-14). Gilber (1990) has mentioned the attractions of the tourists, viz. zoo, heritages, sport activities, entertainment, relaxation, health, shopping and business activities. Actual conservation of natural environment and exploitation in proper way is known as ecotourism. In this context, Lumbinī is enriched for pilgrimage, cultural and ecotourism. In course of study scholars have concentrated on only archaeological area, but not in tourism. Some of the authors of concerned field have mentioned slight scene of tourism of Lumbinī. In 1995 a mini research project was awarded on the topic Religious Sites of Lumbinī Zone by TU Research Division. After revision that report was published on the topic Cultural Tourist Sites (Giri, 2059). Important archaeological as well as religious sites are incorporated on it. Tourism planning concept in case of Nāgarkot has also pointed out the basic phenomena for this region (Pradhan, 1997). In the process of study of Nepāl, Satyāl has pointed out pilgrimage sites, i.e. Lumbinī, Kapilvastu and Niglihawa in brief (Satyāl, 2002:41-43).

Cultural tourism is the focus point of mass tourism at present. Mass tourism can contribute unique benefits to the exploiting of the cultural heritage of a nation and can serve indirectly to improve the individual cultural level of both nationals and foreigners. 51.9% of the total visitors of Lumbinī came in group during 2003-4, which has particular implications for visit management such as the availability of sufficient toilets, orientation to the hoteliers etc (DEVA, 2004: VI). Due to the historical, archaeological, cultural and natural significance of Lumbinī many visitors visit at this sacred site. The survey of Lumbinī visitors has pointed out the types of visitors, purpose of visit, source of visit information, planned period of the visit and route. Maximum number of visitors was 16-30 age-group and 70 % among them visited first time at Lumbinī. Lumbinī is the main attractive site for first time visitors than repeaters'. Among repeat-visitors 55% were from Thāiland. Single, couple, family and group visitors usually come here in proper season. Large number of visitors involved in-group, which indicates the increasing position of mass-tourism at the site. 56 % tourists had visited Lumbinī for religious purpose and remaining 44% for other purpose (DEVA, 2004). Family and friends were main their informative sources for their visit. Visitors to Lumbinī from as far away as Jāpān, Tāiwan and South Koreā decide to come with the planning period of less than one month. Almost the tourists decide to visit Lumbinī referred by the travel agents, hotels and other related authorities after entering Nepāl. It means that there is lack of proper profile networking of Lumbinī information in these markets. Cultural heritages as well as important sites of Kapilvastu and Devadaha were studied from the touristic point of view (Giri, 2005)

According to the report of Nepāl Rāstra Bank the number of Nepālese and Indiān tourists in Lumbinī was 68272, 67545 and 81650 in 2000, 2001 and 2002 respectively. In 2003 and 2004, the number of the tourists was 78553 and 93269 respectively (NRB, 2005:112). The ratio of Indiān and Nepālese tourist was 71% in 2004. In 2004, 16.6% in the total foreign tourists for Nepāl entered from the route of Siddharthanagar Belahiya. Among them 13% visited in Lumbinī complex. 66.7% tourists come for pilgrimage tour in this region (Ibid: 3). Majority of the tourists use air route for their visit at Lumbinī and do not use the services of Tour Company and Travel Agencies. Lumbinī and Bhairahawā have provided 59 and 26 percent accommodation to them respectively.

Only 11 percent has got accommodation in Indiā. About 25 percent tourists accommodated in the monasteries and 16 percent in lodges. In 2007 Hotel Association had opposed the accommodation in monasteries. Remaining visitors mostly used hotel accommodation of various categories. Length of stay of about 90 percent visitors was up to 3 days their average length of stay. South-Koreān and Thāiland have the most willingness to extend their stay with 16 percent of the tourists each from these countries preferring to stay for longer period (Ibid). The tourists who enter from Indiā in Lumbinī stay only 1.5 days in Nepāl. Tour and travel agencies of Indiā come directly Lumbinī and return after some hours at the same day without night rest here (NRB 2005:3).The most interesting thing at Lumbinī is recorded Māyādevi temple to the tourists. Beggars and fake monks' activities have created least interesting feeling to the tourists during their visit at this complex. In 2004, the over all impression of the internationalal tourists about Lumbinī was found to be encouraging as the majority of the tourists expressed that their impression was very good and excellent.

One month field survey and sampling was carried out work to find out the quantity and quality of the tourists in August 2005 (Ghimire:2006:101). In course of this study needs, wants, expectations, travel patterns, facilities, accessibilities and attractions of the tourists have pointed out in brief. Tourist of Śrilanka, South Koreā, Jāpān,

Taiwan, Thāiland and Myānmār usually come in mass. Lumbinī, the birthplace of Lord Buddha, is the main motivating factor to them. From the Buddhist countries many visitors come in group. Role of TRPAP at the seven VDCs' in the periphery of Lumbinī has analysized in case of poverty alleviation (Bhatta:2006:190). Pilgrimage, cultural and mass tourism has simply analysized in course of research on the topic **Sacred Complex of Lumbinī** (Giri, 2008). NTB has published brochuers and proper information of local production including cultural and archaeological sites of Lumbinī and its peripheral sites (NTB, 2008:92). In course of Trade, industrial and tourist Expos of Siddharthanagar, Butwal, Taulihawa and Parasi, special issues have also incorporated the articles of Lumbinī tourism (Giri, 20011).

The significance of Lumbinī as a pilgrimage site has also mentioned in an article on the topic Lumbinī the fountain of Peace and the Holiest Pilgrim Centre of Peace Loving people of the world (Shrestha, 2010:1-9). It is concentrated on the details and published in brief the archaeological remains of the site. In course of field study of UNESCO team tourists movement had also incorporated in their report (Coningham, 2011:1-8). All of the articles are surfacely written only for propagation. Important archaeological, historical and natural heritages are studied with the support of LDT, DDCs' and Industrial organizations on the occasion of Lumbinī Visit Year, 2012 (Giri, 2012). In this work only the detail of the sites has incorporated. But statistical data of the tourists is not analysized from the view point of top origin countries, income source ratio and sector wise analysis. Among the five pillars (agriculture, service sector, tourism, infrastructures and manufacturing's) Tourism is known as the sustainable pillar for economic development of Nepāl including Lumbinī area (Shah, 2069:1).

Lumbinī has the potentials of being the most important centre of cultural tourism. Māyādevi temple, Aśoka pillar, Puskarini tank, various ancient stūpas, vihar structures and finding relics have attracted many pilgrims and other visitors at this sacred complex. In ancient period kings, nobles and other renowned persons had visited Lumbinī in course of their pilgrimage. The tradition has been continuing in an unbroken chain. On special occasion a large number of devotees visit from the various parts of Nepāl and foreign countries. Lumbinī represents not only monuments, but also the requisites, viz. unique life-style of the Hindu, Buddhist and Muslim people, local art, craft and indigenous religious activities. Lumbinī, the birthplace of Lord Buddha, is a sacred complex not only for the Buddhist, but also for the Hindu as well as other religious people due to the peace land. Siddharthanagar, the headquarter of Rupandehi district, is the main entrance gateway of Lumbinī. Immigration office of Belahiya, Bhairahawā has been recorded the number of foreign tourists except Indiān. Due to the open border and cultural similarity between Nepāl and Indiā, it is difficult to find out discrimination and actual data. According to Immigration Office, 46174 tourists entered in Nepāl from Belahiya gateway in 2000. In 2001, the ratio of tourist was decreased in 22.17% and next year was decreasing in 26.43% ratio. In 2003 and 2004 its' numbers increased in 50.80% and 19.93% respectively. In 2005, the ratio of the tourists was increased only 8.03% than the last year. In 2006 the number of tourists increased in 21.34% than 2005. The rate of growth was 44.47% in 2007 than 2006. Increasing 3.70 % ratio is not satisfactory. But in 2009 the ratio decreased in -4.31.

Tourists by plane are not recorded here. Peace and political stability are the major issue for visitors. Because tourists like free, peace and safe in their visit. Six months from October to March are very suitable for tourist industry in this area. The arrival flow of tourists is high in March, November and October respectively. June, May and April are dry months for Lumbinī visitors. Visiting schedule and proper programs should be managed on the basis of tourists' wants and interest by the authority. Main visitors of the sacred complex are of Śrilanka, Thāīland, South Koreā, Myānmār, Jāpān, UK, USA, Israel and Germany. In 2002, visitors were only 26438 due to Maoist movement in Nepāl. After the seize fire of the Maoist, visiting ratio of the foreigners rapidly increased in 2005 and 2006. In the comparison of 2002, the number of visitors was increased 137% in 2006. From 2003 to 2008, the ratio of the tourists is increasing in positive way (LDT, 2010:36). But, in 2009 its ratio has decreased. In 2010 and 2011 its ratio was increased.

The travel trend of both domestic as well as internationalal tourist is soaring in the recent days. 4, 26,250 Nepālese and 65,150 Indiān nationals have visited Lumbinī in 2010 whereas, the number of visitors of the third country reached 99,508 this year. The official data from Lumbinī Development Trust, Information Centre shows a mounting rate of tourists in Lumbinī with increment by 20.69 % in comparison of 2009. The pilgrims and tourists from 94 countries visited Lumbinī this year. Sri-Lanka kept its top position with the total number of 37,645 visitors whereas other Buddhist nations Thāīland, Myānmār, South Koreā, China, Vietnam and Jāpān stood in the second, third, fourth, fifth, sixth and seventh positions with number of 22833, 5701, 5469, 4712, 2317 and 2151 visitors respectively. Among the tourists were least in number from the countries like Albāniā, Boliviā, Croatia, Guatemala, Jamaica, Jordon, Kenyā, Morocco, Sudān, Zambia etc in Lumbinī in 2010 (LDT, 2012). In 2011 And 2012 total tourists were 587538 and 758268 in Lumbinī . In 2013 thee number of the tourists has increasing than last years. Indiān and Nepālese tourists were also counted from 2011.

Rapid development of Lumbinī area is the main reason of tourist growth rate to the birthplace of the Lord Buddha. The publicity of Lumbinī by LDT and various national and international organizations and institution is however other important reasons to increase the visitors. Annual increment of pilgrimage to the birthplace of Lord Buddha, the Apostle of Peace clearly indicates towards people's wish for global peace and universal brotherhood. Ven. Acharya Karma Sangbo Sherpa, Vice Chairman of the Trust expressed his happiness and thanked all pilgrims and visitors for visiting holy birthplace of the Buddha. Member Secretary of LDT opined that the gradual increment of tourists to Lumbinī has added more responsibilities to the Trust for a speedy development of Buddhist sites in the peripherals of Lumbinī along the circuit route and proper site management for the facility and convenience of the visitors. All staffs of LDT had expressed their strong commitment for the maximum exploitation of all possible resources for quality services, works and overall management of the sites. Visitors of Myānmār and Israel are decreasing and the ratio of the visitors of Netherland, France and Spain is increasing. Japānese and Thai visitors are less than last years. Apart from the above mentioned countries, tourists of Australiā, Canādā, Cambodiā, Malaysiā, Chinā, Vietnām, France, Dutch etc are also visiting here in proper season. Their main target of visit is the sacred complex of Lumbinī.

The ratio of tourists was 26.85% increased in 1996 than last year. From 1997 to 99, its ratio was decreasing at least -51.56%. Next year ratio was increased in +31.92%. In 2001 and 2002 arrival ratio of tourists is not satisfied. In 2003 and 2004 were satisfied because of increasing rate +210.42% and +35.07% respectively. The ratio of 2003 was rapidly increased due to seize fire of Maoist Movement. The entry ratio of the foreign tourists except Indiā is increased + 5.01% in 2005. In 2006 and 2007 the ratio of the tourists rapidly increased in +24.63 % and +43.26 % respectively. The ratio of the visitors is 15.51 % and 0.45 % in 2008 and 2009 respectively. Last year was not satisfied. Tourists of third countries had increased in 2011. Nepāl Government and LDT had decided the 2012 as **Lumbinī Visit Year**.

It was a motivation factor to the visitors. Peace, political stability, physical facilities, global communication and toleration among various political party, group, religion, sex and communities are the major factors to promote tourism. Srilanka, Jāpān, South-Koreā, Thāiland, Taiwan and China are the main tourist generator countries for Lumbinī. Sixteen years scenario presents the attraction of Srilankan and Japānese tourists due to the Buddhist religion and philosophical influence. In 1996 and 1998, the number of Japānese was 9405 and 8247 respectively. In 2002, its number was decreased into 937. In 2003 and 2004, its ratio had increased in +41.40% and +20.42% respectively in the comparison of last years. Its vast differentiation was the main cause of national and internationalal violence and terrorism. The arrival ratio of the foreign tourists was decreased in -28.30 and -10.84 in 2002 and 2001 respectively. Tourists of Japān and Taiwan are in decreasing ratio due to peace and security. After killing to Nawa Tame at Nipponzan Myhoji complex in Lumbinī Master Plan area, Japānese tourists are in decreasing position. Messages of proper peace, security and friendly should be released in the concerned areas through Nepālese Embassy and private sectors.

The ratio of Chinese tourists has been increasing in last years than previous years due to the touristy-relation between Nepāl and China government. Thāīland and Taiwan are also generating visitors in the promotion of cultural and pilgrimage tourism of Lumbinī. March is the most favorable month for the visitors in Lumbinī. From August to March the flow of tourists is very high and local people also get chance to earn a lot of money by tourism industry. In 2003 the number of the tourists was increased in 210.42 % than the last year. After 2003 the ratio of the visitors was increasing each year. In 2006 the rate of the visitors was increased in 24.63% than 2005. In the March there were 12214, 14149, 11927 and 16471 foreign tourists at Lumbinī respectively. In 2007, 2008, 2009 and 2010. 817, 606, 830 and 933 tourists had visited at Lumbinī in June of previous years respectively. April, May, June and

July are dry months for the internationalal visitors due to hot weather and rainy season in the region. Due to the internal conflict, violence and unlawful activities the internationalal visitors were not encouraged to visit Lumbinī and its peripheral area in the past. After the seize fire of the Maoist the flow of the visitors is increasing in per year. According to the wants and needs of the visitors GO, NGO and civil societies should manage and provide various facilities and services to them. The trend of the visitors supports to plan and manage the facilities to the authorities in proper time and situation. Nepāl Government has declared Lumbinī Visit Year 2012. Many programs were launched during the period. Within five month period internationalal tourist flow is increased more than 60% and domestic tourists also visited more than 90% in the comparison of last years. But unstable political situation and strike of the political parties and civil societies are disturbing to meet the target of this Visit Year.

Almost the previous activities of the sacred complex of Lumbinī have been concentrated into archaeological excavation and physical development. Due to the sacred value and world peace centre more than one million visitors usually come here per year. Among them one hundred thousands pilgrims had visited from ninety three countries except Indiā and Nepāl in 2011. Government and civil society members are directly and indirectly benefited from their visit. It is supporting to provide government revenue, employment, cultural and social changes. It will be major issue to upgrade the life style of the local people. But the researchers as well as stake-holders are not conscious for this work. Here is one of the problems that Indiān Tour and Travel Agencies take the tourists in their buses and go back within two or three hours after visiting only Māyādevī temple of Lumbinī. In some cases pilgrims do not know that Lumbinī is located either in Indiā or Nepāl.

Their dirty should be managed by the LDT staff and local people without any fee. In this critical situation academic and applied work is not done about tourism of Lumbinī. Except some articles about the tourism of Lumbinī is not studied in systematic and scientific way. This study has attempted to point out the ways of promotion of pilgrimage tourisms. It will be clear that tourism industry has played a vital role in the promotion of life ways of the local people. This study is useful for both in academic and applied value. It will help us to find out the proper way to solve problems of tourism of sacred complex and in great Lumbinī area.

Lumbinī area.

Research Methodology

Main data and information required for the study are obtained from field study and tourist data are used recorded at Lumbinī Development Trust, Immigration Office of Belahiya Siddharthanagar. Primary data are supplemented by secondary sources of data from various reports, papers, maps and photographs. The main categorised of the tourist statistic is based on volume, expenditure and characteristics. In course of this study mainly direct observation, interview, questionnaire and literary methods and techniques are adopted. Stages of the study are as follows:

Pre-field study

Literature review and preliminary activities are conducted during this stage. Data are collected from the record of Lumbinī Development Trust, Immigration Office Belahiya, Lumbinī Regional Tourism Promotion Office Bhairahawa, Nepāl Rastra Bank Bhairaahawa, Nepāl Tourism Board Belahiya, Siddharthanagar Association of Travel and Tour, Lumbinī Association of Travel and Tour, Hotel Associations of Butwal, Siddharthanagar and Butwal as well as research reports and books which are mentioned in bibliography are also used. Relevant data are recorded and interpreted in a proper way to fulfill the objectives, giving attention to the proper collection, logging, interpretation and evaluation of available data. Observational checklist, structured–questionnaires, structured interview, scheduled and other relevant field formats are used to prepare it. All the required information is easily available during the field study. On the basis of desk study required information and proper data for the program of field study, a comprehensive report is prepared.

Field Study

During the field survey, information on location characteristics is obtained through participant observation, interview and questionnaires. Field data are collected from Lumbinī Development Trust, Monasteries, Vihars, Industries on the way of Bhairahawa-Lumbinī, Lumbinī International Research Institute, Hotels, Guest House etc of Lumbinī, Taulihawā, Siddharthanagar and peripherical VDCS' of the region. The observation is followed by interviews using structured questionnaires. Random and judgmental sampling is carried out from January 2012 to June 2013 on the basis of pick and low season of the visitors. This research is followed in proper situation.

Flow Diagram of the Methodology

	Remarks
1. Objective	
2. Literature Review	
3. Identification of Existing Data	
4. Identification of Study Area	
5. Selection of Methodology	
6. Questionnaire Finalization	
7. Field Survey	
8. Monitoring and Analyzing	
9. Planning Implication	
10. Planning Strategies and Recommendation	

Table 1.1

Questionnaire Distribution and Return

S.No	*Respondents*	*Distributed No.*	*Returned No.*	*Returned Percentage*	*in Remarks*
1.	Domestic visitors	75	60	80	
2.	Passport-holder Pilgrimage\Tourists	100	95	95	
3.	Indiān ,, ,,	50	46	92	
4.	Hotels	45	30	66	
5.	Residents	50	42	82	

During the field work, local agents are involved in course of interview programs. In particular projective tests, observation, open-ended questionnaires, opinionnaires and interviews are used in quantitative way. In order to understand different dimensions of the pilgrimage programs, interdisciplinary and holistic approach are appropriately used in course of field study. Library of Lumbinī International Research Institute is highly enjoyed during this period. Questionnaires are fulfilled at entry, exit and on the way of the tourists. Number in mass, average length of stay at the destination, measurement of spending by the tourists, expenditure at transport and shopping are also directly observed.

administrators, UNESCO, Rupandehi District Development Committee and other related person in the area to obtain more information concerning various issues. Any useful information arising during the field study is also recorded precisely to understand and interpret the response of person in their real context.

iii) Post-field study

During the period of post-field study, all technical and statistical data are recorded in computer in proper order. The desk data are up- dated and new field data are added. Essential comments on desk report are mentioned in proper order. Proper information of field study are re-evaluated and mentioned in systematic way. A systematic approach is adopted for analyzing the quantitative and qualitative data. A careful efforts is taken to ensure accuracy in noting down from the records. After the tabulation of required data and information, first draft is prepared on the basis of chapter organization. Incorporating comments on the draft report, a final report is prepared to submit. Final report has prepared after detail discussion with experts and University Grants Commission Monitoring Committee of Research Division.

Limitation of the Study

This study is limited at the periphery of Lumbinī complex, the birth place of Lord Buddha, and from Butwal to Tilaurakot, capital city of ancient Kapilvastu, route about 25 km east and west from Lumbinī and Butwal. Library method is limited in the reports of Lumbinī, Buddhist texts and tourist literature. In this study Lumbinī International Research Institute Library, Tribhuwan University Central Library Kirtipur, Bhairahawa Multiple Campus Library, Rupandehi Campus Library, Gyanmandir Library Bhairahawa, Nepāl-China Friendship Library Siddharthanagar and Sahidahh Library BP Patha Siddharthanagar are used. Field work has launched from Butwal, Bhairahawa to Lumbinī in course of interview, questionnaire and direct observation. Direct observation and questionnaire fulfillment activities are concentrated at entry, exit and on journey of Lumbinī complex, Belahiya, Buddhachoka Siddharthanagar, Khunuwa of Bhgawanpur, Bus park as well as Gautam Buddha Airport Bhairhawa. Tourist data, recorded at Lumbinī Development Trust, Immigration Office Belahiya, field survey report of Cross Flow Nepāl (CFN), Tourism for Rural Poverty Alleviation Program (TRPAP), DEVA, Hotel Associations of Lumbinī and Siddharthanagar; International Buddhist Society (IBS),

Poverty Alleviation Program (TRPAP), DEVA, Hotel Associations of Lumbinī and Siddharthanagar; International Buddhist Society (IBS), are used in course of this study. Pilgrimage, cultural and ecotourism; mass tourism and domestic tourism are major issues of this study. Basic elements for the promotion of pilgrimage, endemic and sustainable tourism are also incorporated. Field survey and observation was carried out in low and high seasons in 2012. Opinion expressed by the respondents has verified in course of field observation.

In this study home-stay visitors are not counted. Concerned banks of this area have not accurate data information of exchanged foreign currency and cashing travelling cheques. It is also a challenge to find out the motivation factors of the pilgrims and visitors. Border workers, nomads, transit passengers, refugees, member of armed-forces, diplomats, representative of consulates, temporary immigrants and permanent immigrants are not mentioned here. School and campus excursionists in mass are also observed in field work.

Organization of the study

Chapter

I. Introduction of Research
II. Geography and History of Lumbinī
III. Buddhist Heritage of Lumbinī
IV. Tourism Development
V. Pilgrims and Pilgrimage
VI. Modes of Transportation
VII. Tourists Accommodation
VIII. Tourism Promotion
IX. Conclusion
Bibliography
Appendices
Illustrations

CHAPTER TWO

GEOGRAPHY AND HISTORY

Location and physical features

Lumbinī, the birth place of Lord Buddha, is situated about 22 km. from Bhairahawā (Siddharthanagar), below the Churiā range, the foothills of the Himālayas, on the western bank of Telār River in Rupāndehi district of Lumbinī zone in Nepāl. 28 km. west of Lumbinī lies Tilaurakot, the capital of the Śākyas and 38 km. east of Lumbinī is Devadaha, the capital of Koliyas. It is about 34 km. from Naugarh Railway Station on the North Eastern Railway of Indiā. It is about 100 MSL. Buddha, known as the Lord of Asia, was born in Lumbinī during the full moon day in the month of Vaiśākha in 563 BC. He was born under a *sal (Shorea robusta)* tree when Māyādevī was going to her maternal town on the occasion of delivery. *Suttanipata* has mentioned the earliest description of the birth of Buddha in Lumbinī. After the birth of Buddha he took seven steps towards north and, looking in all directions, he declared that "I am the foremost of all creatures to cross the riddle of the ocean of the existence, this is my last birth and here after, I will not be born again.

The site is spelt as Rummindei or Rupandei (beautiful lady), the perverted form of Rupā devi, the queen Anjana of the king of Devadaha which was situated to the east of Kapilvastu in ancient time. The site is called Lun- min and La-Fa-Ni by the Chinese pilgrims Fa- Hien and Hiuen- Tsiang respectively. In course of exploration of the ancient Buddhist sites General Cunningham has mentioned La-Fa-Ni is Sanskrit Lavani, a beautiful lady (Cunnigham, 1990:350). In Buddhist literature it is known as *Pradimokṣa vana* blessed with various trees and flowers, which is compared to the *Chittalata* grove of Indra's paradise in heaven (Führer, 1972:4). The earliest Pali text *Suttanipata* has mentioned that, "The wisdom-child that Jewel so precious, that can not be matched, has been born at Lumbinī, in the Śākya land for well being and joy in the world of men". A Muslim historian of Indiā named Abul Fazal has called Mokta (Cunningham, 1990:351).

It is also known as Paderiyā (Parariyā) where the Aśokan pillar is located in the Nepālese Terāi. The name of the site is spelt Lumminigāme and Lumbinī vaṇa in the Aśokan pilllar Edict still standing at the same place (Führer, 1972:31-33). Mukherji has also mentioned the name Rummin-dei in his report. In the Magadhi language, being used in the north-eastern pillar edicts in Indiā and Nepāl, 'la' is invariable substitutedd for 'ra'. The location of Lumbinī is pointed out in the Buddhist literature, as well as, in the records of the Chinese pilgrims who visited Indiā in the fifth and seventh centuries AD. As mentioned in *Jātaka* story this *sāl* garden was in joint possession of the Śākayas and Koliyas during the life time of Buddha. The *Mahāvamsa*, a Ceylonese chronicle, and *Nidāna kath*ā have also located it between Kapilvastu and Devadaha. During the reign of the Śākyas of Kapilvastu and the Koliyas, Lumbinī was a small dwelling site from where the visitors of two states use to walk through there.

Due to the use of bullock carts for the common people and horse chariots with palanquin for the richer people and royalties they travelled about 20 km in a single day. In that situation they might have spent a night in Lumbinī (Bidari, 2003:6). The *sāl* garden was the place of recreation during the reign of the Śākayas and Koliyas. *Buddha charita of Aśvaghosa* describes Lumbinī as "gay like the garden of *caitra ratha* with trees of every kind. According to Fa- Hien it is located about 50 *li* east of Kapilvastu (Giles, 1981:38). Hiuen- Tsiang had also pointed out that it was about 80 or 90 *li.* (21.729 or 24.445 km.) north-east of arrow-well (Beal, 1994:24). It was linked through popular *'Uttara path'* to Kapilvastu, Rāmagrāma and other important cities during the Buddhist period. The present location of Lumbinī, the exact birth place of Lord Buddha, is absolutely clear in the western Terai region of Nepal. The narrow ridge of the Churiā range runs parallel to the *Mahābhārat* Mountain from east to west.

The Siwālika Range

The *Mahābhārat* range is composed of loose non-metamorphic rocks in the western Nepāl (Hashimoto, 1973: 286). Almost the Neogene rocks in

Nepāl are the molasse deposits of the Siwālika group which forms the Churiā hills. The lower Siwālika, regarded as late Miocene in age, are the Chinji formation consisting of reddish clay stones with minor sand stone. According to Hagen most of the exposed Siwālika ranges in this region belong to the middle Siwālika of mio-Pliocene era (Hagen, 1959:3-48). Due to rapid increase in human activities in this region rather gently inclined bad land areas had developed, especially in the area between Butawal to Nepālguñj along the southern side of Dāṅg valley. It is formed of grey to pale-brown medium to coarse grained sandstone and pale-brown mudstone. Its basement is formed by a thick bed of ill sorted conglomerate of more than fifty meters in thickness. This belt shows a few scattered houses made of wooden pillars and dry-grass as a protection-tower against wild animals. Sandy soil with boulders of the region is not so fertile for regular cultivation.

The Terai Zone

On the south of the Siwālika range the Indo-Gaṅgetic plain named the Terai is distributed with an elevation lower than two hundred meters MSL from Nārāyaṇī to Rāpti River in the region. The Terai is composed of gravels and sands and of the late Pleistocene to Holocene age (Ibid). The fertile and sandy alluvial soil in the region is formed by the great river system, viz. Rohiṇī, Tināu, Koṭhī, Bāṇagaṅgā and their tributaries. In course of his pilgrimage Hiuen-Tsiang has pointed out that the soil of the region was fertile and farming operations were regular in suitable weather (Watters, 1961:1).

The Forest and Weather

In this region thick forest contains *Shorea robusta (sal, sakhuwa) pinus longifolia (chir)*, elephant grass, *acacia catechu* (khair), *Salmalia mala boica* (simal), *Dal bergia Sissa (Sisau)*, *Zyiphus Jujuba (Bair)* even now, especially in the northern belt from east to west in the region (Sharma, 1973:2-3). In the sixth century BC *plaksha* tree (*Ficus lacor*), mango tree (*Mangifera indica*), pipal tree (*Ficus religiosa*), *sal* tree (*Shorea robusta*) and Aśoka tree (*Saraca indico*) were associated with the indigenous trees of the area (Bidari, 1996:11-24). According to *Bhadda-Sala Jataka* there were trees in the park for making columns of the palace; but transportation was impossible due to rough road (Cowell, 1901:91-97). This evidence reveals that natural forests as well as parks had been developed in the Buddhists period. *Mahavana* and *Lumbinīvana* were associated with this region (Upadhyaya, 2018: 293-299).

This region has hot and humid climate. Lumbinī (elevation 100 m) has a tropical monsoon climate characterized by a cold season, hot season, monsoon and transitional periods. The core of the cold season extends from the beginning of December to the end of January with temperature occasionally dropping to +5.5^{0}c (Coningham, 2011:3). Rainfall is minimum and relative humidity may reach 100% and 40% humidity of the interior of the temple and the Marker Stone chamber is very similar to the outside humidity (Ibid,4). There tends to be a spell of 7-10 days of foggy weather in December and another such spell in January otherwise sunshine prevails.The hot season from the beginning of March to last June. During the peak of the hot season (May) temperatures may rise to +39^{0}c with a low relative humidity and minimal rain fall. Some times strong winds blow across Lumbinī. HMG Department of Meteorology cites June 12 to September 23 as the period of the annual monsoon in Nepāl. The highest rain fall (approximately 300mm.) is recorded in July and August. The maximum temperature in June (Approximate +37^{0}c) gradually comes down to slightly above +30^{0}c doing July, August and September. Minimum Temperature was 5^{0}c and maximum 43.5^{0}c respectly in January and May 2012. The monsoon remains active between June and September. Being alluvial and fertile area, it is known as the granary of the western Nepāl.

The Rivers

The rivers flow southward and meet Gaṅges in Indiā forming wide beds (Sharma, 1977:39-40. During the Miocene the Churiā range was under the shallow sea and its river system was responsible for the deposition of soil. Due to the deposition of sediments from the rivers, flowing from north to south, Indo-Gaṅgetic plain was created. The rivers related with Himālayan, Mahābhārata and Churiā ranges, were responsible for the formation of the Terai region. The level of the plain land rose due to the sedimentation of Indo-Gaṅgetic forming new river channels in this area for the drainage. Rivers flow from the north to the south slope in this area The Tināu, Dāno, Tilār, Bāṇagaṅgā (Bhāgirathi) and Koṭhi have their origin in the Himālayan and northern hills. The position of the Rohiṇi, Tilār, Bāṇagaṅgā (Bhāgirathi) and Anomā is more precisely indicated by the Chinese pilgrims and Ceylones chronicle. During the modern period, after the eradication of malaria, many people of the hills have migrated in this Terai region.

Ancient Pilgrimage and Trade Routes

The region of the present study and Indiā has been culturally closely related due to the open border between two states. The trade routes between Indiā and this region of Nepāl pass through western hills and the Himālayas.During the lifetime of Siddhartha Gautam his followers, especially monks and nuns, used to pass through these routes (Rhys Davids, 1971:44). As stated in the ancient Buddhists literature the Brāhamaṇ and ascetics used to travel from Kausambi to Vaisali passing through Sāketa, Śrāvasti, Setabhya, Kapilvastu, Kuśinagar, Pāvā. *Vinaya piṭaka* refers to a direct road from Kapilvastu to Vaisāli. Buddhist monks and followers used to travel in the ancient period to Tibet and Mongoliā through a route passing through Kapilvastu, Butawal, Pālpā, Ridi, Kāga-beni and Muktinātha. On 21-30 September, 1995 Buddhist Route Expedition conducted by UNESCO surveyed this area (Pandey, 1985:2). It was frequently travelled by the Buddhist pilgrims through the Terai to the Himālayan region, particularily Muktinātha, Tibet and Mongoliā. The other important route was Surāhi-nākā, at the north west corner of Kapilvastu district, from where the traders as well as pilgrims frequently travelled to Surkheta, Dailekha, Rukuma and other sites to the Western Nepāl.

Emperor Aśoka had come to Lumbinī and Kapilvastu with his spiritual teacher Upagupta in the twentieth year of his reign. Chinese pilgrims Fa-Hien and Hiuen-Tsiang had entered in Lumbinī, Kapilvastu and its vicinity during the 4th, 5th and 7th centuries AD respectively through Śrāvasti. They have mentioned the direction and distances of the places, viz. circuit of the capital town of Kapilvastu, various Buddhist monuments and images of Kapilvastu, Royal field, Arrow-Fountain , Lumbinī, birth place of Lord Budhha, and Rāmagrāma which help us to identify the ancient ruins of those places today. It is being identified with some ancient sites in the periphery of Lumbinī , whose geographical feature and situation are known through the accounts of the Chinese pilgrims as well as Buddhist literature.

In the eighteenth century Prithvi Nārāyaṇ Shah had also come through Varāṇāsi, Gorakhpur, Nautanawā and Butawal to Gorkhā. These routes are regularly followed by the pilgrims and traders even now. The region is plain and fertile and is known as the granary of the western Nepāl. The northern portion of Lumbinī area is formed mainly by sandstone and pale-brown mudstones of the Śiwālika range, as such, is not fertile. To the south of Śiwālika range the fertile and alluvial soil is also covered with *Chara kose jhadi* [about thirteen kms. deep]. Tigers, leopards, lions, elephants and rhinos live in the dense jungle. Rice, wheat, corn and mustard crops are cultivated by the people in the fertile lands. Bāṇagaṅgā, Telār, Ghāgharā, Rohiṇi and Koṭhī rivers are ancient rivers mentioned in Buddhist period. All the commercial goods are taken to the hill region of the western Nepāl from the southern Terai region as well as from Indiā. Thus, these ancient routes are still important to the traders and pilgrims as it was in the past.

HISTORY

A brief historical survey of Lumbinī is mentioned in order to follow the chronological framework of the study of sacred complex. Preliminary stages of the history of Śākyas and Koliyas are catagorised under prehistoric and proto-history remains are also obtained in the periphery of Lumbinī. Thereafter, the historical age begins in the area as we start getting evidences in the form of epigraphic evidences, seals and sealings. The history of the area is divided into ancient, medieval and modern periods. The purpose of this short description is to delineate the cultural history, the life style of the people in the area, and to trace the dynamic cultural process of Lumbinī.

Pre-history

On the basis of variation in shape, size, polish and their usage of stone tools, the period is divided into traditional three ages.

Paleolithic Age

Pre-historic men used to live in the foothills of the Siwālika ranges in this area. Most of the valleys of this range are formed of the sedimentary rocks of the Miocene and Pleistocene era containing shale, sand and pebble beds. Due to deforestation and landslides the range has no human habitation and is naked at present. River terraces are composed of gravels. Stone tool industries found in the gravels are of considerable importance to the pre-historian. A river cuts away its banks and carries the material along with it upto the sea where it is deposited. But all this depend on the velocity and volume of the flow. Some of the material are left only on the way. In this context, the rivers Koṭhi, Ghāgarā, Tināu, Rohiṇi, etc. are very important as the pre-historic dwelling sites in the region. In December 1980, a team of scholars from U.S.A. and Nepāl, under the leadership of J.H. Hutchison, of which other members were James Munthe, K. Munthe, R.M. West and Vishṇu Dāṅgol, T.U., fossil remains of *Ramapithecus* were found in a place near Butawal on the bank of the river Tināu attached to the rocks cliff. A piece of the upper left jaw which is 1 cm. in width and more than 1 cm. in length is kept in the Natural Museum in Kathmandu. It was dated approximately eleven million years old on the basis of paleomagnetic dating method. This hominoid finding is one as the oldest in Asia and the second oldest in the world. Its life style and civilization have similar to the *Kenyapithecus* and *Brahmapithecus* of Asia. Having been great forest area the pre-historic men used to live by hunting and gathering wild fruits in the neighbourhood of Lumbinī.

Mesolithic Age

The stone tools of the Mesolithic age are available in limited number in Nepāl. However, some evidences of this phase have come to light in the region. In course of excavation and exploration to the north-west of Kapilvastu district, Surāhi-nākā area, G.Corvinus, a German scholar, has discovered many prehistoric sites in the beds of the Surāi kholā. There were workshop sites, camping sites, simple flaking and small activity spots. A lot of plant fossils of leaf impressions, fossilized carbonized wood and leaf material were found in the fine clastic deposits of claystones and mudstones in the older period. In course of rock-cutting, a large bedding plane of a mudstone was exposed, on which a set of animal footprints of some smaller artiodactyl animals were seen. In course of the examination of these findings a profile column of 5500m. of Siwalik deposits was recorded with all the details of palaeontological and sedimentological data . Palaeontological and magnetostratigraphical studies along the Surāi kholā, north-west of Kapilvastu district, suggest dates on the basis of major lithological units that it is not so different from those found in Pākistan by Johnson, et al. and in western Indiā by Ranga Rao. Above-mentioned evidences reveal that microlithic industries as well as Mesolithic tools had been used by the prehistoric men on the northwest of Lumbinī.

Neolithic Age

The Neolithic culture of the Terai region is presented by surface collection. The warmer climates of the sheltered valleys of the Terai region were ideally suited for the habitat of the prehistoric man. The Neolithic culture presents a change. Permanent habitation, start of agricultural activities, animal husbandry, industries of pottery and polished microlithic stone tools were the main features of the Neolithic man. The culture associated with food-production and self-dependence was also developed in the western Terai region of Nepāl.

Proto-history

Lumbinī was a part of Kapilvastu of the Śākyas in the western Terai region of Nepāl. The Śākya kingdom was formed here by the vanished sons and daughters of the Kosala king Okkaka. According to the *Divyadana* the town of Kapilvastu was situated by the side of Bhāgirathi (Bāṇagaṅagā), close to the *āshrama* of Rishi Kapilmuni. According to the *Lalitavistār* in course of ages it was organized into a big town as other people came from other sites to do well in the new settlement. Two theories have been propounded regarding the origin of the tribal name Śākya-the first is based on the name of the *sāl* forest (*Shorea robusta*), where Kapila used to live, and the second theory is based upon the legend of the banished sons and daughters who married each other to protect the purity of their blood. The four brothers married the four younger sisters and appointed the eldest sister as queen mother (Rockhill, 1972:11). When the father of the children came to know about them, it is said, he delightedly exclaimed: "*Śākya vata-bho-kumara-parama Śākya-vata-bho kumara*" (Aha! smart men indeed, Śākya indeed are the princes, very smart men)'. So the endogamous tribe is known as Śākya. Different sources have incorporated different names of the Śākya kings. According to *Lalitavistara*, Opura was the first king of Kapilvastu and Suddhodana belonged to this dynasty. He became the king in the seventh generation (descent) after him (Oldenberg, 1971:94-99). *Mahāvamsa* has mentioned that Ulkamukha was the first king of Kapilvastu and after several generations, Jayasena became the king of Kapilvastu. He was succeeded by his son Simhahanu, father of Suddhodhana. Simhahanu had five sons namely Suddhodana, Dhautodana, Shakradana, Sulkodana and Amṛitodan and two daughters named Amrita and Pramita. Princess Amṛita was married to Prince Suprabuddha of Devadaha, the father of Yasodhār. *Mahāvamsa refers* that Māyādevi and Prajāpati were the daughters of Anjana, Koliya chief of Devadaha (Rockhill, 1972:19-21).

Suffering from leprosy the queen mother, Priya, resided in a cave in the forest, where the king of Varāṇāsi, Ram, also resided as he was suffering from the same disease. After sitting under a Kolan (*nauclea Cordifalia*) tree they got cured and both of them were married. To the east of Kapilvastu they organised the town named Devadaha and created the race of Koliyas. It is known as Devadaha, Vyāghrapur, Kolinagara or Rāmagrāma.

The Śākyas of Kapilvastu and the Koliyas of Devadaha had established matrimonial relations in future as well. King Suddhodana of Kapilvastu had married Māyādevī and Gautami, the princess of Devadaha. Siddartha Gautam was born from the womb of Māyādevī in Lumbinī. Thus, the ancient Buddhist literature reveals that the present study area was inhabitated by the Śākyas. In course of exploration and excavation of Lumbinī area, a lot of art remains, structural remains as well as habitational depositions are found. In 1964 Deo has discovered a few rammed-up clay walls of plain huts from the low flattish heavily eroded mounds of Bañjarāhi, near Lumbinī. Habitational deposits on the opposite bank of the Dāno river has yielded similar evidences indicating that the ancient habitational deposits were bifurcated by the river. According to the excavator it is dated from 700 to 600 BC. The pottery of P.G.W, Red ware and N.B.P.ware are also found in course of excavation from the site (Deo, 1968:3-7).

In the sixth century BC, Siddhartha was born in Lumbinī garden under a sāl or Aśoka or *pipal* tree, which is comparable to the Chittalata grove of Indra's paradise in heaven in the Śākya land. Lord Buddha himself had advised the monks and followers from his death bed at Kusinagar to visit the four places, viz. Lumbinī, Bodhagayā, Sāranātha and Kusinagar. So, Lumbinī remaind not only as a pleasure garden, but it also developed as a place of pilgrimage after the birth of Lord Buddha (Führer, 1972:63). Structural remains as well as artifacts found from Lumbinī reveal that monks and his followers used to stay here from the beginning of the Buddha's enlightenment. The excavation conducted in 1970-71 has indicated that the earliest human habitation in ancient Lumbinī *grāma* must have started in N.B.P. period (Rijal, 1975-77:30). The site seems to have been occupied from the time of Lord Buddha, i.e. the sixth century BC. The successive human deposit in the southern mound of Lumbinī dates from sixth century BC to the Gupta period on the basic of its antiquities.

King Vidudhabha of Kosala had attacked Kapilvastu four times. Buddha saved three times from the attack; but, at last, Buddha did not interfere. During the attack several Śākyas were massacred and stone slabs of the mote hall was washed with their blood. The Śākyas, who saved their lives, fled in different directions, some to Nepāl (Kathmandu), some to Rājgṛiha and Vaiśāli, some to Vedi, ṣome to

Pippalivan. Thus, the city of Kapilvastu came to an end during the life time of Buddha, i.e. 500 BC (Upadhyaya, 2018:291).

The Mauryan Period.

According to the *Kundavadana* of *Divyavadana*, having led king Aśoka in the Lumbinī *jungle*, the Venerable Upagupta pointed out with his right hand and said, "oh!great king here the Buddha was born ". Thereafter king Aśoka made an offering of one hundred thousand gold coins and established the first pagoda (*ceitiya*) in the twentieth year of his reign Thus, the above-mentioned documentary and circumstantial evidences reveal that Lumbinī region was absolutely developed as the Buddhist pilgrimage site during the Mauryan period. Mauryan terracotta-human and animal figurines, stone sculptures and structural remains, viz. vihār, temple foundation, stūpas and bricks are found here (Giri, 2003:206-232)

Condition After Aśoka.

Almost all the habitational sites had been deserted, but the religious complex and some portion of Lumbinī area had been actively mobilized during the Suṅga, Kushāna and the Gupta periods During these periods terracotta human and animal figurines, stone sculptures, beads, bangles, seals, sealings as well as architectural monuments, viz. vihār, stūpa, Buddhist temples and loose bricks are found. Various art remains of the region are assignable, on the basis of comparative study with the Magadha antiquities, to the fourth century AD.

Accounts of the Chinese Pilgrims

In the 4th and 5th centuries AD Toung Toai and Fa-Hien had seen some monks and a few families of the common people living at Kapilvastu. Fa-Hien mentions that "Fiftyli to the east of the city (Kapilvastu) is the royal garden called "Lum-min" (Lumbinī); it was here the queen entered the bath to wash herself, and, having come out on the northern side, advanced twenty paces, and then holding a branch of the tree in her hand, as she looked to the east, brought fourth the prince. When born he walked seven steps; two dragon kings washed the prince's body, the place where this occurred was afterwards converted into a well, and, here, as likewise at the pool, the water of which came down from above for washing (the child), the priests draw their drinking water (Beal,1983)."About 80 or 90 *li* (21.729 or 24.445km.) to the north-east of the Arrow Fountain there were bathing tank, Aśoka flower tree, two stūpas, a great stone pillar surmounted with a horse figure on the top and river of oil were seen in Lumbinī by Hiuen-Tsiang in the seventh century AD at the birth place of Lord Buddha (Watters,1961:15).

Lumbinī can be clearly indentified with the site near present Bhagawānpur in Rupāndehi district. 300 *li* (81.486km.) to the east of Lumbinī, he reached to the ruined town named Lan-mo (Rāmagrāma) where the accounts of these pilgrims are reliable excepting some events mentioned by them. There are a few differences in the details of the descriptions, such as the direction and distance of it; but such discrepancies are very negligible. Lumbinī, which is the main key to identify other sites even now, has been identified on the basis of the descriptions available in the Chinese accounts. In addition, the details given in the accounts entitled Shui-Ching-Chu describes Aśoka tree, Siddharth's birth under the tree, sweet-smelling flowers and Aśoka had shielded the imprint of Siddhartha's feet on long slab of lapis lazuli (Petech, 1950:34-35). With the help of this description it was possible to prove the real position of the conglomerate stone, discovered in the foundation of the old Māyādevī temple in Lumbinī.

Early Medieval Period

In the early medieval period the older convention of art began to be replaced by new conceptions in the the ninth century AD. After the rise of the Rajaput states in different parts of the country colossal creation and cosmic conception was refined in the field of art. A lot of stone sculptures belonging to the Pāla-Sena school of art of eastern Indiā, are found from the surface of the region, and are dated in the ninth and tenth century AD. King Ripu Malla, Saṅgrāma Malla, Nagarāj's descendant of Karṇāli region, had visited and got engraved their inscriptions on the Aśokan pillar in Lumbinī (Führer, 1972:33). The visit indicates that this region was under the soverignity of this dynasty and that this region was still widely known as holy place of pilgrimage. In this context various antiquities and monuments reveal that Lumbinī was continuously inhabited from the sixth century BC to the fourteenth century AD. The surface collections of the site include some beads of terracotta and semi-precious stones, fragments of iron nails and small bits of bronze objects.

In the fourteenth century AD after the termination of the Nāga dynasty, the region was ruled by Malebom and his successors. During the period of *Chaubīsī* it was under Tanahu principality of Magar rulers, in the fifteenth-sixteenth century (1489-1517AD). Sikandar Lodi, then Sultan of Delhi, might have conquered the weak Magar kings of Tanahu. In this connection, Lodi Sultan might have destroyed the stone sculptures as well as monuments at Lumbinī and Kapilvastu in the process of propagation of Muslim movement in the region (Pradhan, 1979:30-35). A number of stone sculptures are found without leg, hand, nose, mouth, cheek, forehead, shoulder etc. It seems that they were broken by force. Muslim rulers might have been instrumental in this destructive actively in the area as it has been a case in the Northern portion of Indiā during the period. The king of Pālpā had conquered the Magar principality of Tanahu during the period of Mukunda Sen I. After the partition of the Sen kingdom, Vināyaka Sen became the king of the Terai region of Pālpā, the site of the area. Mukunda Sen I had built a seasonal palace *Raṅga Mahala* at Butawal *Phūlabāri* area. During the reign of Mukunda Sen II [1750-82AD] a conflict arose with the Nawab Vazier of Oudh. But the king of Pālpā had got some terrian lands, to the west of Gaṇdakī river, on lease due to their friendship with them later. Mahadatta Sen, son of Mukunda Sen, had also received more terrain lands including its peripheral area. The rate of the lease was cheap because it was an unhealthy, unproductive and swampy area. In1801 the Company Government of Indiā and Nawab Vazier of Oudh had imposed a treaty under which Gorakhpur, Rohilakhaṇd and the area under study became a part of the British rule. In 1806 Pālpā, including the Terai region, was conquered by the Government of Nepāl. Thus, Nepāl Government became the lessee and the British Government was a lessor of the region.

Modern period

After the unification of the region the Government of Nepāl had established the administrative Headquarter of the region at Pālpā from where all the disputes were decided and creative activities for the welfare of the people were undertaken (Mishra, 1999:129-35). The Terai region of Kapilvastu and Rupāndehi, including Butawal area, became the issue of debate between Nepāl and Company Government of Indiā for suzerainty over it. This led to the Anglo- Nepāl war in 1814-1816. At last the Treaty of Sugauli was signed on March 3, 1816, which provided the ownership of the region to the Nepāl Government. This region was under the jurisdiction of Butawal, Siurāj and Khajahni districts under the overall charge of the Governor of Pālpā before 1962. In rearrangement of the administrative districts, this area was incorporated in Rupāndehi district of the Lumbinī zone. Some monuments and sculptures are also seen in the region built under the dynamic leadership of the Sena kings of Pālpā principality. Being far from the capital, a Governor from Kathmandu was appointed for the regional administration during reign of the the Rāṇās. During all these periods kings, nobles as well as people of the area had contributed to make artifacts for the purpose of their domestic and religious life, which provide us a glimpse of the social activities of the region.

Due to the located on the south of the Siwālika range the Indo-Gańgetic plain named the Terai is distributed with an elevation lower than 105 meters MSL. The Terai is composed of gravels and sands and of the late Pleistocene to Holocene age. The fertile and sandy alluvial soil is formed by the great river system, viz. Rohiṇī, Tināu, Koṭhī, Bāṇagaṅgā and their tributaries. Chinese pilgrim Hiuen-Tsiang has pointed out that the soil of that area was fertile and farming operations were regular in suitable weather. Hot weather is influcing the daily life ways of the people. Tigers, leopards, lions, elephants and rhinos live in the dense *jungle*. Rice, wheat, corn and mustard crops are cultivated by the people in the fertile lands. Bāṇagaṅgā, Telār, Ghāgharā, Rohiṇi and Koṭhī rivers are ancient rivers mentioned in Buddhist period. All the commercial goods are taken to the hill region of the western Nepāl from the southern Terai region as well as from Indiā. Ancient trade routes are still important to the traders and pilgrims as it was in the past. Asoka, Chinese pilgrims, Khasa kings as well as devotees had visitd here. Tourist from more than 80 countries usually come to visit per year at the complex. Its archaeological as well as Buddhist heritages are the major attractions to the Buddhists and non-Buddhists people.

CHAPTER THREE

BUDDHIST HERITAGES

Lumbinī, being the birthplace of Gautam Buddha, have been visiting by many VVIP, VIP, monks, nuns and general devotees from ancient period to modern period. In course of this movement, late King Mahendra had visited Limbini on the occasion of the Fourth World Buddhist Summit in 1956 (Falgun7, 2012). He had shown keen interest in developing Lumbinī as a sacred complex for all the human beings. After the visit to Lumbinī in 1967 U-Thant, then Secretary General of United Nations Organization had suggested to HMG of Nepāl that Lumbinī should be developed as a place of pilgrimage and tourist centre equipped with accommodations. A three member team of UNO Mission had specific instructions to advise the Government on the infrastructural requirements, viz. transportation facilities, drinking water, energy and appropriate accommodation for the visitors from the tenth December to 9th January 1968. In 1970 an International Committee was constituted with the support of the United Nations known as "International Lumbinī Development Committee" under the chairmanship of the permanent representative of Nepāl (CDL,1970: Introduction). The committee constituted of the representatives of Śri Lankā, Pākistan, Indiā, Myānmār, Thāiland, Afghānistān, Cambodiā, Indonesiā, Laos, Malayasiā, Jāpan, Siṅgāpore and Nepāl. Bhutān and South-Koreā later joined the committee. The committee had the representatives of 15 nations under the chairmanship of UNO. UNDP had contributed through them one million dollars in order to prepare the Master Plan for the development of Lumbinī including archaeological and engineering activities (UNESCO, 2013.b:18).

The Master Plan was prepared by Kenzo Tange and Urtec. The first phase of the outline design for Lumbinī development was completed and the report was circulated in September 1972. The Plan was completed in 1978. With a total area of 25 sq. miles, only 3 sq. mile is main core area of Lumbinī plan. One sq. mile in each sector on south, east and west is separated as restricted area. After the restricted area one sq. mile on east, one sq. mile on west and two sq. mile on south is planned Agriculture Zone (Buffer zone) It is to be remarked that 21st meeting of World Conservation Society held during 1-6 December, 1997 has mentioned Lumbinī as one of the World Heritage Sites. Project Area is divided into three zones (1 sq. mile each), viz. New Lumbinī Village, Monastic zone and Sacred Garden. To start with, the first phase of Master Plan was land acquisition because earlier only the area of Māyādevi temple belonged to the Master Plan.

Sacred Garden

The Sacred Garden is the focal point of Lumbinī as it is the exact birthplace of Lord Buddha (UNESCO, 2013.b:21-22). Its form of a circle enclosing square is a universal symbol of purity, peace and simplicity. The squares have proposed by a network of raised walkways between the landscaping and archaeological areas. The Garden is surrounded by the ponds and a circular levee as mentioned in plan (LDT, 2067;18-23). In order to preserve the historical integrity and combination of the location, new construction is strictly prohibited. Philosophically and symbolically when the visitors will cross a bridge over the circular levee from the Monastic zone to Sacred Garden they will feel the spirit and simple approach of Buddhism after entering there. According to Master Plan there should be no temple or monument, but a simple garden kept much as it was when Siddhartha Gautam was born.

Aśoka pillar, Māyādevi temple, Puskarini pond, ruined structures of ancient vihar and stūpas have been exposed in course of excavations. JBF, DOA and LDT have obtained an important findings, i.e. Marker Stone, Siddhartha Yasodhara terracotta panel, in course of restoration of Māyādevi temple. According to the provision of Master Plan a Circular levee link to protect the sacred site from flooding, especially north-west side of this zone, and to preserve the archaeological sites. The plan has designed four ponds around the circular levee. Earthworks, retaining structure and slope turfing for the pond in the north-east quadrant have been completed. The depth of the pond is

3.25m., the bottom level is 96 cm and the water level is 97 cm from the sea level (LDT, 2012:26). The four ponds will maintain the perennial source of at least 1 m water level to enhance the beauty of the entire holy site as per the Master Plan.

Aśokan Pillar

Lumbinī, the birth place of Buddha, was discovered on 1st December 1896 in course of exploration under the leadership of Rana and Fûhrer. The most interesting piece of antiquity, the sandstone pillar carrying characteristic Mauryan polish and having tiny blackish specks, was found here which provided a documentary evidence of Emperor Aśoka of third century BC The pillar is made of Chunar sandstone, as are other Aśokan pillars in Indiā and Nepāl. The height of the extant part, above the rough hammer-dressed surface meant to be buried below ground, is 7.391 m. The crowning elements of the pillar, which were unknown, are lying on the paved platform in front of the Māyādevi temple. At the height of 3 m 41 cm above the rough surface of the stone pillar is engraved an inscription in five lines of *Priyadarsi* (Aśoka) recording that after twenty years of his coronation he had come to the spot where Buddha was born. He had also erected a stone wall around the place as well as a commemorative pillar. Aśoka exempted the village of Lumbinī from paying taxes except only one\eight of the product (Fûhrer, 1972:33). The pillar tapers slightly upwards. Its circumference at the base is 2 m.51cm. and near the inscribed portion, it is 2m. 25 cm. At the top of the pillar it is 1 m. 97cm.

The pillar has vertical fissure down to the pillar and its top is broken off, probably, by lightening, as noted by Hiuen-Tsang. The capital of the pillar was bell- shaped. Its base, broken into two halves, still exists. The capital shows the usual festoon in the face of the big cyma under which there was one 30.47cm. deep hole of 12.5 cm. diameter in which was fitted the copper mortice that was fixed above the shaft. Its slender tapering towards the top, mirror like Mauryan shining polish and sophisticated chiselling indicate that it was made by the skillful Mauryan masons. The horse surmounting the top was broken into pieces due to lightning flash which penetrated into it from above, the effect of which can be seen at the top even at present. Mukherji has also noticed the bell-shaped capital of Aśokan pillar, broken into two halves and stored in the temple compound (Mukherji, 1969:34). In course of excavation of the site many pieces of chunar sandstone, with and without Aśokan polish, and some of the pieces of the Aśokan pillar-capital were also recovered. It proves that after the erection of the pillar by Aśoka it was destroyed, possibly by thunderbolt and lightening. In course of excavation at the Māyādevi temple foundation two pieces of the pillar were found in the central chamber and one piece in the side chamber (Uesaka, 1997:8). Rijal has claimed that 15 chambers were filled in third-fourth centuries AD. Three pieces of the Aśokan pillar were found in the filling of the first temple complex. They carry evidences which indicate lightening stroke that fell the Aśokan pillar in about third or fourth centuries AD. Hiuen-Tsang, therefore, had seen it in the seventh century AD. However, Fa-Hien did not mention any information about the Aśokan pillar and Māyādevi temple.

Fûhrer and Rana did not excavate the basement of the monolithic stone pillar at the site. They measured Aśokan pillar and found 91.3 cm. of it below the surface of the soil and 2 m. 95 cm. above the base of the pillar. Mukherji also could not go down to the foundation. Mitra wanted to reach at the bottom of the pillar to know the height of the hammer-dressed portion and its contrivance. She could not go beyond 51cm. below the polished portion because of the intervention of the Commissioner. Railing attached to a building is the basic component of the Buddhist architecture from the ancient period. Its popularity soared to the climax in the post-Mauryan epoch by about the second century BC, when important stûpas like Bharhut, Sānchi, Mathurā, Sāranātha, Bodhagayā and Amarāvatī were built or enlarged. This architectural feature might have begun during the period of Aśoka as we find a mention of "*Silā-vigada-bhicha*" in the Rummindei (Lumbinī) pillar inscription which indicates, most probably, the presence of some kind of railing around the Aśokan pillar installed at the birthplace of Lord Buddha. An inscribed *harmika*-railing with typical Mauryan polish was brought to light from Saranatha. During the Suṅga period, every portion of the stone railing was richly carved in bas-relief portraying incidents of the Jātakas, or scenes connected with the life of Buddha (Brown, 1976:14). The openings in the stûpa railing form the entrance where imposing gateway were erected.

Māyādevi Temple

Lumbinī has been associated with Buddhism and is known as "Buddhist Land". Many structural remains as well as unexcavated mounds are scattered all over the area in Lumbinī. However, because of limited archeological activities, the evidence of separate existence of temples is quite limited, except the Māyādevi temple of Lumbinī. The Sikhar style temple of Māyādevi was not found in its original shape and size because it was never reconstructed for a long time, i.e. from the Mauryan period to the eighth century AD. The original basement of the temple was 26 m. east-west and 21 m. in north-south direction from outside of the walls. It's inside walls measure 20 m. east to west and 16 m. north south. There are 15 chambers arranged in five rows in east-west and three rows in north-south direction. All the chambers are rectangular in size except chamber 2, 5 and 8 which are square in size. A conglomerate stone (a pebble sand stone of the Siwalik hill) was found at the center of second row in chamber 2 on the west side of central row on the east west axis. Various antiquities including punched silver coins and numerous NBP ware pieces were found here. From the *kundus* polished pieces of Aśokan pillar of Chunar sandstone were also found (Rijal, 1997:3). The temple is in *saptaratha* pattern and made of moulded bricks. Five phases of the temple construction, viz. the Mauryan, the Suṅga, the Kushana the Gupta and the late Gupta have been noticed in course of excavation. The box chamber of the structure is called *maṇdala*.

The *maṇdala* structure was built as high platform to erect the earliest Gupta temple to install the nativity image of Māyādevi. In the third phase, the stone marker was covered by a square votive platform in front of the nativity sculpture. During the fourth stage, a *saptaratha* temple was erected over the Gupta temple in 8-9th century AD. From 1200 AD the site was gradually forgotten by the pilgrims due to the decline of Buddhism and Muslim invasion in the region. According to Tulsi Ram Vaidya, former Vice Chancellar of Lumbinī Bauddha University, all these structural remains might have demolished because of devastating earthquake during the period. During his exploration and excavation Mukherji mentioned the structure of the ruined temple of Māyādevi in Lumbinī. It was in curvilinear style and a *saptaratha* type in plan, measuring 3.65 x 3.04 m. A sanctum was provided at the rear back with six flight of steps from the east. The size of the temple was 14.62 x 9.14 m. in length and breadth respectively. Mukherji had noticed four successive phases of construction. The lowest position of the wall was plain with two courses of bricks being ornamented and carved in circular design. A floriated cyma was seen standing above it. Lotus-petals, *gala* (neck), *dasa*, cyma and *kumbha* were

He is of the opinion that there should be remains of the old temple structure below the present temple. Rijal exposed the eastern plinth of the temple, but he did not mention any detail of it in his report. The temple was linked up with the Śākyan tank by a cause-way for taking a bath by the devotees before worshipping in the shrine. The foundation of Māyādevi temple has deteriorated due to the unusual growth of roots of a Linden tree. JBF and LDT have signed on an agreement in September 1990 to restore Māyādevi temple. In June 1991 another memoranda for the same purpose was signed. The tribunal team of LDT, DOA and JBF has conducted archaeological work in the Māyādevi temple complex during 1992 to 1996 (UNESCO, 2013.b:7). During this work six phases of the various periods of the structure were exposed. In the first phase, Aśokan bricks were found on the north- west corner of the temple. On this spot, Rijal had found an oblong brick structure with rammed floor measuring 4.72×3.78 m. during 1976–78. An oblong structure below the Mauryan square stûpa was found there. The bricks measure 38×25.3×7.6 cm. in size. The pre-Aśokan structure was, perhaps, destroyed during constructions in the Mauryan period.

During the period of Aśoka the construction with burnt bricks and perhaps, with stone fragements, was done around the Nativity site. Antiquities related to the Mauryan period-coins, punched silver coins and numerous Northern Black Polished (NBP) sherds and earthen ware were also found. In the second stage, a rectangular shaped chamber on east-west axis, measuring 1.87m, 1.22 m. in north- south direction, was located directly above chamber 2 of stage I. In the center four pieces of sand stone were found of which two were rectangular in size. The whole temple was again encircled by a compound wall with brick-paved floor for circumambulatory path. The third phase of the temple was encircled with five irregular pits in which stone pieces of the same proportion might have been erected in the style of an *Apsidal* square cell. The important architectural element is the corbelled niche with a few stone pieces in it. The conglomerate stone (70x40x10 cm.) was found in this part, having a corbelled niche.

Being very important monument of the sacred site of Lumbinī, the old temple is protected and preserved in its original shape and size as recommended by Tange in the Master Plan. In course of excavation during 1984-85, Mishra had exposed two basements of Buddhist brick temples and a 12.1916 m. long wall. Most probably, a compound wall running east to west had also been found in the southern side of running east to west had also been found in the southern side of Māyādevi temple which was repaired. In course of excavation Mauryan, Sunga, Kushana and Gupta remaims had also exposed during the period of 2011-2013 (LDT, 3013:16-18).

The Nativity Sculpture of Buddha

A nativity image of Buddha from the Lumbinī measuring 167x106 cm shows Māyādevi giving birth to Buddha from her right side under the *sāl* tree and grasping its branch with her right hand while the left hand is resting on her waist (*katyavalambita*). The deity (she) wears a solid earlobe (*ratnakuṇdala or mukta-phala kuṇdala*), armlet in her right hand, and one piece of heavy anklet (*Tulākoṭi or Hansaka*). Curly hairs on both sides of her head are visible in the relief. Her waist is held by Prajāpatī (Gautamī) from her right side as is usual during delivery. Her oval face and curly hairs are depicted in a beautiful manner. On extreme right in the relief is executed a figure of Brahmā, wearing *karaṇdaka mukuṭa* catching the body, perhaps on a cloth, having been delivered by Māyādevi. Behind Brahmā, Indra (Sakra) is depicted wearing a *kiriṭa mukuṭa* and watching the birth scene. Down the centre of the panel is executed the figure of prince Siddhartha probably standing on a lotus flower with a circular halo (*prabhāmaṇdala*) behind his head. Broken into three parts the panel has been divided into three horizontal sections on which the latest figure of *Māyādevi* is executed in the first line in the upper part. In the second and the third lines figures of Prajāpatī (Gautamī), Brahmā, Indra and Siddartha Gautam are depicted. Scholars have dated of the panel on the basis of its style. Führer was first to inform this sculpture. However, he did not mention the details of this panel. Mukherji is of the opinion that the sculpture may be associated with the time of Aśoka as he found similarity in material and workmanship of Yaksha with the door-keepers of Pātaliputra belonging to the Mauryan period.

V.S. Agrawal is of the view that it may belong to the Kushāṇa period as the style of the *dhoti* of *Māyādevi*, wavy flowing locks of hair of Gautami, projecting high crown of Indra and *mukuṭa* of a male figure seems to be in a style of that period. Mitra however placed the sculpture in the Gupta period. Krishṇadeva, an eminent scholar of art history of Indiā, says that this sculptural panel may be dated in 400 AD. Mishra places this panel in about 300 AD. Pandey agrees with the opinion of making of this panel. Venerable Bhikkshu Sudarsan is of the view that the term *silā vigadabhica kālāpita* in Aśokan pillar refers to this *Māyādevi* image. Execution of Buddhist images, including the nativity sculptures of Buddha, began in first century AD at two art centres-Mathurā and Gandhara.

Sculptures originating in Mathurā were sent to sacred places at Sāranātha, Kuśinagar (Kasiā), Śrāvasti and Lumbinī from where the present Nativity groups of sculpures are available Agrawal, 1965:163). Chinese Yech-Chi monk Shengtsai saw it during the course of his visit between 250-375 AD at Lumbni (Petech, 1950:35). It proves that the sculpture was established there before his pilgrimage of the site. Thus, the present sculpture belonging to the second-third century AD. is the earliest and the best of all the Nativity panels so far discovered from the sub-continent.

Vajravārāhi image

Vajravārāhi image from Lumbinī in *sthānaka* pose, measuring 122x 55cm., belongs to the Gupta period (Pandey,1985:58). Two-armed deity holds a discus in the right hand and the left one is broken. The deity wears waist-band, *sādi* upto the heel and other usual ornaments. Two circular lines are executed at the back of the head. Halo of the panel is decorated with floral and geometrical designs. The relief is broken into two halves across the breast (Mukherji, 1969:36). Other parts are not clearly visible due to its damaged-condition.

Dharmachakra

Before the representation of Buddha in human form, he was represented through one or more symbols with decorative themes in the Buddhist art tradition. He was represented by *Chaitya-vṛiksha, Bodhi- druma,* stūpa, *Dharmachakra,* deer park, lion, bull, cow, halo, foot-prints, coffin, riderless horse and turban associated with a story in the life of Buddha, his message and events connected with this history of Buddhism. According to Buddhist tradition a *Bodhi* tree, a wheel, a stūpa and a *sāl* tree symbolic the memory of holy places connected with the life of Buddha, viz. Bodhagayā, Sāranāth, Kuśinagar and Lumbinī. Nativity sculptures of the region may be representation of Kapilvastu.

Dharmachakra is also available from Lumbinī. The sculptures of Buddha in various forms were executed first during the Kushāṇa period at Mathura, dominating the northern part of the country, and influenced as well as inspired other subsequent schools of art (Giri, 2003). Stone sculptures of Buddha used to be brought back from the holy places as a small material souvenir of what they had there seen.

Buddha Images

A head of Buddha, measuring 7.5 cm. high and 5 cm. wide, is executed with a plain bump like *ushnisha* and *urna* marked on the forehead, open eyes and smiling face (Mitra, 1972:199). The sculpture is of red sandstone which came from the atelier of Mathura. On the basis of style, it is ascrible to the Kushāṇa period. One other Buddha sculpture of chlorite from Lumbinī, measuring 17cm.x 12cm., is in *bhumi-sparsa-mudrā*. He is seated in *vajra-parayaṅkāśana* on a damaged *visvapadama* below the *Bodhi* tree. Another fragment of Buddha of chlorite measuring 11.5 cm. high in *bhumi-sparsa mudrā* is seated in *vajra-parayaṅkāśana* on a fully blossomed lotus. Two badly defaced figures including a hooded-*naga* are supporting the lotus. On the basis of art style the figure representing the Miracle of Śrāvasti, belong to the Gupta period. The sculpture from Sainā mainā, now placed in Lumbinī Development Trust office in Lumbinī, measuring 78x65 cm, is seated on lotus in *bhumi-sparsa mudrā* (Giri, 2003:205). A portion of the head is broken.

The deity seated crossed-legged in *dhyāna-mudrā*. The right hand displaying is in earth-touching pose and the left hand is broken. Buddha wears usual dress and ornaments ascribable to the Gupta period.

A sculpture of eight great miracles presents the figure of Buddha in *Vajra-parayankāśana* on a double petalled lotus and his damaged right hand shows *bhumisparsa-mudrā*. The deity wears *dhoti* and a scarf; the latter with ends tucked on the left shoulder has left the right chest and shoulder bare. Around the figure of Buddha are represented the seven other great incidents of Buddha's life. In the birth scene, Buddha is seen on the right side of his mother, holding a branch of Aśoka tree (?) and left hand resting on her hip. Above the birth scene of Buddha is seated in *Vajarparyankāśana* on a double lotus displaying hands in *dharma-chakra-pravartana-mudrā*. The sculpture measuring 18cmx17.5 cm. from Lumbinī is made of greyish sandstone (Miṭra, 1972:200). Remaining figures of the birth and the first sermon are offering of honey of the sinister.

figures of the birth and the first sermon are offering of honey of the sinister.

Maitreya

22×14 cm. high greyish sandstone sculpture of Maitreya from Lumbinī is crudely executed in *lalitāśana mudrā* (Mitra, 1972:200). Bodhisattva depicted in *vyākhyana-mudrā* wears a *hāra* and a *jatā mukuṭa* with, possibly, a stūpa in it. The branch of a *nāgakesara* with three leaves and a flower passes through the left armpit. Another branch with four leaves and a flower is also shown on the right side of the figure. Thus, Maitreya is shown in traditional ī *śana mudrā* with a stūpa figure on the *mukuṭa*. The image agrees with the description of the *Sādana mālā* as well.

Bodhisattva

Two-armed image of Bodhisattva of buff-coloured stone from Lumbinī is 7 cm in height and 4.8 cm in width. It is seated in *lalitaśana* pose. It is shown resting with one leg on a double lotus pedestal and the other one is placed on a two-tiered pedestal. The deity is wearing a long *dhoti* a girdle diaphanous scarf like object in *upavita* fashion, an *upavita* and a tall *jatā-mukuṭa*. The Bodhisattva in *vyākhyana-mudrā* is shown with half-closed eyes, graceful flexion and sensitively modelled limbs. The stalks of the flower pass through both the armpits. On the top of the relief, the corner is encircled with a row of petals. The panel belonging to the eighth-the ninth century is in the *mudrā* of *Manjushri* and *Maitreya*

Ratnasambhava

A head of Bodhisattva measuring 12 cm high exhibits the features of Ratnasambhava (Ibid). The figure of *dhyani*-Buddha is executed with half-closed eyes and a short crown with a decked triangular piece at the bottom of the long *jatāmukuṭa*. On the basis of the features of the fragment its right hand seems to be in *varada-mudrā*.

Padampāṇi Avalokiteśvar

A bronze figure of Padampāni measuring 11 cm. in height from Lumbinī is shown holding a stalk of a fully-bloomed lotus in the right hand (Mitra: 203). The deity wears *dhoti* without *kachchha*, a folded scarf around his waist elaborated double bangle, a plain *hāra, kundalas*, a waist-band and a short *mukuṭa*, probably a part of a turban. The attribute in the left hand is seen like a *vajra* with its both ends in the form of prongs. The figure belongs to the late Kushāṇa period type of stone greenish black stone belonging to the tenth century AD. The deity holds a full-blossomed lotus stalk in his left hand and the other one is missing. The high *jatā-mukuṭa* is decked with a tiny figure of Amitaba, a fan-shaped projection and a stūpa on the head.

Puskariṇi

Ring wells were built in many residential complexes, vihārs and the Royal complex to provide drinking water in ancient period. Its method, model, technique and materials were used according to the geographical location and interests of the builders. In Lumbinī ring well is made of kiln-burnt bricks. The ring well is significant from the utilitarian as well as religious points of view even now. The Śākya tank of Lumbnini was originally oval–shaped. In the Buddhist literature it is called *Puskariṇi* or *Siddharth kupa*. Māyādevi was provided with hot and cold water before and after the birth of Siddhartha (Beal, 1994:25). The Chinese pilgrim Fa-Hien had also mentioned that in Lumbinī garden, queen (Māyādevi) entered the pond and bathed there. It denotes the significance of the sacred pond. On the south of this tank is standing a sacred old Pipal tree. It is the symbol of peace and harmony. In the seventh century AD Hiuen-Tsiang had also pointed out the bathing tank of the Śākyas which had bright and clear water like mirror and its surface was covered with mixed flowers. This tank undoubtedly represents the bathing tank of the Śākyas as mentioned by Huien-Tsiang (Mitra, 1972:198) As the legend goes, on the occasion of the birth of Lord Buddha, dragons had poured down first cold water and thereafter warm water from their mouth to wash the prince.

These details prove that the tank was in existence until seventh century AD. The tank must have been buried or filled up with rubbish in course of times. In 1939 Rana got it cleaned and made it *pakka* by using kiln-burnt bricks. 15.2395 m. square tank shows six terraces and a flight of steps far descending upto the water level. After the birth of Lord Buddha in Lumbinī garden the tank got changed into a sacred pond, which was being used by general public before this event. Within the archaeological site of Lumbinī a terracotta ring-well as well as some antiquities belonging to sixth century BC were found from the lowest level. A large number of Kushāṇa figurines are also reported from the habitation-mounds, as well as, two brick-walls from the upper level. During 1970-71, three more such type of the new wells were exposed in the area. A brick-well, datable to the Kushāṇa period, was discovered from the nursery field of Lumbinī in 1983. It was exposed upto the bottom with 29 courses of solid concave bricks which were well elaborated with the symbols of horse, elephant, boar, palm tree, conch etc. At the bottom of the well a few Kushāṇa spouted pots as well as faceted pots used for *Nāga* worship were found.

Stûpa

The word stûpa refers to a Buddhist monument, generally of a pyramidal or dome like form, erected over the sacred relics of the great Buddha. In Pāli *thuipikata* means heaped up or heaped of an alms bowl. Ṣtûpa thus became a symbol of supremacy and stability of an order. Stûpas commemorate essential moments of the life and famous miracles of Lord Buddha. It is an ancient architectural element in the Buddhist world. Originally, it contained the relics of Buddha and represented *Pariniravāṇa*. It became religious component to those who wanted some concrete form to worship before the image. The practice of erecting stûpas over corporal relics is of pre-Buddhist tradition. Earlier stûpas or chaitays, either in the shape of a tumulus or made of perishable materials, must have been in existence before Aśoka. It is clear from the declaration and instructions given to Ānanda by his master, Lord Buddha that his bones and other remains were to be kept under a dome after cremation. It is thus clear that stûpas were popular in the Buddhist religion and society right at the time of the death of Lord Buddha.

The Buddhist stūpas are categorized into four groups, viz. (a) *Sāririka,* those erected over the corporal relics of Buddha, his disciples, Buddhist teachers and saints (b) *Paribhogikā*, erected over the objects used by Buddha, like robe, begging-bowl, cloths etc. (c) *Uddesika,* commemorative of the Buddha's life, (d) Votive, those which were small in size and mostly erected by the pilgrims when they visited the sacred places. Main components of the stūpas have been changing according to the interest of the builders and situation from the ancient to modern period. In the beginning, the stûpa used to be a low hemispherical dome (*aṇda*), raised on a basal cylinder (*medhi*). Circumambulatory path was provided around the *aṇda* and on the top of the *aṇda,* a *harmika* was made enclosing the *chhatra* or a series of *chhatras*. Later on lower circumambulating path of the stûpa was constructed and the railing was made of wood, stone or brick adjoining the elaborate entrances.

circumambulating path of the stûpa was constructed and the railing was made of wood, stone or brick adjoining the elaborate entrances.

The exterior components of the solidly-constructed stûpa was smoothened with lime, clay or concrete plaster. Later the *medhi* was filled-up with appropriate packing materials to provide additional strength to the stûpa to bear the weight of its huge hemispherical top. Due to the influences of Hindu temple architecture various components of the stūpas were decorated and other additional parts were also added to it.

Unfortunately, the main (original) shape, size and features of the ancient stūpas are not available because of later reconstructions from time to time. In the beginning earthen funeral mounds were made of layers of mud which used to be separated from one another by thinner layers of *kankar* and ashy clay. The earliest definitely dated stupas were made by Mauryan Emperor Aśoka. They are provided with hemispherical dome of brick- work with *medhi* as its base. It is surmounted by a dome or umbrellas with square railing. The top of the drum was also utilized as an elevated processional path during this period. Brick stûpas of Aśoka with veneer of hammer-dressed stone, was converted in the second century BC into an almost hemispherical dome flattened near the top, crowned by three superimposed umbrellas, *yasthi*, *harmikā* and *vedikā*. *Medhi*, *sopanā* and circumambulation path were also added as the elements of the stūpas. The earliest stūpas were built solid. But in later times, when ostentatious stūpas of great height came to be erected by filling the core used to be filled with earth or rubble in order to economize the building materials, i.e. brick or stone as the case may be. During this period box-chambers built by network of walls were also filled with earth.

From the Kushāṇa period onwards the drum (*medhi*) grew in height as compared to its diameter and turned into a tall cylinder dominating the dome. Projected niches were made, as in temples, to install the images of Buddha or other divinities of the Buddhist pantheon. During the Gupta period four images of Buddha were kept at four cardinal points of the stūpas. In the Gandhara period, the drum was built in diminishing terraces and the facade was elaborately embellished. The low hemisphere of the earliest stūpas was changed into a tall figure with ornamental tower on the platform, drum and *chhatravali*. The shape and size of the stūpas were so radically changed that it became difficult to recognize the original form and its importance without the knowledge of the intermediate stages. The changing modes as well as the stages in its development could not be studied without the support of the stone and metal miniatures, rock-cut specimens due to the absence of the preserved complete superstructure. All the structures cannot be clearly classified into various periods in chronological order due to reconstruction and repair from time to time. Each stûpa shows the impact of many periods.

Buddha had forbidden his disciples to make his images. As such stûpas were built after his death at the spots related with him during his life time to commemorate him. His followers in Lumbinī might have built many stûpas in the fifth century BC (Pandey, 1985:54). Pre-Mauryan stûpas were enlarged by Aśoka during his visit of the place in the third century BC. This stûpa was buried under the plinth of the brick temple, which was excavated under the aegis of the LDT and JBF during 1992-97. The earliest structure of the site had been exposed to the north-west corner of Māyādevi temple. The texture of the brick used to build a rectangular room was very rough as it contained much husk and straw. These rough bricks could probably be dated tentatively in the pre-Mauryan period. Thus, it is clear that building activities had already been started in Lumbinī area during the lifetime of Lord Buddha himself.

Pre-Mauryan stûpas were repaired and rebuilt during the Mauryan period features and tradition of which are clearly seen in the structures available in course of excavation. Thirty-four stûpas of Lumbinī are directly associated with this period. The stûpas during this period were plain with two steppings at the basement. These monuments seem to have been built with kiln- burnt bricks and their interior chambers being filled-up with lumps of clay. The lid of the vessel was broken into pieces, most probably in the course of excavations conducted between1933-39 and the remains in it were found scattered over the ground (Rijal, 1975-77:32). Various phases of the monuments have been described when discovered in archaeological excavations (Mishra, 1996:42). Mauryan stûpas of the region are plain with their basements having two steppings.

These seem to have been built with kiln-burnt bricks. The interior portion of these stûpas was filled up with clay-lumps. They carry low hemispheres on their squarish drums including *harmikas* on the top. In course of excavation, Mukherji had postulated that the foundation of the original temple of Māyādevi is embedded in the mound This could foundation of the present temple was exposed. The foundation of Māyādevi temple is based upon fifteen square chambers in the grid of five rows from east to west and three columns from south to north. Two kinds of NBP (Black and Brown), typical red ware, punch-marked coins and copper coins were recovered in the chambers belonging to Mauryan period. A piece of natural rock (a hard conglomerate) having dimensions of 70 cm x 40 cm x10 cm. with its axis running in south to north direction was found in the central chamber.

It has been interpreted that Aśoka had built a square *Bodhi mandal chaitya* consisting of nine box chambers with the stone marking the 'birth spot' in the first central chamber. In the second phase six more chambers were added to make a total of it 15 within the centre of a concentric square huge Bodhi stûpa at the spot. In course of excavation, Mishra had discovered some very important stûpas among the ninten big and small stûpas in the complex of Māyādevi temple in Lumbinī. They belong to different periods. They were of various sizes and shapes. Thus, it is clear that the shape and size of the original stûpa was changed from time to time (Mishra, 1996:42).

Vihār

In the beginning, followers of Buddha used to stay in a forest, under a tree, on a hill side, in a glen, a cemetery, a mountain cave, in the open air, a forest glade and on a heap of straw. During three months of the rainy season, they took shelter in the caves or under trees or in sanctuaries, begging around the periphery of their abode. Thus, a monastery or vihār was a hostel of the Buddhist monks during the lifetime of Gautam Buddha. Verandah, bathroom, drain, shrine, courtyard, kitchen, refectory, privy, storeroom, assembly–hall and scullery are provided in the structure of the vihār. To both sides of the entrance gate cells are built. One of them is used as a guardroom and the other for Goddess *Hāriti*. In the courtyard of the complex a well is built to supply drinking water to the monks and nuns residing in the vihārs. Verandah is used as the waiting place for the guests, monks and nuns visiting to the complex. Places of residence in the east were generally with the rooms opening on to an interior quadrangle making plain outside walls to secure both privacy and protection. However, the construction of the vihār may differ according to the interest, needs of the sects and changing modes of the architectural styles of different ages.

During his visit Aśoka built a huge stûpa and installed a monolithic stone pillar to commemorate the spot of nativity of Lord Buddha. On this occasion monks and nuns required vihāras to retire in the night and to stay during the day at Lumbinī. Some of the ruins of the monasteries have been exposed in course of excavation (Mishra, 1996:40-42). In 1898 Mukherji had exposed the square structure of a low mound to the south-east corner of the Māyādevi temple. The mound yielded a mass of solid brick-work. Its original structure was not exposed due to incomplete excavation of the site. About 33m.52cm. south-east of the temple there was another mound (monastery) of which some walls were running north-east and south-east. The complete structure was, however, not exposed on this occasion. Although Mukherjee could not expose all the monuments, he expressed hope that the site is enriched with the ancient mounds.

During excavations in 1984 and 1985, Mishra discovered four vihārs to the south of Māyādevi temple. These monuments are built in a row from east to west. Exposed monuments reveal that might have been encircled by stûpas as well as the Aśokan stone pillar, which are partially exposed even now. 1m. 21.9cm.west of the vihār No.1 is situated vihār No.2 dated in the Mauryan period. There are living rooms in four directions and a meeting hall in the center. Rebuilt Kushan structure has yielded fourteen rooms in three directions, except to the east where there existed a courtyard (Ibid). In the western portion of the complex there is a verandah facing to the east.

Exposed walls also overlapped due to the repair and reconstruction from time to time at the same place. The earliest position of the perishable materials, i.e. wood, bamboo and dry-grass, are not clearly known. However, generally vihārs where built on a quadrangular plan consisting of a series of cells being enclosed on three sides and the remaining open side was used as a gateway. Cells of different size and shapes were built around the courtyard providing communication to the monks and nuns in the complex. Verandah, bath-room, drain, kitchen, meditation-room, store-room, assembly-hall and other apartments were provided in the structure of the vihārs. In this structure the image of Buddha was housed to be worshiped by the devotees during their leisure period. After the collapse of the structure of the vihār, remaining fragments of Buddha images are found in courses of excavation from the site, especially from the Lumbinī complex. Modern structures of Lumbinī vihārs represent its significance and throw light on the nature of ancient vihārs.

Circular Levee

Circular Levee link is made to protect the sacred site from flooding and to preserve the archaeological structural remains. Four ponds are dug around the Sacred Garden. Depth of the pond is 3.25 meter, Bottom level and water level are 96 and 97 meter from the sea level rerspectively.

Peace Flame

Then Prince and Chairman of LDT Gyanendra Bir Bikram Shah lit a torch of eternal peace in Lumbinī in commemoration of the International Year of Peace in 1986. The Eternal Peace Flame in Lumbinī is still burning as a symbol of World Peace.

Peace Bell

Immediately west of Peace Flame a Peace Bell is hung on horizontal bar. It is donated by Nyigma Meditation Centre USA and 2.5 ton in weight.

Central Link Canal

Central link canal is 1464 meter in length from north to south, 1.55 meter in depth, four boat stations and 16 meter in width between the eastern Theravada and western Mahayan Monastic zone. This central link establishes the sanctity of the sacred Garden. It will be used for boating to disabled, old visitors as well as foreign pilgrims to feel peace and harmony (UNESCO, 2013.b:24).

Monastic Zone

Monastic zone is situated in the centre within the forest area, north of the Sacred Garden complex which is divided into two halves East and West Monastic zone, with a canal originating from the Eternal Peace Flame a symbol of peace and prosperity of human existence. There are 42 plots for Theravāda and Mahāyān monasteries, Stūpa and meditation centres on east and west respectively. According to Master Plan central canal should be constructed in beautification with water-lilly flowers on its bank, soundless leg-boating system to the interested visitors, green-field on both sites and resting chairs. Facilities of public-toilets, cold-drinks etc. are also proposed in Master Plan. Ever green varieties of plantation in 16 lines of 14 types of plants have been proposed. Eastern zone is for Theravadi (Hinayan) and Western zone is separated for Mahayan and Vajrayān Stūpa, Vihar, Monaseries and Bahāls Central bridge for adjoining the eastern and western complex is also mentioned in plan (Fig.10). Monastic zone is also divided into three parts on the basis of a coverage area, consisting 80, 120 and 160 meter in area.

Table 3.1

Plot-Division

S. No.	*Area of Plots.*	*Western (Mahayan) Zone, No. of plots.*	*Eastern(Theravada) Zone, No. of plots.*	*Total of Plots.*
1.	160 × 160 m.	2	-	2
2.	120 × 120 m.	6	3	9
3.	80 × 80 m.	20	10	30
4.	Meditation centre	1	1	2
	Total.	29	14	43

The governmental and non-governmental organizations of 15 nations have been alloted for the construction of monasteries in the international monastic zone. The east monastic zone has 13 plots and one site as meditation centre while the west monastic has 28 plots and one meditation centre. Ten western plots are assigned to five countries, i.e., Myānmār, Nepāl, Śri Laṅkā, Indiā and Thāiland each with two. Myānmār and Nepāl have taken plots in eastern as well as western zone. The government of China and Myānmār, the Mahabodhi Society of Indiā, the International Nun's Association, the Manang Sewa Samaja Geden International of Austria, Lotus Stupa of Germany and the Lama Monastery of Dharmodaya Sabha, Nepāl and have completed the construction and is operating to the visitors. The governments of Thāiland, Srilanka, the Linhson of France, the temple of Viettnam , the Mahabodhi Society of South Koreā the Sokyo of Jāpān and Nepāl Baudha Sangha have been constructing proper monasteries, stūpa and meditation centres. The governments of Bhutan and Mongolia as well as various organizations of Nepāl have also shown keen interest to construct vihar, Stūpa and monasteries in this sacred complex of Lumbinī.

The east and west monastic zones set aside for the two major sects of Buddhism. Theravada (Hinayan) and Mahayan have witnessed a number of developments by friendly states and institutions. These Stūpa, vihar and monasteries have developed Lumbinī as "A Mini

Stūpa, vihar and monasteries have developed Lumbinī as "A Mini World of Buddhism". Each of them has constructed its building own their national tradition and techniques, based on architectural and religious trends. Some of them have been providing accommodation to pilgrims as well as visitors upon payment in different forms. Koreān, Myānmār, Vietnamese and International Bhikshuni Sangh have providing such services to the visitors at present. 6 *lakha* trees were planted in monastic and New Lumbinī area. Planting and re-planting of trees along the central canal, roads, around Bus Park, car park and as specified in the Master plan. Many *kadamba* trees and bottle brush trees along the central canal are missing and need to be replanted.

Cultural Zone

Friendship bridge over the Harahawa river is the borderline of monastic zone and cultural zone. LIRI, museum and U-Thant auditorium hall are the proposed components at this complex. Research centre, library and museum are operating for public services. Auditorum hall is under construction with the financial support of Indian Government.

Friendship Bridge

Bridge of Harhawa River was construction by World Federation of Buddhism and partly loan from bank. It is the linkage of monasty and cultural zone of Master Plan.

Lumbinī International Research Institute (LIRI)

It is contributed by Reiyukai, Jāpān and situated at Master Plan grid-points, X-13 Y-37; Cultural complex (Fig.20). It is running under the operation of Reiyukai, Jāpān as Research Institute Library and scholar residence. It was inaugurated by Late King Birendra and Queen Aishwary on February 6, 1996. It has providing various facilities to the scholars. The building contains about 50 rooms, which includes the library stocks, a meeting and microfilm-room, book-acquistition, restauration-room, three administrative offices, several study and research rooms, a dormitory, a cafeteria, the main kitchen, some tea kitchenettes and two lounges. There are also Lecturer rooms, Professor's room, Director's room and central Foyer. The main entrance hall is open to the general public, and here visitors will find introductory material viz., books, booklets, brochure and and Buddhist illustrations in Newari Buddhism.

Library

There are approximately 35,000 volumes and to ca 100,000 items in digitized forms, which all donated by the Reiyukai on the basic of ten years agreement between Reiyukai Jāpān and Nepāl Government in March 2005 (Cueppers, 2012:78). Besides the Buddhist texts, there are collected art and language tools for the relevant language for Buddhist studies, viz. dictionaries grammars of Pali, Sanskrit, Tibetan, Burmese, Thai, Manchu, Mongolia, Chinese, Japanese, Ceylonese and Indo-European languages (Ibid, 79).

Acquisition

Collection of Religious studies, philosophical studies, comparative religion, Buddhist studies, Pali texts, Historical maps of Buddhist countries, Buddhism in Nepāl, Journals, Microfilms of rare research material, CD-Rom of research material etc. A project to establish an internationalal documentation centre is proposed to collect and preserve important historical documents, data, and images, which would be accessible to visitors, researchers and concerned authorities to Lumbinī , the birthplace of Lord Buddha, world property. (UNESCO,2013.b:29).

Lumbinī Museum

Museum building is made up of a central exhibition hall, surrounded by the four mezzanine spaces and the ground floor space. The two mezzanine spaces on the west side and ground floor are used for administration, workshop and laboratory for archaeological research. The building had repaired and beautification with the support of Indian government. Artifacts of Lumbinī complex, viz. photos, manuscripts, coins, fragment of Siddhartha, Yasodhara and Rahula, fragments of Aśokan pillar's horse capital, scroll paintings, xerox of valuable manuscripts and Buddhist dress are displaying here (Fig.21). It supports to the research scholars, experts, visitors, students as well as general public in course of its regular duties. The number of the visitors is increasing day by day. In vs. 2062, only 1,223 tourists had visited. In 2067 vs, there were 53,891 tourists had visited at this museum (Pandey, 2013:34-35). The quality of the museum will support to increase the number of the tourists in Lumbinī .

Auditorium:

A multi-purpose hall, to be used for national and internationalal conferences, including balconies, technical facilities is a uniquely stylized architectural motif of the Lumbinī Master Plan. For press and observers balconies, peculiar balcony with annex facilities and upper back wall of the hall for interpreters are major components. Proposed U-Thant auditorium hall is under construction, which has signed between Nepāl government and donor (UNESCO, 2013.b.:20).

New Lumbinī Village

Division of project area into three zones is symbolic and based on philosophical concept. Components of settlement, Education and Culture, religious and *nirvāṇa* have managed from north to south from philosophical point of view respectively. In course of this planning four types of resting houses viz. luxurious hotel of 100 beds, middle-class hotel of 150 beds, pilgrimage rest house of 200 beds and camping-grounds for general visitors are proposed in this zone. Two hundred residential-houses for two hundred households, high school, electricty, drinking-water, communication, drainage system etc. have stated on plan. Asian Highway is also proposed from the north of this zone. The village will be the location of the administrative offices of the Lumbinī complex. Architecturally, the village is divided into eight blocks aligned with two parallel arcades. The buildings on the north of the road will be utilized as the administrative centre, while those on the south of the road will be occupied by the tourist centre.

The completed project include standarded hotel Hokke in1990 and in operation, middle class accommodation, ie. Hotel Kasai is also providing services to the internationalal as well as internal tourists, pilgrimage rest house; viz. Śri Laṅkān pilgrimage rest house is completed in 1986. DPC of high school is also completed. A scheme for protection of cranes is operating with the patronage of International Crane Foundation. Construction of high school, camping ground, administrative blocks and water tank are incomplete. The three major buildings, viz. museum, library and research institute have completed in1989, 1989 and 1996 in respectively and in operation. The construction of auditorium is not yet started in 2013. The World Peace Stūpa named Nipponzan Myohoji of 156 feet in height is completed in November 2001. It is the symbol of world peace and prosperity. Many components of infrastructure have been running and some of these are not yet started due to lack of proper fund. Major Pedestrian space, road service, staff-colony, meditation centres and school building are partially completed. Boundary wall of the south portion, south of Parsa to Taulihawa road, has been completed. Due to the open boundary the animals are gazing in project area as well as the security of the project is also poor. Secondary pedestrian, water management, water supply system, sewerage system, electrical power system, telecommunication system (under ground), tourist information building, administrative building, medical centre, retails and service facilities, colonade and auditorium are even incomplete (LDT, 2013).

In order to monitor the development programmes in Lumbinī Complex the Lumbinī Development Committee was constituted in 1971 and since 1974 it was given the change of the total area with all the activities working under different departments of HMG to be co-ordinated in consultation with it. (LDC, 1975:Nos.17-18). In 1985 Lumbinī Development Trust was created as an autonomous and non-governmental organization for the creative and concrete action in the region instead of LDC. Lumbinī Development act, 1985 was amended according to the interest of the working team. The trust had focussed on to develop and mobilize the physical facilities, viz. water supply, communication, electrification, transportation, road construction, land acquistition, land scaping, afforestation, as well as, to promote academic and archaeological activities from time to time. According to the condition of master plan besides these infrastructures Bhairahawā airport extension and plantation on road side from Bhairahawā to Lumbinī were also completed in preliminary base. UNO had taken the responsibility to prepare the Master plan with the technical support of HMG Nepāl. Governmental and non-governmental agencies of various nations were requested to build their monasteries, Stūpas and vihars in their interest. LDT has been conducting world summit and conferenc Declaration to provide valuable guidelines and financial supports to complete the Master plan as soon as possible. Then His Royal Highness Prince Gyanendra Bir Bikram Shah Dev, Chairman of LDT, paid a visit to the United Nations and addressed the International Committee for the Development of Lumbinī in 1986. Gyanendra had also visited Jāpān and Koreā to promote awareness and to develop friendly relationship with each other. He lit a torch of eternal peace of Lumbinī in commemoration of International year of peace in 1986. The Eternal Peace Flame in Lumbinī is still burning as a symbol of World Peace.

Land charge should be increased only after consulting with the concerned monasteries and institutes, which is 150, 200 and 300 $ of 80,120 and 160 sq.m.in area respectively at present.

Apart from these suggestions other conferences and meetings have also recommended certain components to revise in Master Plan on the basis of synchronous times. About 55 percent of the total works of Master plan have been completed in two and half decades. Political instability of the country has been on obstacle to the progress of the plan. Lumbinī International Development Committee (LIDC) should be activated to mobilize in proper direction. The authority should be free, fair and unbias to impliment and offer the components of Master plan. The total cost of Master Plan was ascertained US $ 55 million. Donor agencies should be encouraged to provide cash and materials to develop Lumbinī. At the preceding ratio of development indicates that the plan is going to take another four to five decades to complete it. If it is so late the first developed part will already reach a state of restoration.

Santi Stūpa (Peace Stūpa) Jāpān

Santi stūpa, north of Lumbinī water distribution tower has built by Nipponzan Myohoji (Fuji Guru) after signing on contract letter with Nepāl government on 6-8-1993. Its height is 41.5 m & 59 m in diameter. It,s design was prepared by Dr. Minoru Ohoka of Jāpān. Here are Buddha statue and kita: Heian Bijutsu, bronze plated with gold, images of Birth, Enlightenment, First Sermon and Nirvana of Lord Buddha. It was opened in March 1995. 1st January: New Year prayer, full Mon Day: Buddha Jayanti, 3rd July, Rev. Y. Nabatame's death anniversary, 6th August: Fuji Guruj's birth anniversary and Hiroshima Day, 3rd November: Peace pagoda Anniversary and 1st-8th Dec.: A weak fasting (ROHACHI-SESSION) are major festivals, which are celebrated each year. During these occasions Japanese guests come to participate on.

Saras (Crane) and Blue cow

Saras (Crane) are found in the wetland and cultivated fields in Lumbinī area. A few years ago, it disappeared from the eastern region of Nepāl. Saras (Crane), the tallest flying bird in the world, reside outside the protected area of Nepāl. To conserve them Lumbinī Crane Conservation Centre, affiliated with International Crane Foundation, USA, has done work on crane conservation sector at Lumbinī. We must careful for saving our endangered cranes, blue cow and precious wetlands.

According to the Master Plan of Lumbinī development tourism is one of the major issues to change the life styles of the people of Gandki Region (from Rapti to Narayani river). Archaeological, historical and cultural heritages of Lumbinī are not only the property of Nepāl, but also property of the world, structural as well as artifacts should have preserved in proper way. Aśokan pillar, Māyādevî Temple, Puskarini Tank, vihars and stupas are located in Sacred Garden Complex. The Nativity Sculpture of Buddha, Vajravarahi image, Dharmachakra, images of Buddha, Maitreya, Bodhisattva, Ratnasambhava and Padampanī Avalokitesvar are remarkable pieces of art. Theravada and Mahayani Vihars; LIRI, Museum, Shanti Stupa and Crane Foundation areas are the major attractions for the national as well as internationalal tourists. All the heritages should be conserve and preserve in scientific way and transfer to new generation in condition. If the tourists visit at these sites their length of stay will be extended at Lumbinī, which will be fruitful to gain foreign currency. Components of Master Plan of Lumbinī have not completed even now. According to the authority its about 70 % works have completed. UNESCO has requested to assist from both national and internationalal stakelolders in course of completion Lumbinī Master Plan and its peripheral sites (UNESCO, 2013.b.:34). It should be completed in schdule time bound. LMP should be revised on the needs and Nepālese capacity of construction budget. Buffer Zone and Restricted Zones are encroaching day by day. These components should be preserved according to the provisions of Ancient Monuments Preservation Act, 2013 (Revised portions too). The construction of the huge concrete buildings should be immediately stopped by the authority. In course of construction and repair of the buildings permission is needed on the basis of Ancient Monument Preservation Act. It should be strictly followed by the stakeholders. Industrial polllution and land encroachment should be controlled on time. Other wise it will be great problem in near future.

CHAPTER FOUR

TOURISM DEVELOPMENT

In modern period tourism is a very important source for foreign currency earning. It is an unrisky procedure for transfer of real resources from industrially capital surplus developed countries to developing countries. Tourism is a labour intensive industry offering employment to skilled, semi-skilled and unskilled manpower. The problems of unemployment and underemployment are more acute in the developing countries. It employs large number of people and provides a wide range of jobs. A large number of specialist persons are required to work as accountants, housekeepers, cooks, waiters, and entertainers; semi-skilled workers, viz. porters, kitchen-staff, gardeners and chambermaids. Furnishing and equipment industries and others, farming and food supply as well as souvenir industries provide indirect employment to the local people. In course of effective implementation of tourism industry, a systematic plan is needed.

Planning means proposed method of action to achieve aims and objectives of any concerned sectors. Objectives, action programs and measurement of the objectives are the main elements of a successful planning.

Objects must be transparent and measurable in course of implementation and measurement process. Planning process follows an orderly sequence of actions in series. Two economy systems i.e. planned economy and market economy influence to it tourism industry (Bhati, 1997:296). Human resource, material and equipments are related with production in planned economy. Market economy is controlled by the forces of market, i.e. demand, supply, prices, transport, production and policy of the authority. The planning for tourism is the main sector of planned economy. After the end of World War II, many countries increased their interest towards the planning of tourism. After knowing the significance of tourism industry as a source of income, employment generation, regional development and major source of foreign currency many countries have been attracting towards the promotion of tourism industry. Rome Convention held in 1963 had pointed out that developing countries should be given high priority in the field of tourism and short term as well as long term plans should be estimated after serving of existing and potential tourist traffic. UNCTAD and IUOTO had also emphasized the tourism industry in the promotion of local, regional and national economy of the developing countries.

The basic infrastructure of tourism, i.e. roads, water supply, airport, public utilities and accommodation units provide jobs for thousands of workers. The promotion of tourism can be a great encouragement to economic development. Cultural motivation has always stood as a unique vehicle for the cultural propagation through the process of tourism. It has always been an essential medium for broadening the limits of human knowledge. Tourists travel to cultural enriched states to participate in entertainment through usages, custom, fair, festivals, art, architecture, food and drinks of the host country. Tourism is an important medium of social and cultural development and also of promoting lasting goodwill and friendship among the nations of the world.

Lumbinī being the birth place of Lord Buddha thousands of Buddhist as well as other religious people come to visit in every year. It provides direct and indirect benefit to the people of this region. Pilgrimage, cultural, nature, mass, sustainable and domestic tourism can promote in Lumbinī and its outskirt. Lumbinī Development Trust, the authority, has co-ordinated many physical, cultural, natural and architectural perspectives in course of increasing the ratio of the foreigners and to increase the growing rate of the tourists (LDT, 2013:39-41). In the nineteenth century the people had started to move in large numbers to the far off from their usual places of residence. Railways, steamships, motorcars and aeroplanes link interrelation among the people of developed, developing and under developing countries. Rapid development in the means of transport and communication has changed the whole world one neighborhood and has made travel an easy affair. Leisure, pleasure pilgrimage and recreation are the motivating factors of mass movement of people. Thomas Cook, the pioneer of mass tourism in England, had said that the earth in all its fullness and beauty is for the people (Bhatia, 1990). Now-a-days a large number of people move from one country to another due to the cultural and natural attractions. Cultural tourism is the main focus point of mass tourism in Lumbinī. Mass tourism can contribute unique benefits to the exploiting of the cultural, archaeological and natural heritages of the site and can serve indirectly to improve the individual cultural level of both nationals and foreigners. Lumbinī, the birthplace of Lord Buddha, is the main motivating factor to them.

Lumbinī has the potentials of being the most important centre of cultural tourism. Māyādevi temple, Aśoka pillar, Puskarini tank, various ancient Stūpas, vihar structures and finding relics have attracted many pilgrims and other visitors at this sacred complex. In ancient period kings, nobles and other renowned persons had visited Lumbinī in course of their pilgrimage. The tradition has been continuing in an unbroken chain on special occasion a large number of devotees from the various parts of Nepāl and foreign countries. Lumbinī represents not only monuments, but also the requisites, viz. unique life-styles of Hindu, Buddhist and Muslim people, local art, craft and indigenous religious activities.

Lumbinī, the birthplace of Lord Buddha, is a sacred complex not only for the Buddhists, but also Hindus as well as other religious people as peace land. Siddharthanagar, the head quarter of Rupāndehi district, is the main entrance gateway of Lumbinī (Coningham, 2011:7). Immigration office of Belahiya, Bhairahawā has been recorded the number of foreign tourists except Indian. Due to the open border and cultural similarity between Nepāl and India, it is difficult to find out actual data. Belahiya is the main road entry to Lumbinī, which is located on the south of Rupandehi and 25 km south-east from Lumbinī. Immigration office of Belahiya has recorded the number of third country tourists but not Indian tourists. Due to open border it is difficult to count accurately Indian tourists. At the border there are also transit passengers as well as crue passengers. In 1998 only 38670 tourists were recorded at the office. After that Maoist movement disturbed due to internal strike, unlawful activities and feeling of insecurity of the tourists. Internal conflict and insecurity also influenced to the tourists.

In 1999 and 2000 tourist ratio from Belahiya, Siddharthanagar entry gate was increased +8.19 and +10.36 percentage respectively than previous years. In 2001 and 2002 the flow of the tourists decreased in -22.17 and -26.43% respectively (Giri, 2008:169).

Table 4.1

Tourists of Belahiya

S.No.	*Years*	*Total*	*%*
1.	2003	39869	+ 50.04 than last year
2.	2004	47813	19.93 ,,
3.	2005	51655	8.05 ,,
4.	2006	62680	21.34 ,,
5.	2007	90516	44.40 ,,
6.	2008	93958	3.50 ,,
7.	2009	89880	4.34 ,,
8.	2010	102120	13.61 ,,
9.	2011	133285	30.49 ,,
10.	2012	144468	8.39

Source- Immigration Office, Belahiya 2013

Table 4.1 shows the ten years scenario of the foreign tourists excluding Indians. In 2003 the ratio is increased drastically 50.4%. During ten years period 44.40% has increased in 2007. But it is not satisfactory in next year 2008. 3.80% is not good. In 2009 their flow became 4.34% only. In 2010 it was improved in 13.61% than 2009. In 2011 it was increased 30.49%, which was declared "Nepāl visit year 2011" by the Nepāl Government. In 2012, Lumbinī visit year was declared by the authority. National as well as international Medias were used for its advertisement, but the ratio of the tourists was increased only 8.39% in 2012, which is not achievement. It is only regular ratio by nature. In the process of reaction of the concerned authority Yadavraj Pandey, Chief of Immigration office Belahiya, has said that third country tourists are coming due to the motivation of Indian and other country tour guides and package policy of the Indian tour and travel agencies. Nepāl Tourism Board office of Belahiya and Nepāl Government Tourism office have not any role to motivate and to provide proper services to the tourists. These agencies, tour and travel agencies and local communities must be active and reinforce to improve good relation and understanding in foreign countries.

Table 4.2

Tourists at Lumbini

S.No.	*Years*	*Total*	*%*	*Remarks*
1.	2003	28053	+21.42	compare to last year
2.	2004	37892	35.07	"
3.	2005	39792	5.01	"
4.	2006	49595	24.63	"
5.	2007	71053	43.26	"
6.	2008	82075	15.5	"
7.	2009	82445	0.45	"
8.	2010	95508	15.84	"
9.	2011	128259	34.29	"
10.	2012	136001	6.03	"

Source- LDT, Information Section, 3013

Information section of Lumbinī Development Trust has recorded the volume of the foreign tourists. In 1996 the number of the tourists was +26.85% increased than last year (Giri, 2008:172). Due to the Maoist movement the volume decreased respectively. In 1997 and 1998 the ratio decreased in -8.35% and -4.99% respectively. In 1999 only 10715 tourists had visited in a year. It was -51.56% than last year. In 2000 its ratio increased in +31.92%. But in 2001 and 2002 their ratio decreased in -28.30% and -10.84 than the previous years. In 2002 only 9037 had come in Lumbinī. Table 14 shows the ten years ratio and change of the visitors. In 2003 its number was drastically changed into +210.42% from 2003 to 2012, the ratio is increasing per year. But the ratio is not rationalism. It is low and high without reasonable cause. During this period +43.26% and +35.07% had increased the number of the tourists in 2007 and 2004 respectively. In 2011, +34.29% is promoted than last year 2010. In 2005 and 2009, its number was +5.01% and +0.45% only. 6.03% was promoted in 2012 than last year 2011.

In the comparison of the land entry of Sunauli-Belahiya and Lumbinī the changes ratio is not so different. In 2006 the ratio of Belahiya and Lumbinī is +21.34% and +24.63% respectively. In 2007 increasment ratio of Belahiya was 44.40% and the ratio of Lumbinī was 43.26%, which is similar to both sites. In 2009 the number of the tourists at Belahiya entrance decreased in 4.34% than last year. In Lumbinī complex it was only 0.45% progress than previous year. In 2011 30.49% increased in Belahiya and 34.29% in Lumbinī complex, 8.39% and 6.03% have increased in Belahiya and Lumbinī in 2012 respectively. In course of declaration "Lumbinī Visit Year 2012" it was not fruitful due to lack of prerequistics to promote it (NRB, 2013:2). The number of the tourists at Belahiya and Lumbinī reveals that Belahiya is the main land transport for Lumbinī. The number of Belahiya indicates the ratio of the tourists in Lumbinī. Both are connected in a tourist chain and lean.

Besides the road transport air transport has also played a vital role in the promotion of the tourism in Lumbinī complex. Gautam Buddha Airport was operated especially focusing to the birthplace of Lord Buddha (Tange, 1978:7). Its main structure was completed in 1977. This airport has provided easy and comfortable services to more than twelve hundred thousands people in a year.

Table 4.3

Ten Years Passengers' Scenario at Gautam Buddha Airport, Siddharthanagar

S.No	*Years*	*Arrival Number*	*International (Excluding Indian)*	*% International Tourists*	*Index +100*	*Remarks*
1.	2003	24806	2569	10.35	110.35	App. +5 % Indian by Air
2.	2004	44060	4030	9.14	119.49	
3.	2005	61981	4504	7.27	126.76	
4.	2006	35024	3860	11.02	137.78	
5.	2007	30468	1782	5.84	143.62	
6.	2008	33868	5335	15.75	159.37	
7.	2009	43316	5492	12.67	172.04	
8.	2010	56239	6668	11.85	183.89	
9.	2011	59532	9014	15.14	199.03	
10.	2012	59922	9697	16.08	215.11	

Source- Gautam Buddha Airport, 2013

Table 4.3 shows the number of coming tourists at Gautam Buddha airport, Siddharthanagar Bhairahawa. During the ten years period 61981 tourists have arrived at this airport in 2005 and departure ratio is the highest in the same year. On the basis of the illustrated table in 2003 among the total passengers (24806) there were 2569 third country tourists. Its ratio is 10.35% of the total passenger by air transport. In 2005 the number of the tourists excluding Indians is 4504 among 61981. Their ratio was 7.27% than last year 2004. Its annual ratio among the total passengers is in increasing position. In 2006, 2008 and 2010 its number had increased in 11.02%, 15.75% and 11.85% respectively. 15.14% and 16.08% have grown in 2011 and 2012 respectively.

These Tables 4.1,2 and 3 shows that 44.40% tourists had come from this entry point, Belahiya in 2007. In 2004, the ratio of the tourists was 35.07 % in Lumbinī than Belahiya. 9677 third country tourists had landed at Gautam Buddha Airport in 2012. These figures are the highest in number during those ten years. In the comparison during this period third country tourists were only 1782 in 2007 and the entry ratio was decreased at Belahiya and Lumbinī in 4.34% and 0.45% respectively. Among the total tourists (pp holders) of Lumbinī about 8% come by air transport, Gautam Buddha Airport, Siddharthanagar. In 2003 only 9.15% tourists had come by airline among the Lumbinī visitors. The ratio of the Lumbinī tourists by air transport is 10.63%, 11.31% and 7.78% in 2004, 2005 and 2006 respectively. In 2007 it is only 2.5% and nearly 6.5% in next three years. It is 7.02% and 7.08% in 2011 and 2012 respectively. There is no vast difference in the ratio of this year. In average 8% tourists come to Lumbinī by air transport excluding Indian. Adding about 2.34% Indian tourists by plane, it will be 10% by air transport in Lumbinī. In Lumbinī Master Plan it was projected that 20% would have come by plane, which was not possible in 2012. It was proposed in 1985, but it is not completed even 27 years later (Tange, 1978:11). Annual increasing rate is 15% per year in the plan, which is not completed even now.

Table 4.4

Monthly Tourists arrival Trend at Belahiya

S.N.	*Months*	*2000*	*2001*	*2002*	*2003*	*2004*	*2006*	*2008*	*2010*	*2011*	*2012*
1.	January	3446	3242	2122	3364	3379	4530	7690	5855	7551	7958
2.	February	6749	6041	3035	5568	6849	8717	14026	13814	17630	22269
3.	March	7933	6321	5001	5553	8412	9342	16036	16862	20642	23309
4.	April	3484	2377	1552	1990	2163	1289	3742	3679	5231	7140
5.	May	1554	1030	733	985	876	925	1670	1133	1943	1657
6.	June	684	453	479	493	566	804	871	864	1004	1475
7.	July	1054	989	654	1269	1405	1464	2195	2257	2982	2707
8.	August	4368	4073	2673	3768	4572	7059	11649	14089	18765	18060

S.N.	Months	2000	2001	2002	2003	2004	2006	2008	2010	2011	2012
9.	September	2785	2620	1585	2633	2615	4504	6403	7644	8946	8968
10.	October	4653	3621	2455	5092	4938	8917	11031	9730	17211	13393
11.	November	5851	3503	3723	5518	6585	8988	12470	15921	19977	21085
12.	December	3613	1666	2426	3686	5453	6141	6175	10267	11603	16447
	Total	**46174**	**35936**	**26438**	**39869**	**47813**	**62680**	**93958**	**102115**	**133285**	**144468**

Source-Immigration Office, Belahiya, 2013

Table 4.4 presents ten years scenarios of monthly tourism arrival trend from Belahiya, Sunauli gateway of Siddharthanagar. During the period of 2000 to 2012 October to March month show the flow of the tourists in Lumbinī. March, November and February are the highest tourist months. In March the number of the tourists is 7977, 6321, 5001, 5553 and 8414 in 2000, 2001, 2002, 2003 and 2004 respectively. In February there are 6749, 6041, 5568, 6849 and 8717 in 2000, 2001, 2003, 2004 and 2006 in respectively. May, June and July are low tourists months. Due to the hot air and heavy rainy season, tourists do not visit here.

Table 4.5

Monthly Tourists arrival Trend at Lumbini

S.N.	Months	1994	1996	1998	2000	2002	2004	2006	2008	2010	2012
1.	January	2025	3958	4297	1177	1498	3160	3751	7250	6222	6591
2.	February	1620	2079	2213	1810	1903	5690	7508	11941	12348	20045
3.	March	858	1620	862	1576	2352	6298	7655	14149	16471	20519
4.	April	733	760	1188	399	47	1321	546	3095	3705	8295
5.	May	464	615	456	352	06	492	406	1236	1051	1316
6.	June	329	387	198	112	18	350	454	606	933	1366
7.	July	370	249	348	180	48	782	831	1406	1828	2651
8.	August	687	766	724	787	321	3590	5948	10288	12437	17924
9.	September	1045	1533	784	586	432	1889	3602	5680	6802	7955
10.	October	2561	2103	7951	1418	247	3220	6962	9411	9380	13099
11.	November	6677	8303	1133	3576	983	5186	6762	11219	16964	21740
12.	December	3603	3027	1965	2162	1182	5914	5170	5765	11367	14566
	Total	**20972**	**25400**	**221[illegible]9**	**14135**	**9036**	**37892**	**49595**	**82075**	**99508**	**136001**

Source-LDT, Information Section, 2013

Table 4.5 represents the number of tourists during the ten years period in monthly wise ratio. The record reveals that November, December, March, February, October and January, six months in a year, are very favorable to the foreigners. March is the most favorable month for Lumbinī visit. At the beginning years November is at the top. Later years the flow changes to March month. May, June and July are very low tourist months. Remaining is in average on the basis of peace, security and plan of the authority.

Tourists of more than 80 countries visit Nepãl each year. Holiday recreation, trekking, mountaineering, and business, pilgrimage, official works; conference, convention research and rafting are their main purpose to visit in Nepãl (MoCTCA, 2011:2). They come from Indiã, china, Bangladesh, Belgium, Bulgaria, Colombia, Denmark, France, Finland, Greece, Ireland, Italy, Jãpan, Malaysia, Netherland as well as Pakistan. In such a way they usually visit from Poland, Republic of Koreã, Singapore, Spain, Śri Lańka, Switzerland, Thãiland, Turkey, U.K. and USA. Among the visitors of Nepãl some are frequently coming more than three-four times.

Table 4.6

Top Five Countries of Nationality Arrival in Nepãl

Rank	*Nationality 2011*	*Nationality 2012*	*Remarks*
Rank 1	Indiã	Indiã	
Rank 2	PR China	PR China	
Rank 3	Sri Lanka	Sri Lanka	
Rank 4	USA	USA	
Rank 5	UK	UK	

Source-MoCTCA, 2011

Table 4.6 represents the top five country of nationality. Indian tourists are at the top level all of them. It takes first rank and northern neighbor Republic china has second position in both years, i.e. 2010 and 2011. Śri Lańka is in the third position among the country of nationality. USA and UK tourists are in the fourth and the fifth position to visit in Nepãl. The table indicates that Indian, Chinese and Śri Lańkan are motivated by the natural, cultural, religious and pilgrimage motives. USA and UK tourists are motivated by the natural as well as cultural life style of the various groups of Nepãl. Remaining both is not motivated by pilgrimage concept. In course of visiting in Nepãl, many country-tourists enter from Sunauli-Belahiya by motor-car, tourist bus or other vehicles. Their main target is the pilgrimage of Lumbinī, the birthplace of Lord Buddha.

Table 4.7

Top Five countries of Nationality at Belahiya

Position (Rank)	*2000*	*2001*	*2002*	*2004*	*2005*	*2006*	*2009*	*2010*	*2011*	*2012*
1	Sri Lanka	Śri Lańka	Śri Lańka	Śri Lańka	Śri Lańka	Śri Lańka	Śri Lańka	Śri Lańka	Śri Lańka	Śri Lańka
2	Jāpan	Jāpan	South Koreā	Thāiland	Thāiland	Thāiland	Thāiland	Thāiland	Thāiland	Thāiland
3	UK	South Koreā	Thāiland	South Koreā	S.Koreā	S.Koreā	Myānmār	Myānmār	Myānmār	Myānmār
4	Thāiland	UK	UK	Jāpan	Jāpan	Myānmār	Koreā	S.Koreā	S.Koreā	S.Koreā
5	South Koreā	Thāiland	Jāpan	Myānmār	Israel	Jāpan	UK	UK	UK	Dutch

Source-Immigration Office, Belahiya, 2013

Belahiya is the main entry gateway of the third country tourists in the western Terai, especially for Lumbinī by road ways. Their entry record is up to date at Immigration office Belahiya, Siddharthanagar in course of their passport check. Foreign tourists come by the tourist bus, taxi and cars from Indian-gateway. According to the Table 4.7 rank of the third country visitors from 2012 sampling of ten years shows that Śri Lańkan tourists are in the first rank in the years. During ten years of the sample study Thāi tourist are also within top five countries. Seven years in second position, third, fourth and fifth ranks are gained respectively in other years. But Thāiis are not first in rank. South Koreāns are also always within fifth position among the third country visitors of Lumbinī. They have taken second rank in one year, third rank in four years, fourth rank four years and fifth rank in one year. Their ratio is in parllar position. It is neither drastic induced nor reduced during these years. They have taken ranked position in ten years. In 2002 it was ranked in second position. After that their number is also decreasing than previous year. This table shows that Śri Lańkan, Thāii and Koreān (South) are more motivated and devoted to visit Buddhist sacred complex Lumbinī in course of their Holy *tirthas* in Buddhist sites. Almost the Śri Lańkan, Thāii and Koreān tourists go Lumbinī, who come from Sunauli-Belahiya entrance.

Jāpanese tourists are also motivated to pilgrimage in sacred complex of Lumbinī, the birthplace of Buddha. They enter from Sunauli-Belahiya gateway by bus through the guidance of Indian Travel and Tours. In 2000 and 2001 AD. Jāpanese have taken second position among the third country visitors from this entry. After 2001 their position is decreasing due to Maoist movement. They did not feel secure due to unstable political situation of Nepāl. The fourth and the fifth position had secured in twice years among the foreign visitors. Jāpanese had also secured within the fifth rank during six years. Myānmār and British (U.K.) visitors had also taken rank in six years. In four years it is ranked on 3rd and 4th and 5th positions in each year. Their entry ratio is also not satisfied with in 13 years. Tourists from UK are also coming to visit Buddha's birthplace. They had taken third rank one year, fourth rank two years and fifth rank in three years during the study period. Dutch and Israeli are also coming from Belahiya entrance to know the geography and cultural life style of the Nepālese. This table indicates that Śri Lańkan, Thāiland and Koreān are motivated to visit Lumbinī due to harmony and good relation with them. Their ratio has not drastically changed. The authority and civil society must be active to increase the length of their stay in Lumbinī, motivating by cultural or natural heritages of this area. Relation with the Jāpanese civil societies and government should be promoted in diplomatic sector. They should feel secure to visit Lumbinī by heart.

Tourists from more than 80 countries come to visit in Lumbinī each year. Among them Śri Lańk, Thāiland, South Koreā, Myānmār, Jāpan, Netherland, UK, Israel, USA, Germany, Indian, Taiwan etc are the major origin countries. Table 4.8 shows the position of the tourists in nationality wise. In 1994 Jāpanese, Śri Lańkan, South Korean, Thāii and Taiwan had taken rank 1 to 5 respectively. Jāpan took the first rank in 1994, 1996, 1998 and 2000. At the beginning of the 21th century Śri Lańka took the first rank from 2002 to 2012.

Table 4.8

Top Five countries of Nationality at Lumbini

Position (Rank)	*1994*	*1996*	*1998*	*2000*	*2002*	*2004*	*2006*	*2008*	*2010*	*2012*
1.	Jāpan	Jāpan	Jāpan	Jāpan	Sri Lańka	Śri Lańka	Śri Lańka	Śri Lańka	Śri Lańka	Śri Lańka
2.	Sri Lanka	South Koreā	Thāiland	Śri Lańka	Thāiland	Thāiland	Thāiland	Thāiland	Thāiland	Thāiland
3	S.Koreā	Taiwan	Taiwan	Koreā	Koreā	Koreā	Koreā	S. Koreā	Myānmār	Myānmār
4	Thāiland	Śri Lańka	Koreā	Taiwan	Jāpan	Jāpan	Jāpan	Myānmār	S.Koreā	China
5	Taiwan	Thāiland	Śri Lańka	Thāiland	China	Taiwan	China	China	China	S.Koreā

Source- LDT, 2013

Jāpanese were more attractive before 2001. After the massacre event of Ven. Nawatame, the frequency of the Jāpanese became slow and in decreasing position. In 1994 Śri Laṅka was in second rank, which changed its position in 4th rank in 1996. In 1998 and 2000 its position was in the fifth and the second respectively. After that it has taken the first rank before twelve years. Śri Laṅka has gained the first rank and within the fifth rank during this period. South Koreā is also a motivated national for the pilgrimage of Lumbinī. Almost of them are inspired by the teaching of Buddha and Buddhism. Their main purpose is to visit in Lumbinī. It has taken third rank in 1994, second rank in 1996, and fourth rank in 1998 and second rank in 2000. Tourists of South Koreā have taken place within fifth position of the third country visitors. Due to the influence of Buddhism, Thāi people are also coming to visit Lumbinī. During the ten years sample years it has taken position within five. Taiwan, Myānmār and Chinese tourists are increasing day today. Nepāl Government has contracted with China to increase the number of Chinese tourists. Nepāl Tourism Act, 2035 (Amendment include), Tourism Action procedure, 2067 and Tourism Rules and Procedures have encouraged to promote the number of foreign tourists. To increase the number of tourists, viz. Chinese, Jāpanese, Taiwan, Thāiland, Śri Laṅkan, UK, USA and other European countries should be reinforced providing proper information of Buddhist religion, philosophy, culture and unique cultural life style of the local people in Lumbinī area. In the comparison of the national wise tourists in Nepāl, Belahiya and Lumbinī, Indians are always in the first rank. Indian tourists did not have recorded before 2010 in Lumbinī and Belahiya have not recorded the Indian tourists. But the motion and frequency of the Indian tourists is active and in the first position. Chinese, who have taken the second rank in the national context, have not taken rank at Belahiya. They have always visited in Lumbinī in order to offer devotion towards Buddha and Buddha *dhamma*. China is very potential for promoting internationalal tourism in Nepāl. Śri Laṅka has always taken position within fifth rank. They visit Kathmandu, Lumbinī and other sites of Nepāl. Myānmār, Jāpan, Taiwan, UK and USA tourist are also in ranking position.

One of the aims of Master Plan is the development of tourism. In the report of this plan has mentioned that 10% of total tourists by air and 80% by land to Nepāl were expected to visit Lumbinī. At the tourist high season i.e. October, November, December, January and February 70%

of total tourists of Lumbinī would have come. Only 25% would have come in tourist low season i.e. March, April, May, August and September. It was also projected that 70% of the total tourists in Lumbinī would be stayed overnight in Lumbinī (Tange, 1978:11).

Table 4.9

Projection of Tourists in Lumbini Master Plan

S.No.	*Details*	*In 1980*	*1985*	*Remarks*
1.	Foreign Tourists in Lumbini	44700	89700	
2.	Tourists in High Season	31300	62600	
3.	Tourists in Low Season	11200	22400	
4.	Daily Average in High Season	208	418	
5.	Daily Average in Low Season	75	150	
6.	Daily Average of over night in High season	156	314	
7.	Daily Average of over night in Low Season	57	113	

Source-Tange, 1978.

According to the Table 4.9, 44700 and 89700 foreign tourists would have visited in Lumbinī in 1980 and 1985 respectively. Within five years it is expected that it would be 100% growth. The number of high season tourist is 31,300 and low season number 11200 is projected in 1980 in the project profile. In 1985 average number of tourists in high season and low season had proposed 418 and 150 daily respectively. Among them 314 (75%) and 113 (75%) in high and low tourist season would be stayed overnight in Lumbinī. But the assumption has not met the target in previous years. After 18 years latter the tourists were 28053 in 2003. Excluding Indian tourists there were 82445 in 2009. After 25 years the assumption ratio has not met due to passive intention of the authority. In 2010 the number of the total tourists in Lumbinī is 583442. Among them third country tourists are 95508. If the projection was prepared without counting Indian guest, it seems to be completed after 25 years later. It is also a challenge to the authority to implement in proper time and situation.

LDT Information section has recorded third country, Indian and Nepālese tourists separately from 2010. Before this only third country tourists were recorded.

Table 4.10

Nepālese, Indian and PP Holder Tourists at Lumbini

S.N.	*Years*	*PP Holder*	*Percent*	*Indian*	*Percent*	*Nepālese*	*Percent*	*Total*
1.	2010	95508	16.4	57675	9.88	426250	73.06	583442
2.	2011	128259	21.82	63709	10.84	395570	67.34	587538
3.	2012	136001	17.94	120583	15.98	539210	71.11	795794

Source- LDT, 2013

Table 4.10 presents that passport holder tourists are only 16.16 %, 21.82 % and 17.84 % in 2010, 2011 and 2012 respectively in Lumbinī. Indian tourists are in the ratio of 9.88%, 10.84% and 15.98% in 2010, 2011 and 2012 respectively. Remaining more than 70% tourists are internal. All of them are day visitors. They go back after few hours. They do not spend money in Lumbinī. They create pollution and crow from the commercial point of view. This ratio can not effect and change in Nepālese socio-economic and cultural life style of the local people. In course of management and pollution free policy, nominal entrance fee may be reasonable for internal tourist on the basis of Nepāl government tourism procedure policy 2067.

Indian tourists always can visit in Lumbinī because of the environment similarities. They can easily visit and go back from the southern border of Nepāl. If they come at tourist low season, there should be concession or especial discount or any especial attraction in Lumbinī visit. They can support to promote endemic and sustainable tourism in Nepāl.

Table 4.11

Monthly Annual Indian visitor at Lumbini

S.N.	*Months*	*2011*	*2012*	*Remarks*
1.	January	2827	8678	
2.	February	3478	4263	
3.	March	4737	3275	
4.	April	3753	63266	
5.	May	8386	6099	
6.	June	4889	4222	
7.	July	2691	1713	
8.	August	2683	2607	
9.	September	2467	3297	

S.N.	Months	2011	2012	Remarks
10.	October	5949	5512	
11.	November	12778	9022	
12.	December	8071	8629	
	Total	**63709**	**120583**	

Source- LDT, 2013

Indian tourists are regularly coming from ancient to modern periods. But accurate data has recorded from 2011 in Lumbinī. This table shows that November, May, December, April and June months are potential or attractive for Indian. If the ratio of Indian tourists can improve at the third country tourist's low season it will be fruitful in Nepālese economy and employment. Nepālese are also motivated to visit Lumbinī. Seminar, workshop, conference and excursion teams usually come from Mechī to Mahākālī, east-west Nepāl. Their visit supports to promote good relation among Nepālese to generate income to the stalk-holders of Lumbinī and to create employment.

Table 4.12

Monthly Internal (Nepalese) Tourists in Lumbini

S.N.	Months	2010	2011	2012	Remarks
1.	January	39411	45376	41146	
2.	February	35418	27531	34230	
3.	March	50419	23490	34129	
4.	April	35372	58006	147669	
5.	May	24112	16666	21128	
6.	June	19830	20057	20938	
7.	July	14455	13107	11447	
8.	August	15658	14475	12986	
9.	September	12371	13352	16179	
10.	October	36485	34538	26409	
11.	November	74954	78247	74444	
12.	December	67765	50725	98505	
	Total	**426250**	**395570**	**539219**	

Source-LDT, 2013

Table 4.12 presents that 73.06%, 67.34% and 71.11% were domestic tourists in 2010, 2011 and 2012 respectively. Their flow is high in

November, December, January, March and April. June, July, August and September months are dry months or season. On the basis of Nepāl Tourism Action Procedure 2067 if provided the concession and especial facilities to the public service staff, teacher and other agency staffs, it will be promoted at low season of foreign tourists.

Museum art gallery and archives are also the attractive centers for the tourists. Museum provides unique and important information in a limited time, place and movement. In this process Lumbinī museum, Kapilavastu museum, Khudabagar Tharu museum and Sainā-mainā museums in the vicinity of Lumbinī have played a vital role in the promotion of tourism. National as well as international tourists come to visit these museums. Stone sculpture, terracotta figurines, beads, bangles, dabber, flesh-rubber, coins, Buddhist dress, replicas of the sculptures as well as manuscripts are also exhibited these sites. These are not only promoting tourism, but also enhancing the glory of the Nepāli society all over the world. One of them Lumbinī Museum has played a vital role for tourism promotion.

Lumbinī museum located at the cultural sector of Master Plan is also one of the attractions of Lumbinī sacred complex, where the internal as well as international tourists come to observe. Artifacts obtained in course of excavation of Lumbinī archaeological garden, photos of Kapilavastu, and replicas of national museum Kathmandu and received by the Indian Embassy are displayed here. Buddhist dress, vessels and audio-visual facility are also provided to the tourists. In course of visit of Lumbinī about 7% visitors to Lumbinī come here. Ticket charge is fixed Rs. 50, 10 and 5 to the third country visitors, Indian-Nepāli and students respectively.

Table 4.13

Tourists at Lumbini Museum

S.No	*Fiscal Years*	*Internal Tourists*	*International*	*Total*	*Remarks*
1	2064-65	13000	795	13795	
2	2065-66	22000	937	22937	
3	2066-67	30200	931	31131	
4	2067-68	47745	1846	49591	
5	2068-69	-	-	53891	

Source- LDT, 2013

Table 4.2 shows the total scenario of the visitors in Lumbinī. In 2011 only 5.3% visitors to Lumbinī had visited at the museum. Lumbinī museum visited number of the third country tourists is 0.72%. In 2012 among the 136001 third country tourists to Lumbinī, only 3113 persons had observed this museum. It was only 2.28% among the PPH visitors to Lumbinī museum entry was collected Rs. 280050 and 481615 in 2011 and 2012 respectively. Camera fee is extra charge. Museum is immediately eastern site at the bus park. It is easy to enter. But the almost the tourists go to the Sacred Garden exact birthplace of Lord Buddha. The opinions of the tourists, who visit at the museum, are artifacts are not sufficient, conservation and preservation are not scientific only Indian photos and replicas are displayed here. To manage it reference library, scientific laboratory and scientific display technique should be adopted on time. After promoting its quality the ratio of the tourist will be upgraded in proper ratio in future.

Lumbinī known as the Buddhist world there are Theravadi, Mahayani, Vajrayani monasteries, museum, research centre, archaeological structures as well as natural heritages at the complex. The ratio of the tourists is seen high, but they do not approach at all the components of the Master Plan. Almost the pilgrims and day visitors come at the Māyādevî complex and go back with in a short span time. First of all they are unknown about the various components, viz. monastic zone, circular levee, central canal, peace eternal Flame, Peace bell, Research Institute and natural beauty of this Sacred complex. Special plans should have operated for this challenge.

Table 4.14

Places Visited in Lumbini complex

S.No	*Sacred Sites*	*Visitors' Number*	*Position in Percentage*	*Remarks*
1.	Māyādevî Temple	180	90	
2.	Nepāl Vipassana Centre	80	40	
3.	Gautami Bhikkhuni Sangh	110	55	
4.	Myānmār Temple	112	56	
5.	Sri Lankan Monastery	60	30	
6.	Mahabodhi Society Monastery	120	60	
7.	Royal Thaii Monastery	122	61	

S.No	Sacred Sites	Visitors' Number	Position in Percentage	Remarks
8.	International Panditaram Mediation Centre	20	10	
9.	Mananga Sewa Samaja	30	15	
10.	Chinese Monastery	130	65	
11.	Korean Monastery	130	65	
12.	Dharmodaya stupa & Vihar	80	40	
13.	Lotus Stupa, Germany	140	70	
14.	Museum	14	7	
15.	Lumbini International Research Institute	10	5	
16.	Nipponzan Myhoji Peace Stupa	130	65	
17.	Natural Scenic Birds, Crane etc watching	40	20	
18.	Tharu Museum, Khudabagar	10	5	
19.	Kapilvastu	8	4	
20.	Gaidahawa Lake	2	1	

Source-LDT, 2013

In course of field study of this complex 225 questionnaire were distributed to the tourists, on which 200 were returned after fulfillment the required answers. Their visit ratio at the above mentioned table shows that Māyādevî temple is the main focus point to them. Due to the sacred pilgrimage site almost the devotees come to pay devotional feeling at Māyādevî temple complex. 90% of the total Lumbinī visitors observed the Māyādevî temple. In course of the visitor's survey only of the sacred complex, 44% had observed the Mayadevi temple during 2001-2002 (Coningham, 2011:1-7). At that time the temple was under construction. After completation of the construction work its attraction drastically changed. In 2001-2002, Asoka pillar was judged most important by 15.3% and Nativity sculpture of Buddha was observed by 11% during that period. Puskarini tank and Pipal tree, immediately west of the tank were also watched by 4.3 and 2.7% respectively (Ibid). In 2012, 70% tourists had visited to the lotus stupa, Germany Tara Foundation on the Western monastic zone. Thāi complex and Mahāmāyā Mahābodhi monastery were also visited by 61% and 60% among them. Gautami Bhikkhuni Sangha and Lokāmuni pagoda of

Myānmār were also observed by 55% and 56% respectively. The ratio represents that domestic as well as international tourists easily visit at the eastern monastic zone.

Chinese monastery and Korean monastery were visited by 65% of the total tourists of Lumbinī. Shanti stupa of Nipponzan Myohoji is also visited by 65% tourists. It is one of the attractions of Lumbinī complex. Only 30% visitors reached at Śri Laṅkan monastery due to backside of Gautami Bhikkhuni Sangha. Panditaram Lumbinī International meditation centre, Lumbinī International Research Institute, Tharu museum, Dānāpur Lake, Gaidahawā Lake and museum are not easily accessible to the visitors. Meditation centre is concerned only to the mediators, especially foreigners. Research centre is also not related with general public. Due to the office calendar museum is also not access to all the visitors. The tour and travel agencies of Indiā take the tourists for 2 or 3 hours in Lumbinī. They visit at Māyādevî temple and go back within proposed time schedule at Gorakhpur or other sites of Nepāl. A field survey has shown that 68% visitors of Lumbinī spent only less than 30 minutes (Coningham, 2011:6). It is not reliable result. The Surveyor might have seen only the teams of Indian visitors, which are not counted as tourists, but they are only day visitors. They do not get chance to take general information of the sites except Māyādevî temple area. They throw only wastage in Lumbinī and go back with out any benefit to Nepāl. It is a challenge to the authority, who counts the number of tourists to show their high flow of tourists. Only number is not fruitful without income of this risky industry.

Jurisdiction of Lumbinī Development Trust is concerned to Kapilavastu Tilaurākoṭ, Goṭihawā, Niglihawā, Rāmagrāma, Devadaha etc. Some of the pilgrims who come on Lumbinī visit at Tilaurākoṭ mound and Kapilavastu museum to know the real situation and findings of ancient Śākya Republic.

Table 4.15

Tourists at Tilaurākot

S. No.	*Years*	*Nepāli*	*Indian*	*Third Country*	*Total*	*Changed Position*
1.	2009	-	-	13697	13697	--
2.	2010	5160	1361	16216	22737	66 %
3.	2011	3256	1434	23025	27715	21.9 %
4.	2012	4198	1217	33143	38558	40.2%

Source- LDT, Tiaurakot Office, 2013

Tilaurākoţ is the capital city of ancient Kapilavastu. It is extended 1700 feet north-south and 1300 feet east-west including security fort all around it. National as well as international tourists go there. According to the above mentioned table 13697, 16216, 23025 and 33143 third country tourists had visited at Tilaurākoţ in 2009, 2010, 2011 and 2012 respectively. Indian visitors are 1361, 1434 and 1217 in 2010,2011 and 2012 respectively. These figures show that single day visitors from India are not mention in this record. In total the ratio has increased 66% in 2010. But the ratio is low only 21.9% in 2011. In 2012 it is promoted in 40.2%, which is satisfactory. In 2012 archaeological excavation was carried out at Lohasaudiā, immediately about 200 meter east of Tilaurākoţ mound and on the north of Tilaurākoţ mound. Due to archaeological activities tourists were motivated at Tilaurākoţ site.

On the south-west bank of Bāṇagaṅgā river and immediately on the south of Ramaghat at Kapilavastu is situated Kapilavastu museum. Artifacts of Tilaurākoţ, Pipari, Goţihawā, Araurākoţ and of other sites surface findings are deposited in this museum. Terracotta figurines, coins, seals and sealings are also displayed in showcases (Fig. 33). Due to the capital city of ancient Kapilavastu many tourists are visiting here. Lack of proper transport from Taulihawa to the museum many interested tourists can not approach there. Its tourist movement shows the Table-4.16.

Table 4.16

Kapilvastu Museum Visitors

S.No	*Fiscal Years*	*Domestic*	*International*	*Total*	*Remarks*
1.	2063-64 July	3020	393	3413	July 16 to 15
2.	2064-65	2231	530	2761	"
3.	2065-66	3040	565	3605	"
4.	2066-67	3029	637	3666	"
5.	2067-68	4169	651	4820	"
6.	2068-69	5753	558	6311	"

Source- Kapilvastu Museum, 2013

In fiscal years 2063-064, 2064-065, 2065-66 and 2066-67 the number of the tourists was 3413, 2761, 3605 and 3666 respectively. During this international tourist number is 393, 530,565 and 637 from 2063 to 067 respectively. In 2067-68 and 2068-069 total tourists were 4820 and 6311.

In two years internationalal tourists ratio was 651 and 558 respectively. In the comparison of Table 4.15 and 4.16, it is clear that tourists of Tilaurākoṭ do not enter into museum, which is not far. International tourist ratio is only in hundred figures at the museum, which is vast different between two sites. It means that museum observation mechanism is not easy and comfortable. First of all it opens only office days and hours, but tourists usually come on holidays to take rest recreation and relax. Tuesday is holiday at the museum, but it is not known all of them. Information system should be scientific and practical to achieve its target.

Khudābagar Thāru Museum, which is situated about 8 km. north-east of Lumbinī, is also important site to observe Thāru culture and natural beauty i.e., monkey-tree, punnihawā Lake. Some of the tourists who come in Lumbinī have reached there. TRPAP had promoted this museum. It is not systematically operating due to the lack of budget. Saināmainā museum as well as structural remains of Jogiḍāḍā, Baurākholā, Sanopaṭel, Rānikuwā, Patthar kuwā and Patel are unique and attractive. Natural scene of Saināmainā is also beautiful as well as peace zone. Some tourists also visit these museums and sites. But, there is no record system in Sainā mainā. In course of field study, flow of the visitors was seen. It is potential area for tourism development. Package tourism and tourist circuit should be managed in proper way. Its networking among Palpa, Gulmi, Arghakhachi, Baglung, Pyuthan, Rolpa, Mustang, Pokhara and Chitawan must be well- managed by the authorities. Natural as well as cultural heritages of Palpa are motivating to the domestic and international tourists. The ratio of the tourists was 26.73% increased in 2012-13 (NRB, 2013:16).

Tourism being the outcome of combination of the motivations, It depends upon the free consent and curiosity of the visitors. Satisfaction and achievement of goal are the major motivation factors. Leisure, transport facilities, income, accommodation, locale, package tours, climate, business, natural beautification, better education, world exhibition, trade, fairs and cultural heritages are known as motivating factors to visit. Geographical items, historical and archaeological monuments as well as pilgrimage sites are major elements of tourist attraction. In this situation Lumbinī and its neighbour sites are related with cultural, archaeological and pilgrimage status. Lumbinī, the birthplace of Śākyamuni Buddha, is the symbol of peace, compassion, pity and harmony.

Tourists usually visit from Śri Laṅka, Thāiland, Koreā, Myānmār, Taiwan, China and Jāpan at the Sacred complex of Lumbinī. Jāpanese are in decreasing position due to negative impact after the killing of Ven. Nawatame at the vicinity of Nipponzan Myohoji Peace Stupa. Chinese are in increasing position. Nepāl Government has also attempted to motivate them through Chinese Government and civil society sectors. February, March, August, September, October, November and December are high tourist months and remaining is low tourist season. For endemic and sustainable tourism the authority should have provided special concessions, discounts and subsidizes to the hotels, airlines, tourist buses and visitors during the period of low tourist months. To extend the length of stay various cultural programs, Buddhist Circuit-sites visit, religious activities performing and recreational activities should be managed by the authorities in proper time and situations.

CHAPTER FIVE

PILGRIMS AND PILGRIMAGE

Concept and Motives

The institution of pilgrimage plays an important role in generating "a circulation mechanism" in which all the social strata of Buddhist participate. The institution of pilgrimage in the Buddhist world is as old as the life time of Buddha. When Buddha was lying down on the death bed at the age of eighty in Kuśinagar his disciples, monks and nuns surrounded him. Buddha advised with feeling of holy reverence and awe, viz. the place where the *Tathāgata* was born (Lumbinī grove), the place where he had reached perfect enlightenment (Bodha-Gayā), the place where the first time he had proclaimed the law (Deer park near Varāṇasi) and the place of his final extinction (Kushinagar). These facts reveal that Lumbinī was declared as the sacred spot to the pilgrims and was regularly visited by the monks, nuns and devotees at this sacred-place.

In modern period conflict and violence there is much emphasis on the linguistic, geographical, regional and social diversities created by the political activities and dogmatic religious body. They are playing a vital role in integrating the societies of this part of the world into one cognate order. The motives of the earning of the religious merit consist of holy places and *darśana* of the deities. The religious merits support and lead one to attain *Nirvāṇa* at the end.

Tirtha phala and Tirtha practices

According to the orthodox view a pilgrimage is not a pleasure tour, and if undertaken with such motive it fails to become a *tirtha-yatra.* One of such opportunities is furnished by the discipline of pilgrimage which is not an end in itself but only one of the means to the high tested end. The merits of pilgrimage range from immediate relief from *tirtha yatra* troubles to the expiation of sins and gaining the ultimate Reality. There is no automatic spiritual reaction to the mechanical act or rite; the mental *tirthaṣ* are more effective than the physical ones. Sacred complex as well as the activities done by the nuns, monks and devotees also supports to secure a co-ordination between pious life and highest knowledge.

Fasting, sexual abstinence, abstinence from unguents, soft bed and luxuries rejection of the aid of the vehicles or animals for making journey, and walking without shoes in *tirtha* have been enjoined on the pilgrims with a view to producing righteous mind by disciplining the body. The pilgrims worship the deities of the site while chanting the Buddhist *mantras* offering the prayers and different kinds of gifts sand finally doing *darshan*. The throwing of fruits, flowers, money and shaved-hair is also considered to be meritorious. Living at a *tirtha* or *barsāvāss* of at least four month is considered to be an important means of obtaining salvation or *nirvana*. *Parikarma* of the *tirtha* is also an important act. The liberal feeding accompanied by *dakṣiṇā* to monks, nuns and hungry is also a commendable practice during pilgrimage.

Pilgrimage of Lumbinī

According to *Kundala Vadana of Divyavadana* having led King Aśoka into the Lumbinī jungle, venerable Upagupta indicated with his right hand and said "*Asmin Mahārājā pradase bhagavan jatah*", meaning 'Oh Great king! Here the Blessed one was born!" King Aśoka made an offer of one hundred thousand gold coins and established the first *cetiya* or pagoda. In the next chapter *Aśoka vadana of Divyavadan* we find the description of the site. In the Aśokan pillar of Lumbinī it is inscribed that "Here *Bhagwan Śākya*muni was at the Lumbinī village". It is translated by Führer as to mean King *Piyadasi* beloved of the Gods (or dear to the Gods), having been anointed 20 years came himself and worshipped saying: "Here Buddha Śākya muni was born", and he got a stone (capital) representing a horse, and the stone pillar erected. Because here the worshipped one was born, the village of Lumbinī has been made free of taxes and a recipient of wealth. According to Hultzsch it mean, 'when king, beloved of gods, had been anointed twenty years he came himself and worshipped (this spot).' Here Buddha Śākyamuni was born. He got a stone bearing horse made at this place.

Hiuen-Tsiang's remark that the capital of the pillar contained a horse figure confirms to this interpretation. "As quoted by Rhys Davids, Bohler also says that "a stone horse was made and put on a stone pillar". King Aśoka installed the stone column with a clear legend inscribed on it that it is the spot of Lumbinī where the Blessed one was born. In Lumbinī a brick railing was erected at a distance of 48.76 cm. from the base of the pillar and it had dentils also. After the visit of Emperor, many monks and nuns had started visiting the place. A large number of monasteries and vihārs must have been built for their stay in this sacred complex. A large number of artifacts of the Mauryan, Suṅga, Kushāṇa and Gupta periods were recovered in course of various excavations. It is thus clear that it continued to be a place of pilgrimage since the third century BC till to date.

Chinese pilgrims have given a more accurate and authentic description of Lumbinī. Shui-Ching-Chu describes that at Lumbinī the Aśokan tree which was gripped by Māyādeví at the time of Siddartha's birth was still in a living condition and an image of Māyādeví was placed there where devotees used to offer *puja* articles. The spot where Siddhartha's feet touched the earth first, Aśoka got the Siddhartha's foot prints shielded with stones. His description has been ratified by the noticeable findings discovered during the joint excavation of the DoA, LDT and JBF from 1993 to 1997. It is clearly seen that Aśoka had shielded the Siddhartha's footprints with stones in order to secure it. This significant news of the findings of the excavation was publicly declared by then Honorable Prime Minister Sher Bahādur Deubā on February 4, 1996.

The monumental and habitation structures, stone sculptures, terracotta human and animal figurines, fragments of pottery belonging to the Mauryan, Suṅga, Kushāṇa, Gupta, Vardhan and Sena-Pāla periods, found here prove that Lumbinī was well-populated till the early-medieval period and was frequently visited by the monks, nuns and other devotees from time to time. Fa-Hien and Hiuen-Tsiang had visited in Lumbinī, Kapilvastu and Rāmagrāma in the 5th and 7th centuries respectively. They were also motivated from the sacred concept of Buddhism. The names of Jitari Malla (1287-89 AD) and Ripu Malla (1312 AD) were engraved on the stone columns (pillars) at

Niglihawā and Lumbinī garden. It consists of the words, "*Om mani padme hum, shree Ripumallaschiran jayatu, 1234*". The former portion is a Mahayani Buddhist prayer and the later portion means "Prince Ripu Malla, be victorious for long 1234". The year 1234 in the Saka era, corresponding to 1312 AD. Bhuwan Lāl Pradhan has claimed that Sikandar Lodī (1489-1517 AD) and Aurangzeb (1668-1707AD) were mainly responsible for the destruction of cultural heritage and property of the Lumbinī- Kapilvastu region. Prof.Dr. Tulsiram Vaidya, s versions is that this area was collapsed and destroyed due to the devastating earthquake in early medieval period. During the reign of Mukunda Sena I (1540-1575 AD), Mukunda Sena II (1750-82 AD) and Mahadatta Sena (1782- 93 AD) in Pālpā the previous religious condition in the region could not be retained. The site was lost in the dense forest until the discovery of General Khadga Shamsher JB Rāṇā, Governor of Pālpā.

In 1967 U-Thant the then Secretary General of the UNO had visited Lumbinī and after that he offered the help of the United Nations for the development of Lumbinī. Due to the keen interest of UNO, Prof. Kenzo Tange and Urtec of Jāpan prepared the architectural Master Plan of the Lumbinī garden and Lumbinī Development Committee organized various development in this region. Late King Mahendra Bir Bikram Shah had shown keen interest in developing Lumbinī as a sacred complex for all the human beings. In 1985 Lumbinī Development Trust was created as an autonomous and non -governmental organization for the creative work instead of Lumbinī Development Committee. Then His royal Highness prince and Chairman of LDT Gyanendra Bir Bikram Shah paid a visit to the United Nations and had addressed the International Committee for the Development of Lumbinī in 1986. At that time Gyanendra had also visited Jāpan and Koreā to promote awareness and to develop friendly relationship with each other. In 1986, Gyanendra lit a torch of eternal peace in Lumbinī in commemoration of the International Peace Year.

Composition of Pilgrims

To analyse the pilgrimage to Lumbinī in modern times a sample of 200 pilgrims representing the various cross-sections of Buddhist society was drawn up from hotels, monasteries, *dharmaśālā* and lodges. The flow of pilgrims visiting the peace city is almost uniformly large round the year. By the pilgrimage of the Lumbinī, they shall receive all kinds of worldly pleasures, peace, progencies and exemption from different kinds of ailments and obstacles in the life. A large number of people from the ancient period have continued to come here from China, Indiā and other western countries. The pilgrims from more than eighty countries, viz. Jāpan, south-Koreā, Thāiland, Taiwān, China, Indiā etc, come here on the important days of festivals and proper season to offer their prayer and respect to the deities . Buddha *Jayanti*, *Barsāvass*, Chaitra *śukla purṇimā* etc are the main occasions when there are many festivities and much rejoicing in Lumbinī. During their visiting the visitors of the monasteries, temples and stūpas offer prayers and oblations and represent their devotion in traditional manner.

The pilgrims and local people of Lumbinī often hesitated from filling up the questionnaires and within a short span of time to study the number of pilgrims and their features.

Table 5. 1

Showing professions of the pilgrims

S.No.	*Professions*	*No. of pilgrims*	*Percentage*	*Remarks*
1.	Peasant	50	25 %	
2.	Business	44	22 %	
3.	Higher professions (Doctor, lawers, Engineers etc.	24	12 %	
4.	Students	40	20 %	
5.	Monks & Nuns	16	8 %	
6.	Menial Services	18	9 %	
7.	Other professions	8	4 %	
	Total	200	100 %	

Source: Field survey, 2012-13.

Table 5. 1 presents the profession of the pilgrims. It represents that there were 25 % peasants, 20 % students and 12 % of higher professional tourists in course of this field study. Businessmen as well as monks and nuns visited from various countries. Bhairahawa being a main entrance gate of western Nepāl, businessmen who come to Bhairahawa they reach in Lumbinī at their free time. 22% of the business persons visited in course of this field work. Monks and nuns are 8 % during this period. Co-operatives as well as rural development agencies have also take to the farmers in Lumbinī. Almost all the peasants are domestic visitors only for one or two night over.

Table 5. 2

Showing percentage of literacy among the pilgrims

S.N.	*Educational qualification*	*No. of pilgrims*	*Percentage*	*Remarks*
1.	Illiterate	24	12 %	
2.	Literate	60	30%	
3.	Matriculate	22	11%	
4.	Intermediate	38	19%	
5.	Graduate	18	9%	
6.	Post-graduate	12	6%	
7.	Buddhalogists	16	8%	
8.	Professional qualification (Technicians)	10	5%	

Source: Field survey, 2012-13

Table No. 5.2 shows 12% of the pilgrims of Lumbinī were the illiterate persons and 30% of them were only literate. Number of illiterate is decreasing than last years (Giri, 2008: 128). 11% pilgrims among them were matriculate and 19% were intermediate passed. 9% graduate, 6% post-graduate and 8% Buddhalogists had come for pilgrimages during this study period (Figs.28 & 29). Monks and nuns from various countries were experts in Buddhist literature, art and architecture. The educated pilgrims had known the significance of Lumbinī and they came here to visit Māyādevi temple, Aśokan pillar and monasteries. Some of them were interested to see ancient Telār River, described in Chinese accounts. They feel that Buddha's peace has motivated them to come to the sacred complex and offering donations to the poors, Lumbinī Development Trust and proper local NGOs to build building and create peace . At present Lumbinī has become a particular site of attraction for its great natural and scenic beauty, the school, campus and university students of Buddhist countries visit this place for educational tour and pilgrimage. Nepālese students have also come here.

Table 5. 3

Pilgrims by sex and age groups

S.No.	*Age range*	*No. of pilgrims Male*	*Female*	*Total*	*Percentage*	*Remarks*
1.	0-15 years	12	8	20	10	
2.	16-30 years	30	20	50	25	
3.	31-45 years	42	28	70	35	
4.	46-60 years	18	12	30	15	
5.	61-Over years	18	7	25	12.5	
6	Not specified	-	-	5	2.5	
	Total	**100**		**200**	**100 %**	

Source: Field survey, 2012-13

Table 5.3 represents the highest number of pilgrims at Lumbini is of the people between the years 31 and 45, which are 35%. Pilgrims' age of 16 to 30 years was 25 %. At the last phase of life over 60 years, 12.5% among them had visited during this study period. Age of 46 to 60 years group was 15 %. Below 15 years group had come with their family members and teachers. The highest number during the 31-45 was conscious and interested to now about Lumbinī and its international publicity. Almost of them were also professionals and businessmen. This table indicates that this age group must be motivated to preserve and develop Lumbinī. Among the tourists males were more than females. Its main cause is that male can visit in single, but females are scarcely visiting one her without male partner.

Table 5. 4

Team of pilgrims

S.No.	*Visiting team member with*	*No. of pilgrims*	*Percentage*	*Remarks*
1.	Alone	18	9	
2.	Family members	36	18	
3.	Friend and relatives	44	22	
4.	In groups (Mass)	72	36	
5.	Couple	30	15	
	Total	**200**	**100%**	

Source: Field survey, 2012-13

Table 5. 4 shows the pilgrims comprised of various sizes such as single, couple, family and group visitors and the largest number of visitors belonged to group visitors, which include 36%. Pilgrims from Thāiland, Taiwān, South-Koreā, Jāpan, Myānmār and Indiā usually come in groups for three days (Figs.29, 30 & 41). 18% of pilgrims come with their family members, viz. parents, brothers, sisters, grand-father and grand- mother at Lumbinī. Nine percent among them had visited alone age of 18-35. Fifty percent were couple, who had come to pilgrimage and perform some rituals at the Māyādevi temple complex and at other proper monasteris. Their number has increased than last years. Among the pilgrims of Lumbinī 22% had accommodated in the monasteies, 45% in hotel and lodges, 20% at Bhairahawā and 8% in Indiā, border of Nepāl, ie. Sunauli and Nautanawā. Lumbinī is the prime location of accommodation for majority of the visitors. About 10% of the visitors of Lumbinī use air route for their visit. Travel and Tour companies or agencies directly come from Indiā taking pilgrims and return within a short span of time after bird's eye view at the sacred complex of Lumbinī. This study reveals that mass tourism (pilgrims) should be emphasised providing miminum visa-charge, discount, subsidizes and other proper facilities.

Table 5.5

Tourists Arrival by Nationality and Frequency of Visit in Lumbini

S.No	*Nationality*	*Frequency*		*Total*	*Percentage*	*Remarks*
		First time	*More than Once*			
1	Nepāl	45	18	63	31.5	
2	Indiā	22	12	34	17	
3	Srī Lanka	15	5	20	10	
4	Thāīland	11	4	15	7.5	
5	South Koreā	9	3	12	6	
6	Japan	8	2	10	5	
7	USA	7	1	8	4	
8	UK	4	-	4	2	
9	Taiwan	3	1	4	2	
10	Chinā	5	-	5	2.5	
11	Myānmār	9	3	12	6	
12	Others	3	-	3	1.5	
13	Not Stated	-	-	10	5	
	Total	**145**	**45**	**200**	**100 %**	

Source: Field survey, 2012-13

Table 5. 5 present the highest number of domestic tourists. Single day visitors with out night stay in Lumbinī have not mentioned in this study. Farmers, office holders, students as well as monk-nuns usually come here. Seventeen percent were Indian tourists during this study. Due to the border side Indian guests come frequently in all seasons and can go back easily in a day. Some of them from far i.e. Mahārāstra, Gujarāta and Punjāb spent three or more days in Lumbinī and Kapilvastu. Śri Laṅkan tourists are in 10 %. They are completely devoted towards Buddhism and Buddha's teachings. Thai, South Korean and Myānmār tourists are interested to visit Lumbinī due to religious concept and motivation of Lumbinī. Visitors from Jāpan, Taiwān and China had come in the ratio of 5 %, 2 % and 2.5 %. Jāpanese tourist's number was decreasing than last ten years. UK, USA, Denmark, Frānce, Pākistan, Netherland, Finland, Germany, Singāpore, Malaysiā and others visit Lumbinī for their own purpose.

Table 5. 6

Motivation Factors

S.No.	*Motivator*	*Tourist No*	*Percentage*	*Remarks*
1	Advertisements (Radio, TV, FM, Net, Magazines etc.)	48	24	
2	Travel and tour Agents	30	15	
3	Sacred Religious Books	50	25	
4	Friends	45	22.5	
5	Guide Books	15	7.5	
6	Relatives	8	4	
7	Not Stated	3	1.5	
	Total	200	100 %	

Source: Field survey, 2012-13

According to the Table 5.6 Radio, Television, Frequency Modulation, magazines, papers and internet have played a vital role in the promotion of tourism in Lumbinī. In the 21 the century communication is the more effective medium, which can propagate at any thing with in a short span of time. Lumbinī Development Trust has also created *www.Lumbinītrust.org* to provide proper information to the interested individual as well as corporate body in all over the world. It has also supported to provide proper information. Travel and Tour Agents, especially of Indiā have helped to motivate the guests for the visit of Lumbinī. Nepālese as well as Indian Tour and Travel Agencies have informed to 15 % tourists. Buddhist religious books, written in Nepāl and India, have also supported to spread the significance of Lumbinī in Buddhist as well non-Buddhist countries. Friends, guide books and relatives are also motivating to the interested pilgrims to come at this sacred complex.

Table 5.7

Average Length of Stay in Lumbini

S.No.	*Length of Stay*	*Tourist No*	*Percentage*	*Average Days*
1	One day	102	51	
2	Two days	36	18	
3	Three days	36	18	
4	Four days	10	5	
5	Five days	8	4	
6	More than five days	8	4	
	Total	**200**	**100**	

Source: Field Study 2012-13

Statistic number of visit is not satisfactory at their stay in Lumbinī. Third country tourists should have stated minimum 3 or more days in Lumbinī or in the vicinity of Lumbinī. Other wise it is not concrete benefit to the civil society as well as the government of Nepāl. In course of visit to Lumbinī 51 % of the total tourists go back in a day. They pass only 24 hours and use their baggage for food. Only they take rest at the cheapest accommodations. Their activities can not effect in the economic aspect of this area as project in Lumbinī Master Plan. 18 % of them pass two and three days in the process of their visit. 5 % and 4 % among them respectively pass four and five days in Lumbinī complex far their journey of Lumbinī. 4 % visits more than five days, who are Thai, Śri Lańkan, Myānmār and Korean. Before that a survey had conducted with in a span of time, which had resulted that 41.82% and 58.18% visitors had stayed one and more than two days respectively (Ghimire, 2006:109). In course of socio-economic survey of Lumbinī Okada had also mentioned that researchers and general visitors stayed about 3 days and mediators as well as devotees had stayed between 15 to 30 days in Lumbinī complex (Okada, 1969). Several monasteries have been built here for the pilgrims by the national and international donor agencies. Monasteries have not fixed the accommodation charge to the pilgrims, but they can donate on their own will.

This study reveals that monasteries have not captured pilgrims from business point of view. Pilgrims stay at Bhairahawā bazaar, 22 km. east from Lumbinī. Some of them go Indiā across the border after their visit. Only a few pilgrims stay in the houses of their relatives and friends at the time of their stay at Lumbinī, they generally visit archaeological garden, monastic zone, meditation-centers, bird-watching *Sāras* and *Nilgāi* watching, dance, sing and enjoy themselves by undertaking various kinds of entertainments. The number of male pilgrims is always higher than that of the female pilgrims. Almost the foreign tourists usually come from more than eighty countries, especially from Jāpan, South Koreā, Thāiland, Taiwān, Myānmār, Chinā and Indiā. In an attempt to assess the attitude of pilgrims towards the sacred complex in general we enquired about their pilgrim's cycle, their motivators and their knowledge of the sacred complex in Lumbinī. Pilgrims were motivated by their kinsmen, family members and friends.

Peasants, business men and students are motivated to visit in Lumbinī. Peasants usually visit on their off season of farming and annual schedules of local NGOs' and Government Agriculture Office. Female groups, banana farming groups, bee-farming groups, fish-farming groups etc visit Lumbinī in course of their targets. Higher professionals, i.e. doctors, lawyers, engineers, professors etc), monks, nuns, menial services and others' ratio of visit is low. About one third of the tourists in Lumbinī complex are literate and intermediate in qualification are about 20%. Graduate, post-graduate and illiterate persons are also visiting. 31 to 45 aged persons are about 35 % and 16 to 30 aged are 25 %. The ratio of the aged over 61 years is only 12.5%. This study indicates that people of 16 to 45 years old are more motivated than others. More than one third visitors visit in mass and 22 % with their friends and relatives in this sacred complex. About 22% tourists had visited more than the second times. About 78% tourists had visited at first time at the complex. Srī Lankan, Korean, Jāpanese, Myānmār and Thai tourists had come the second and third times. In the survey of 2001-2002, it has shown that Srī Lankan and Indian pilgrims were more about 49% and 75% once more respectively in Lumbinī (Coningham, 2011:6). Radio, TV, FM and magazines have played a vital role to provide proper information to the tourists. Sacred books and friends have also motivated to them. Half of the tourists go back from Lumbinī in a day. In average their length of stay is about 5 days. It is very poor in the comparison of national ratio.

CHAPTER SIX

MODES OF TRANSPORT

One of the basic elements of tourism is transportation. In course of travel of the tourist a mode of transport is necessary to reach at the destination. In ancient period a visitor used horse, horse-cart, bull-carts, hand-carriage and boat to visit at purposes sites. It was not easy affairs during that period. Tourists were attacked by the wild life, misbehaved by human beings as well as no security of health. In the process of invention new mechanical technique for speed railways and motorcar transport were started since the post World War I in the nineteenth century. After the invention of road transport a lot of businessmen, administrators, diplomats, researchers, family visitors as well as interested persons got chance to move from one site to another by road transport. To visit quickly at any remote area or at long distance plane was invented in post World War II.

At the beginning road and air transport were used at the wars. After the war was over they were used as modes of transport for travel. Airports and roads built during war period were used for travelling tourists and transport goods at various sites of the world. Road transport, rail transport, ocean and air were used at the beginning. Among these transport road transport was easy and general. In ancient Nepāl goods were carried on horse, sheep or bull carts. According to Kautilya *Arthasastra* woolen-blankets and *pākhī* were exported from Nepāl to Pataliputra. Huge stone pillar were also taken from Chunargadha to Lumbinî, Niglihawā and Gotihawā during the period of Aśoka. In ancient Kapilavastu roads were connected from north to south, east to west, north to west and north to east in course of travelling and transport goods. Due to the road facilities Chinese pilgrims, viz. Shu-Chi-Chu, Fa-Hien, Huien-Tsiang and Wu-Kung had visited in ancient Kapilavastu, Devadaha and other sites in the 4th, 5th, 7th 8th centuries respectively. In the Lichchhavi period road transport as well as boat system were used during the war period and in order to carry goods. Elephant, horse and camels were used at war. In the medieval period there was not invented other mechanical equipment except the previous modes. In the modern the concept of transport became more popular due to the influence of the neighbors countries. Due to the geographical condition of Nepāl road transport and air transport are the main medium.

Road Transport

At the beginning private car and coach were used for short and medium journey. Roads were not black topped. Mud tracks and motor able roads were only dry season. Motor car took the place of private car and coach for both short and medium range journeys. East-west High way was started in v.s.2019 to connect all the parts of Nepāl. North-south roads were also constructed in Siddhartha High way from Bhairahawā to Pokharā has played a vital role to promote tourism industry in the region. It joins East-west Highway at Butwal. Bhairahawā to Lumbinî road was also proposed in Lumbinî Master Plan to approach domestic as well as international tourists.Three hundred kilometer black-topped road of Siddhartha Highway and East-west Highways are providing services in Nawalparasi, Rupandehi and Kapilvastu district areas (NRB, 2013:18). By the support of UNESCO, UNDP and Nepāl government it was completed in 1985. Kapilavastu to Lumbinî, Nawalparasi to Lumbinî, Highway at the point of Rudrapur to Lumbinî and other internal roads support to approach domestic as well as international tourists in Lumbinî. Kakrahawā (Indiā) to Lumbinî, Chakarchauḍā to Lumbinî, and Sorajagaḍha to Lumbinī and Sunauli to Lumbinî roads are connected. Indian and third country tourists enter from these routes, public bus, private cars, taxi are providing proper facilities to the tourists (Transport Office, 2013). The provision of the good motor roads and road services are important factors in the promotion of both domestic and international tourism. Indian tourists are travelling by road increased as more and more at their holidays away from home. Six lane Belahiya to Butwal International Trade Route is also providing proper tourist services (NRB, 3013:18). Newer and faster road from Bhumahî, Nawalparãsî immediate north of Rãmagrãma to Lumbinî are built which made movement of traffic by road faster and comfortable than last years.

Table 6.1

Distance Chart (Bhairahawã to Lumbinî=22 Km)

	Sunauli	Bhairahawã	Butwal	Tansen	Pokharã	Narayanghat	Mugling	Naubise	Taulihawã	Lamahi	Dang	Tulsipur	Kohalpur	Nepãlgunj	Birendranagar	Krishnanagar	Banbasa	Kathmãndu	Hetauda	Birganj	Jankpur
Bhairahawã	4	0																			
Butwal	26	22	0																		
Tansen	63	61	39	0																	
Pokharã	184	180	158	119	0																
Narayanghat	142	138	116	153	126	0															
Mugling	178	174	152	135	90	35	0														
Nawbise	262	258	236	280	264	150	84	0													
Taulihawã	88	84	62	101	207	178	214	278	0												
Lamhi	142	138	116	155	261	232	268	352	54	0											
Dang	166	184	149	179	285	256	292	376	78	24	0										
Tulsipur	190	186	164	203	309	230	316	400	102	48	24	0									
Kohalpur	262	258	236	275	381	352	388	472	174	120	96	120	.0								
Nepãlgunj	284	280	258	297	403	374	410	494	136	142	118	166	22	0							
Birendranagar	353	349	327	366	472	443	479	563	265	211	137	235	91	69	0						
Krishnanagar	111	107	85	124	230	201	237	321	23	31	55	79	151	173	242	0					
Banbasa	466	462	440	479	585	556	592	676	378	324	300	279	204	182	113	355	0				
Kathmãndu	288	284	262	306	200	146	116	194	326	378	402	426	490	520	589	347	702	0			
Hetauda	220	216	192	233	204	78	114	168	256	310	334	358	430	458	521	279	634	224	0		
Birganj	270	266	244	283	254	128	164	248	308	360	384	408	480	562	571	329	634	274	50	0	
Janakpur	379	375	353	392	363	237	273	357	415	483	493	517	589	603	678	438	793	385	159	157	0
Rajbiraj	450	446	424	463	434	308	344	428	486	540	564	589	660	690	749	503	864	454	230	228	119
Itahari	520	516	494	533	504	378	474	498	556	610	634	658	772	750	819	579	934	524	306	298	189
Dhankuta	588	584	562	601	572	449	482	566	624	678	702	726	718	812	887	647	1002	582	368	366	257
Dharan	538	534	512	551	522	396	432	516	574	628	652	676	788	768	837	597	952	542	318	316	207
Kakarbhitta	614	610	588	627	696	470	526	590	650	704	728	752	824	844	913	673	1028	616	392	380	281
Kodan	502	498	376	420	314	265	224	328	478	492	516	540	612	632	701	461	816	116	378	388	497
Trishuli	356	352	330	374	268	314	178	262	392	446	470	694	566	586	655	415	770	68	282	332	451
Biratnagar	542	538	516	555	526	400	436	520	578	632	656	630	752	772	841	601	956	546	478	476	211

The chart shows the distances from various sites of Nepãl to Bhairahawã, about 22 km east of Lumbinî. Gautam Buddha Airport is also located at Bhairahawã and almost all the public buses come at the site from the various sites of Nepãl. Road transport is available from Biratnagar to Bhairahawã, Pokharã to Bhairahawã and Kathmãndu to Bhairahawã. From western Nepãl buses are providing services to Butwal only. After arrival at Butwal, they usually go by bus to Lumbinî through Bhairahawã. Direct bus from Butwal to Lumbinî is not available.

Table 6.2

Modes of Transportation and Travelling Route

S.No	From-To	Plane	Tourist Bus\ car	Public Bus	Private car\jeep	Taxi	Others	Total
1	Kathmāndu-Lumbinî	6	3 in average	5	4	2	2	22
2	Pokharā-Lumbinî	-	1	1	1	2	-	5
3	Chitawan-Butwal-BWH Lumbinî	-	3	10	3	4	1	21
4	Taulihawā-Lumbinî	-	3	15	2	5	3	28
5	Palpa-BTW Lumbinî	-	2	7	3	3	4	19
6	Indiā-Lumbinî	-	4	2 in mass	4	6	3	17
7	Bhairhawa-Lumbinî	-	2	35	7	11	5	60
8	Other sites-Lumbinî	-	2	3	2	3	3	13

Source- Paschimanchal and Siddhartha Bus Vyavasayi Sanga, 2013

Thirty five buses are allotted from Bhairahawā to Lumbinî and 5 from Kathmāndu to Lumbinî per day. Direct and high speed coaches are lunching at night as well as on day from Kathmāndu to Lumbinî. Above mentioned table shows that buses are regularly running to Lumbinî. Bhairahawā to Lumbinî bus service provides transport to the tourists from Indiā, Butwal, Tansen, Pokharā and from other sites. Mobility is one of the major causes of the development of the motor transport from Bhairahawā to Lumbinî. Speed also economizes on time, which supports to travel to distant places with limited amount of time. At the construction of wide motorways from Bhairahawā to Lumbinî domestic tourists as well as foreigners are also increasing to relax their holidays.

Regular plane service is available from Kathmāndu to Gautam Buddha Airport, Siddharthanagar. About 30 minute's public bus reach in Lumbinî from Airport. Taxi services are also available here. Taxi fare is NC Rs. 1200 /- from Airport to Lumbinî except internal visit charge. If engaged for 8 hours it will be about 3,000/- only. Day visitors go back within 4-5 hours. They are not tourists. In this study is also counted to them. The number of vehicles is fixed on the basic of the flow of the tourists. It is decided by the Yãtãyãta Vyavasa Samities, viz. Paschimanchal and Siddhartha Yãtãyãta Samiti.

The Asian Highway

According to the decision of the United Nations Economic and Social Commission for Asia and the Pacific (ESCAP) and the co-operation of 15 Asian countries, viz. Nepãl, Indiã, Afghanistan, Bangladesh, Burma, Canadian, Indonesia, Singapore, Śri Lańkã, Thãiland etc., the Asian Highway project for a network of about 66,000 kilometers has proposed. Its target is to construct east-west route connecting as possible many countries as possible with proper linkage to other countries. The Asian Highway is proposed to connect Lumbini immediately north of the master plan area (Tinge, 1978). After completion of this road Asian as well as other internationalal tourists can reach Lumbinî in cheap direct and within limited time. It will reinforce to the tourists to visit Lumbinî.

Road Transport of Lumbinî

Lumbinî is situated about 198 km. south-west of Pokharã and 306 km from Kathmãndu. It connects Kapilavastu, Nawalparãsî, Butwal, Bhairahawã, Khunuwã and other sites in the western region of Nepãl. Lumbinî- Bhairahawã road connects Sunauli-Pokharã Siddhartha *Rãjamãrga* at Siddharthanagar Buddhachoka. Lumbinî-Pokharã of Paschimanchal Yãtãyãta Vyavasahi Sanga go one non-stop bus named Sakura in the morning of each day. According to Baburam, Regional Office Staff, fives buses run Kathmãndu and come back from Kathmãndu at the same ratio per day. Bhairahawã to Lumbinî run micro buses of Paśchimãñchala Yãtãyãta and Siddhartha Yãtãyãta Sańgha at the interval about 20 minutes in queue system. If the flow of the passengers are over than scheduled, other additional buses are also permitted to take their quick duty for Lumbinî. Bhairahawã to Lumbinî bus service opens at 6:20 am and last bus of Bhairahawã left Lumbinî at 6:45 at the evening. Approximately 35 buses run from Bhairahawã to Lumbinî per day. At the special occasion i.e., Buddha *Jayanti* and other special meeting or seminars, extra buses are also involved to serve the passengers from Bhairahawã to Lumbinî.

Bus Station of Buddhachoka-Bhairahawā to Lumbinî has not planned in systematic way. Buses are standing on the south corner of the main high way road. Butwal to Bhairahawā bus runs at the interval about 4 minutes from 5 o'clock in the morning to 7:30 at evening per day. Mini-buses are providing services daily at other sites. Kakrahawā (Indian border) Lumbinî about 8 km. distance road has also provided proper services to the Indian tourist). Some of them come from Chakarchaudā-pakadî and Surajagaḍha-Taulihawā to Lumbinî by bus. Five percentage of the Indian tourists enter from Krishnanagar and approach in Lumbinî by bus. It is difficult to distinguish Indian and Nepālese tourists due to some cultural facial and genetic features, especially Terai people. LDT has recorded the number of Indian tourist 57675, 63709 and 120583 in 2010, 2011 and 2012 respectively. Their flow is more than this record due to the nearest neighbour and family relations between the Terai people of Nepāl and Indian good relation, mutual understanding, social interaction and cultural exchanges are running between them from long time, which has supported to promote the tourist activity in Lumbinî.

Butwal to Bhairahawā approximately 218 bus always provide service. Almost all the passengers are local people only for visit for their personal works. Among them about three percent in average approach in Lumbinî. Reserved buses run taking Korean, Thāi, Śri Lańkā and Indian tourists from India-border Sunauli to Lumbinî and return within a short span of time throwing only gargage plastic bags and bottles.

Air Transport

Air transport has a significant role for long distance and intercontinental travel and tour. It was started from the commercial point of view before the world war. Mass tourism was popular from the middle of twentieth century. New aircrafts was introduced in 1952, which was by the large capacity. After invention of large capacity aircraft package holiday's trend was developed around air transport like the global tourism at present. Air transport should be responsible for the introduction of cheaper travel especially visiting far off countries for the purpose of holidays. After introducing Jumbo Jets in 1970 air travel became more comfortable, convenient and luxury by the Boeing 7475, DC-105 and L-10119 (Bhatia, 1997;330).

In Nepāl air transport was started from 1951. Before this period Nepāl was isolated from the side's countries. Indian National Airways

(IAC) had started service between Kathmãndu and Patnã in 1951. Himãlayan Aviation was started domestic services to connect Kathmãndu with Pokharã, Bhairahawã, Simrã and Birãtanagar (Satyal, 2000:48) RNAC was established with the joint venture of the government and private sector in July 1958. At the beginning it had started domestic flights from Kathmãndu to Bhairahawã, Pokharã, Simra and Birãtanagar with DC-3s fleet. RNAC started international services with routes Calcuttã, Delhi and Patna in January 1960 after taking with full ownership of this corporation. It linked air service to Dacca in 1963 with 5 DC-3. Fokker F.27 was started in 1966 and DHC-6, Twin otter (19 seats) was introduced to Pokharã and Simra. In 1972 RNAC had started Boeing 727-100 services to Kathmãndu-Delhi, Bangkok and Calcuttã in 1972. Domestic network is provided to more than 43 district in 14 zones as well as mountain flights and helicopter charters to view many beautiful scences of Nepãl.

RNAC has provided an eminent role in the development of routes during 35 years. Jet service was operated up to Bangkok Thãiland 1972. and Śri Lańkã in 1972 and 1977 respectively. These flights and operations have been supporting to promote tourism industry, international understanding and social co-operation. After operating air transport from Kãthmãndu to Śri Lańkã and Thãiland, it has supported to Buddhist pilgrims and pilgrimage promotion in Lumbinî. Almost the tourists from Thãiland, Delhi, Calcutta, Bangkok, Colombo, Hongkong, Singãpur, Dacca and Śri Lańkã come in Lumbinî due to Buddhist motive. More than 30 airlines including Air Chinã, Korean Air, Buddha Air, Gulf Air, Thãi Airway, International United Airlines, China Southern Airlines, Nepãl Airline etc. are permitted in Nepãl (MoCTCA, 2011:94). All the flights are supporting to take Buddhist pilgrims for Lumbinî. After arriving Kathmãndu, the tourists come Lumbinî either by bus or air transports. All the international flights have been supporting to increase international tourists. RNAC flies more than 12 cities in 11 countries. Due to the liberal aviation policy of Nepãl government private companies have done international as well as national services. Air Dynasty, Agni Air, Air Kastamandapa, Buddha Air, Fishtail Air, Guna Airlines, Gomã Air, Mountain Helicaptor and Nepãl Airlines are operating domestic flights in Nepãl. Shree Airlines, Simrik Air, Sitã Air, Tãrã Air, UN, Yeti Air and others are operating internal domestic air transport (MoCTCA, 2011:96)

Gautam Buddha Airport of Siddharthanagar is the main entry point to Lumbinî by air transport. It is destination airport in the runway of about 150 *bighã* area. Night flight is also accessible due to the well management of runway light at night. About twelve flights are running from Kathmãndu. Mass tourists of Śri Lańka and Thãi charter the plane for visiting Lumbinî. About 11% percentage of the Lumbinî visited third country visitors come by aeroplane. After landing the plane, it takes only 25 minutes by taxi or car and about 40 minutes by public bus.

Table 6.3

Air Transport
Gautam Buddha Airport
Passenger, Aircraft Movement and CargoData

S.No	Years	Tourist		Aircraft		Cargo		Third country Tourists	Third country Tourist
		Arrival	Departure	Arrival	Departure	In	Out	No.	%
1	2002	26327	38447	2402	2402	71526	21407	2027	+
2	2003	24806	36385	2370	2370	45111	8080	2569	10.35
3	2004	44060	45703	2864	2864	49506	64210	4030	9.14
4	2005	61981	66452	2640	2640	46447	29738	4504	7.27
5	2006	35024	36048	2474	2474	26269	24101	3860	11.02
6	2007	30468	30931	1960	1960	36328	19559	1782	5.84
7	2008	33868	35104	2094	2094	39765	17770	5335	15.75
8	2009	43316	44411	1987	1987	58180	16934	5492	12.67
9	2010	56239	58049	2537	2537	82151	20363	6668	11.85
10	2011	59532	62629	2463	2463	82708	36201	9014	15.14
11	2012	59922	61999	2086	2086	93982	39053	9697	16.08
	Total	**475543**	**516158**	**25877**	**25877**	**631973**	**297416**	**54978**	

Source: Civil Aviation Office, Gautam Buddha Airport, 2013

Buddha Air, Yeti Air, Agni and Guna Airs are providing regular services from Kathmãndu to Bhairahawã Gautam Buddha Airport. Private airlines companies have served their domestic flights here. Being a land-locked country air transport is very important for international tourists from the different part of the world. Arrival and departure ratio of aircraft from Kathmãndu to Bhairahawã at the past ten years. Maximum aircraft number is 2864 in 2004 and minimum number is 1960 in 2007. In average 239 planes land in a month and it is about 8 flight per day. But in tourist high season its frequency is more than tourist low season. Maximum twelve planes and minimum four in high tourist season and low tourist seasons respectively. In eleven years scenario the number of aircraft is 25877, which is 2353 per year. Aircraft frequency has not drastically changed. At the beginning RNAC had provided services in later private airlines viz., Buddha, Yeti, Guna and Cosmic also started their service at Gautam Buddha Airport.

During this period third country tourists maximum number is 9697 in 2012 and minimum number is 2027 in 2002. Aircraft arrival number is only 2086 in 2012 but third country tourist ratio is high due to the increased seat capacity of the plane, Buddha Air has operated 36 seated plane for Bhairahawã. In 2012 the third country tourist's rate is high due to declaration Lumbinî visit year. From 2002 the number of the arrival passengers was maximum 61981 and departure 66452 in 2005. During this period the minimum number of arrival was 24806 in 2003. Among these 2569 were international tourists excluding Indian. Ten years Maoist struggle was in pick position in 2005. Strike, road jam and security less situation pressured to the general public to use air transport. After the seize fire of the Maoist part the ratio of the passenger 43.5 % decrease in 2006 by air transport. In 2005 third country tourist number was 4504 and 3860 in 2006. International tourist ratio was only 14.3% decreased. It means that international tourists also came by bus in 2006 due to peaceful environment of Nepãl. In the comparison of the eleven years received number of cargo is a more than out going number. Received number of cargo is 49506 and out going 64210 in 2004. Its ratio is 29.69 percentages different between in and out. Out going ratio is more in 2003 and 2004 due to internal disturbance, strike and war between Maoist and Nepãl Government. Myãnmãr, Burma, Indian Airlines Pakistan International Singapora Airlines, Thãi International, Gulf, China South East, Jet Airlines, Quatar Airlines and Aeroflot etc international airlines are conducting international flight for Nepãl.

The tourists who arrive in Kathmãndu visit Lumbinî by either air transport or road transport. The third country tourists' ratio is low in the comparison of the total passengers. In 2003, 2004, 2005, 2006 and 2007 the percentage is 10.35, 9.14, 7.27, 11.02 and 5.84 in respectively. The ratio in 2008, 2009, 2010, 2011 and 2012 is also 15.75, 12.67, 11.85, 15.14 and 16.08 in respectively. In average it is only 11 % out of total air passengers at Gautama Buddha Airport, Siddhartha agar. In course of projection the ratio of the foreign tourists in master plan of Lumina has mentioned air transport will provide about 20% in 1980-85. But it is only 55 % after about 30 years later. It is a challenge to improve the ratio of the tourists to the authority. Cargo services are also effective and managed. Charter flights are also servicing to the mass tourists in course of seminar, workshop, symposium and pilgrimage tours.

To conduct qualitative and quantitative air transport for Lumbinî the runway of the airport should be extended as soon as possible as mentioned deadline in project proposal. Runway must be grassless at the side from where the animal should not run during the landing period. Tower office building toilets and waiting apartment should be maintained in proper way. Not only this capacity and facilities should be increased to meet the needs of the domestic as well as international tourists. Environment around the airport and immediate out going road sides should be peace, reflection of compassion and authorized accommodation should be managed for the first time coming guest. Tourist information and support unit should be established at the airport complex, which will properly guide to visit cultural and natural sites including Lumbinî, Kapilavastu, Devadaha, Ramagrama, Tansen and Pokharã of this area.

Siddhartha Association of Travel and Tour Agency

Siddhartha Association of Travel Agency, Lumbinî Chapter is one of the the leading travel associations in western Nepãl. It was established at Siddharthanagar including the agencies of the region in 2005. Thirty six agencies are affiliated with this association. Objectives of this association are to provide quality service to the tourists as well as authentic information of Lumbinî and other sites of Nepãl. All the agencies have attempted to provide trained tourist guides in course of the visit of the guests. The main **Objectives of this Agency** are contribute to the healthy development of tourist industry and trade, to develop goodwill among travel agents on all subjects of common interests and welfare & protect the professional interest.

There are also targets to provide co-operation and consultation to Nepãl Government for the promotion of tourism in western Nepãl and work directly or indirectly for institutional mission of all matters pertaining to interests of tourist industry & trade. Its has also proposed to use feelings of close co-ordination and professional ethics among all components engaged in tourist industry and trade as well as to undertake research work for promotion of tourism in Lumbinî complex and its periphery. It has also tried to obtain national & international recognition for the association, and promote and safeguard the interests of other professionals, trade & industries.

Programs

Tourists visited Lumbinî, provide village walk in the periphery of Lumbinî Master Plan, viz. Madhubani, Tenuhawa, Khudābagar, Ekalā, Masinā, Suryapurā, Gajedi Lake, Gaidahawā Lake and other sites. They get chances to buy handicraft product of the local people, i.e. bucket, mat, bag, plate, showcase etc. They get chance to observe local fair, festivals, dance, landscapes, vegetation and life styles of the local people. Travel and Tour Agencies of Siddharthanagar have servicing in Lumbinî and Butwal.

Table 6.4

Siddhartha Association of Travel and Tour Agencies

S.No	*Name*	*Address*	*Contract No. (071)*	*Remarks*
1	Asoka Travel and Tour	Bhairahawā	521440	
2	Nepa Travel and Tour	Bhairahawā	520214	
3	Holiday Travel and Tour	Belahiya	522221	
4	Kalasha Travel and Tour	Bhairahawā	521114	
5	Anuska Travel and Tour	Bhairahawā	527644	
6	Indo-Nepāl Himalayan Adventure Travel and Tour	Belahiya	520251	
7	Gujarati Samaja Sarca Travel and Tour	Belahiya	522715	
8	Swami Narayana Travel and Tour	Belahiya	523940	
9	Saeita Nepāl Travel and Tour	Belahiya	527118	
10	Bonjora Travel and Tour	Belahiya	525237	
11	Bhairahawā Travel and Tour	Bhairahawā	522750	
12	Kshitija Travel and Tour	Butwal	545209	
13	Mahima Travel and Tour	Butwal	543557	
14	Rupandehi Travel and Tour	Butwal	543017	
15	Palpa Bhairava Travel and Tour	Butwal	548464	

16	Rajasthan Travel and Tour	Butwal	540560
17	Ama Travel and Tour	Belahiy	527047
18	Dynastic Travel and Tour	Bhairahawã	527807
19	Link Award Travel and Tour	Belahiya	524446
20	Blue Dimond Travel and Tour	Belahiya	527441
21	Hello Mithila Travel and Tour	Belahiya	522923
22	Badal Travel and Tour	Belahiya	523716
23	Jaya Baba Gurunath Travel and Tour	Belahiya	522603
24	Bindu Travel and Tour	Belahiya	-
25	Nalami Travel and Tour		-
26	Lumbinî Swaminarayana Travel and Tour	Belahiya	-
27	Soft Exchange Travel and Tour	Bhairahawã	-
28	Acharya Travel and Tour	Butwal	-
29	Miyama Travel and Tour	Butwal	-
30	Butwal International Travel and Tour	Butwal	-
31	Anandavihari Travel and Tour	Belahiya	522777
32	Happy Travel and Tour	Bhairahawã	9857021614
33	Clean International Travel and Tour	Bhairahawã	-
34	The Holi Birth Travel and Tour	Lumbinî	9857020064
35	Subhakalasha Travel and Tour	Lumbinî	9857022520
36	Nepa International Travel and Tour	Bhairahawã	526513

Source: SATTA, 2013

These tour and travel agencies have provided services to the internal as well as international tourists in Lumbinî, Kapilvastu,

Devadaha, Palpa, Pokharã, Chitawan and other sites in the interest of the tourists.

Internal Transport

Besides the external transport of Lumbinî internal transport plan is estimated in the Lumbinî Master Plan. Road from Bhairahawã to Lumbinî was completed in July 1978. 1.5 km peripheral road around LMP was built in 1978 and remaining 6.5 was also completed in 1980 (Tange, 1978:7). Drainage canal around the garden area was also completed at the same time. According to LMP it was estimated about 500 buses with necessary parking space in 1977 (Ibid:9). Master plan was proposed to complete in 1985. But it's 50% work has not completed ever now. In this critical situation bus park is under construction which is situated on the west of cultural zone (LDT, 2004). The main entrance gate is proposed at the north side from Parsa to Taulihawã Road. From the bus park tourists as well as day visitors are allowed to enter sacred complex through Friendship Bridge on Harahawa River. Along the central canal a brick paved path called pedestrian path has been planned which connects Lumbinî centre and Sacred garden at south. Pedestrian path is 16 meter wide on both sides of the canal and 1440 m. long. As the part of pedestrian path 'Kadamba' trees are planted at both side of the pedestrian along the central canal. A rectangular open space for resting of pedestrians is built with four soil-brick benches including dustbins, water fountains, and light posts. Lumbinî squares 1 and 2 are the gate ways to the monastic areas. Boat station is provided for each square. There are two bridges at the boat stations to connect the both sides of the canal. Tourists can reach sacred garden by boat at peace Eternal Flame and immediate south on foot through circular levee. Eight meter wide main pedestrian path leads to the monastic plaza and approach to the entrance courtyard of each monastery.

Tourists on foot can visit from both sides along the central canal. If visit to the east zone, first of all reach Thãi Royal monastery, Indian Mahabodhi monastery and Cambodian monastery which is under construction. The black-topped road leads to Myãnmãr (Berm) is beautiful complex as well as Golden Pagoda Stupa. International Gautami Bhikkhuni Vihar is also located at this area. At the backside of this Vihar, Śri Laṅkan monastery is attractive and out going road is also available on its southern side. Immediately at south corner of the central canal Peace Eternal Flame and Peace Bell are standing as the symbol of world peace. South of the Peace Eternal Flame is located Sacred garden where Mayadevi temple, Aśoka pillar, Puskarini tank, remains of ancient vihar and stupas. If the pilgrims want to take something's or the road leads to east at Mahilawar, local market and on west at Paderia village, at the local bus park.

In order to visit in eastern monastic zone, first of all a visitor can reach at International Panditaram meditation centre, stupa of Dharmodaya Sabha and Mananga monastery complex, western road leads at Korean, Chinese, Geden International, Austrian, Vietnam, Seto Gumbā, Linson Lāmā Meditation Centre and Lotus Stupa Germany. After visiting previous sites, Lumbinî Museum and Lumbinî International Research Institute at cultural complex can be visited. At New Lumbinî village Niponzan Myohoji Peace stupa is throwing light of truth all over the world. Hokke and Kasai Hotels are also providing proper accommodation in course of visiting of peace Land.

If a tourist wants to visit within few hours it can take taxi paying charge to LDT. Unables and other interested persons can use rickshaw. More than 135 rickshaw-pullers are providing proper services to the tourists at this sacred complex. Taxi, motorcycle, cycle, Rickshaw and car are permitted to enter the sacred complex including monastic zone. Boating facility is also available from the south ending of Friendship Bridge.

Mahamaya Rickshaw Puller's Union

One hundred thirty five rickshaws are providing internal transport facility at Lumbinî Development Trust area to visit monasteries, central canal, Lumbinî International Research Institute, museum, Peace Stupa and other sites of the area. Three internal entry points, i.e. Eastern gate, north of Māyādevī temple, on the bank of circular levee and Bus Park are fixed to keep rickshaw and provide internal visiting facilities to the tourists. Rickshaw union and duty management committees have divided the total risk into three groups, who provide service in queue system. About 55 rickshaws are allotted at the bus park and remaining is also grouped in two parts. Their daily rotation has fixed on anti clock-wise direction from eastern gate to bus park, Bus Park to Peace Flame and Peace Flame to eastern-gate. About 150 families are depending on this job. According to Nagendra Gosai, chairman of Rickshaw Puller Union, they earn about Rs. 500 and Rs 250 per day in pick season and dry season respectively. According to the Nagendra Gosai, President of the Rickshaw Pullers' Union, due to the permission of the taxi, private car and government vehicles their income is decreasing day today. If the LDT provides solar vehicle in loan, other vehicles should not be permitted into the sacred complex.

Table 6.5

Rate of Rikshaw in Lumbinî Complex

S.No	*Sites to Visit*	*Fare for Internal visitors*	*For International Visitors*	*Remarks*
1	Mahilwar to Mayadevi Temple	Rs.30 /-	Rs. 50 /-	
2	Bus park to East Monastic Zone	Rs. 200/-	Rs. 250/-	
3	Bus park to West Monastic Zone	Rs. 300/-	Rs. 400/-	
4	LDT Project Area	Rs.400/-	Rs. 500/-	
5	Bus park to Eternal Peace Flame	Rs. 50/-	Rs. 80/-	
6	LDT Project Area per hour	Rs. 150/-	Rs. 250/-	

Source- Mahamaya Rickhsaw Sangh, 2013

Between Lumbinî Development Trust and Lumbinî Mahāmāyā Rikshaw Driver Union have fixed the rate of rickhsaw fare in order to visit at Lumbinî Sacred complex. Rickhsaw service is providing bread and butter to more than one thousand people of this region. Their life style and social economic condition is very pitable and poor. Tax entry after paying annual or daily charge offical vehicles and tourist bus are disturbing for their regular income. In the process of pollution free area at Lumbinî, Lumbinî Development Trust is going to provide 125 solar rickshaws to the rickshaw-pullers in subsidies loan. Cost of a rickshaw is about 1, 25,000 except custom. It is donated by the Thāiland Government on the request of LDT. Electric vehicles are very useful in course of pollution control and spiritual peace.

Communication system is also a major part of tourism industry. Tourists information system as well as security mechanism are inter related to each other. Nepāl Telecom, NCell, UTL and Hello Service are providing internet, telephone, telefax and world net working services in the periphery of Lumbinī . Communication of phone is available 2,63,46 general phones, 45,317 sky phone, mobile 3,24,060 and internet

7,783 in four districts, i.e, Palpa, Kapilvastu, Rupandehi and Nawalparasi (NRB,2013:19). Services of CDMA has rapidly increased in 48.61% (Ibid).

When a person leaves own native land for the purpose of visit, he needs the vehicle of transport to another place. Easy, cheap and comfortable transports are more attractive and motivator factors in course of recreational, pilgrimage, cultural and leave tourism. Thomos Cook had visited so long distances due to the facility of mass carrier in cheap and schedule time. In course of invention of rail ways, steamers, steam-rails, air services as well as other high speed carriers, mass tourism industry has been expanding all over the world with in a short span of time. Land transports, sea transports and air transports should be comfortable, easily available and cheap in the promotion of mass, endemic, sustainable and pilgrimage tourism in Lumbinî. According to the Transport Management Act, 2049 direct and standard tourist buses should be operated from Butwal-Siddharthanagar-Lumbinî and Taulihawā-Lumbinî in proper time schedule. Route permit should be provided from Siddharthanagar and Lumbinī . It is difficult to take permission with in a short span of time from Butwal. Heavy industries, including 11 cement industries, along the road from Siddhārthanagar to Lumbinî are creating sound, air, water and land pollutions day by day. Heavy loading trucks are blocking the road to Lumbinî, which is the challenge to cross the polluted and jammed road to the tourists.

For long time factories should be shifted after fixing Industrial Zone and proper indemnity should be provided to the injured parties. There may be an alternative provision of by pass road along the canal from Butwal to Lumbinî area. Direct and special buses for tourists should be arranged at the beginning. For air transport the quality and capacity of the Gautam Buddha Airport of Siddharthanagar should be up graded as proposed plan. Train service should be managed from Indiā to Lumbinî and its periphery. Smokeless electric vehicles should be managed for internal observation in Lumbinî Master Plan. It will support to approach at the each monastic enclave in proper time.

CHAPTER SEVEN

TOURIST ACCOMMODATION

Introduction

In tourist industry accommodation plays a vital and fundamental role in its promotion. A traveler who has left his house requires accommodation at the destination and during journey which can not complete in a single day. For this he needs over night accommodation. Tourists like peace, clean and well facilitated accommodation in course of their journey. It is one of the attractions in order to motivate to them. According to the standard of the tourists international, industrial, resort, residential, floating and capsule model accommodations should be built to attract them. High standard tourists pay more money and cheap hostels are also needed to the poor visitors. After recognizing it as an industry, government should have reinforced to the parties providing various attractive incentives and concessions in order to establishment of accommodation industry. Liberal payment policy for sites, special discount in long term loans, tax relief, renovation of buildings, liberal impart of licenses and reasonable concessions in other sectors should have been provided to this industry. One of the goals of master plan is to promote tourism in Gandak region focusing to Lumbinî.

Thus, LDT has provided special concession and reliefs to the owners of the hotel, restaurant and other residential accommodations. In the master plan land plots are located for this purpose. In the context of Lumbinî Prof Kenzo Tange has mentioned the provision of accommodation in various standards. In the plan in course of projection of the tourists he has calculated their stay days and numbers. According to the master plan High class, Middle class, Pilgrimage and Camping sites were proposed including 100, 100,100 and 150 rooms (Tange, 1978:16). In the Master Plan of Lumbinî it had proposed that tourists would have come 10% by air and 90% by land in Nepāl. 70% of total tourists in Lumbinî will be concentrated in the high tourist season of October through February and 25% in the low tourist season of March, April, August, and September. It has proposed that 418 and 150 tourists would have visited daily average in high and in low seasons respectively in 1985. It is also incorporated that 314 and 113 daily average in over-night in tourists high season and low season respectively (Ibid, 12). In this calculation, approximately 750-900 beds were needed in 1985.

History

The hotel is an enterprise for the production of goods and of services to sell for a profit to remunerate the administration and capital involved. The production of goods is related with foodstuff into dishes and meats to serve the clients. It is also a unit of wholesale trade when it sells alcohol drinks, cigarettes, postcards, books, booklets, photos and tickets to the tourists. The hotel is also a complex productive unit exercising several functions of recreation. Visiting, walking and journey were not an easy affair in ancient and medieval periods. In ancient period many Inns were established which provided food, drinks and entertainment to weary travelers during the Roman Empire (Bhatia, 1997:347). In the usage of coach, travelers were lodged in the Hoteliers, situated at the railway stations, where the travelers and their horses were found rest and foods. Vihars, *dharmasalas, sarais, musaphirkhana* etc were the traveler's shelter in ancient Indiā and Nepāl. Cave, temple, monastery and thatched huts were also accommodations of the travelers. After enlighten of Siddhartha Gautam in Bodhagaya, many followers were travelling with Buddha in course of propagation of His teachings.

During that period monasteries took over the role of providing lodging and other facilities to travelers who were mainly pilgrims. Special monks and nuns were responsible for reception of the visitors and their well beings. Gautam Buddha was invited by the Nobles and also managed of fooding and lodging in the common halls and open gardens in a mass. Due to the influence of Buddha's teachings a lot of followers involved. During this period travelers were often diplomats, philosophers, intellectuals and researchers. There was no lodging especially for the travelers. Guests were invited to stay in the houses of the village-headman, Nobles or Pandit. Lodging, fooding and other facilities were freely provided as the representative of God. In the third century BC, Asoka had visited to the sacred sites related with Buddha. During his visit he had come in Lumbinî with his spiritual teacher Upa Gupta and installed a stone monolithic pillar engraving inscription to remember the exact birthplace of Buddha. On this occasion he might have received by the local people. In ancient period monasteries were located at the important trade centers. The trade traveler with their merchandise and money on these routes and the vihars were their hostels. Chinese pilgrims Fa-Hien and Hiuen-Tsiang had visited Lumbinî, Kapilvastu and Devadaha-Ramagrama respectively. Su-Chi-Chu had also travelled at these sites. They might have used horse, bull, bull-carts. In the fourteenth century Ripu Malla had visited and engraved his name on Asoka pillar. It was risky affairs to travel unknown place and person.

After the tradition of Christianity, churches were the shelter of the travelers. By the fifteenth century AD Inn concept was promoted in France and England. In the seventeenth-eighteenth centuries Inn facilities were improved including thirty or more rooms. According to English law Inns were public houses and their services were regarded as public service. In America taverns were popular meeting places for eating, drinking and entertainment in 1780 AD. In Nepālese culture guests are regarded as a God, which are well respected and not charged of fooding and lodging a few years ago. Hotels are categorized on the basic of providing physical service and infrastructures. Fixed immovable, lodging open to the public and an enterprise, which sells goods and services are main features of the hotels. Motel concept was also developed after Second World War. Motor passengers as well as waiting for a time being to take rest and providing service is known motel. Due to the impact of the neighbors and commercial point of view accommodation became an industry in modern period. In Nepāl hotels are known as instruments of production or an enterprise for the production of goods and of services. At the beginning of the modern hotel Mr. Boris Lissance had started the Royal Hotel in Kathmandu valley in February 1955. Mr. George Lebree, advisor of France bilateral co-operation program to Nepāl has prepared a report about the hotels of Nepāl in 2058-59 (Satyal, 2000:59). In 1964, there were 127 beds in 9 hotels in the Kathmandu valley.

After two years later the number of the beds was 518. Due to the tourist flow hotel industry became popular in the field of industry. Its ratio is drastically changed day by day. In 1997 the number of the rooms and beds is recorded 14214 and 27612 respectively in Nepāl. At that only 12 beds are recorded in Lumina. In course of legal organization Hotel Association of Nepāl (HAN) was established in 1966. During this period there were only eight hotels and all of them were situated in the Kathmandu valley. In the first ten years of its establishment, it could not promote lack of the industrial concept as well as the rigid process of membership. After some time, HAN became able to make its mark on the governmental regulatory and social upgrading aspects of tourism. In course of its dynamic leadership, HAN was able to project itself as a leader in the decision making process pertaining to tourism. Any aspect of tourism strategies and their implementation could avoid the forceful imprint of HAN. During this period, the hotel industry was perhaps one of the most successful industries in the scenario for hardly any other industry in Nepāl.

During the period from 1970 AD to early 1980 AD was remarkable for tourism growth and its spread. At that time all categories of star rated hotels grew not only in the Kathmandu valley, but also spread its wings in Pokhara, Chitawan, Lumbinī and other cities as well as tourist flow points. Tourism was still in the confines of sustainability and hotels helped in the promotion of other segments of the tourism industry. Travel and trekking agents became more professional and their size of the market and its returns grew in manageable levels. In 1980's idea of a borderless world and as such trade and commerce began to flow from one part of the world to the next. The tourism industry, the very heart of the concept of borderless economy, obviously began to get its full share of benefit. On the other hand, the concept of international standard made the need for international network of marketing. In the master plan of Lumbinī standard hotels 100, middle class hotels 100, pilgrimage 150 and camping capacity 100 of the accommodation had proposed in 1980. After five years its ratio is proposed 900 in the plan (Tange, 1978:13-14). In1988, there were only two tourist standard hotels in Bhairahawā, i.e. Hotel Himalaya consisting 16 rooms and 40 beds and Lumbinī Hotel of 15 rooms 45 beds. During this period only on Lumbinī Garden Guest House of 7 rooms and 14 beds is recorded as a tourist standard hotel (Satyal, 2000:67).

Types

Accommodation industry makes an important contribution to the economic development, social contracts and commercial activities. It is a basic infrastructure as well as expansion of tourism. Being the matrix of tourism, accommodation plays a distinctive role in the development of the industry. Cheap and qualitative accommodation motivate to the tourists at any time and situation. Simple restaurants, resorts, hotels, bar, residences and cottages are serving to the tourists as well as day visitors in Lumbinî, Bhairahaw and Butwal. The pilgrims of Lumbinī 22% accommodated in the monasteries, 45% in hotel and lodges, 20% at Bhairahawā and 8% were found accommodating in Indiā, border of Nepāl, i.e. Sunauli and Nautanawa. Lumbinī is the prime location of accommodation for majority of the visitors. About 11% of the visitors use air route for their visit. Travel and Tour companies or agencies directly come from Indiā taking pilgrims and return within a short span of time after bird's eye view at the sacred complex of Lumbinī. This study reveals that mass tourism (pilgrims) should be emphasized providing minimum visa-charge and other proper facilities.

Table 7.1

Modes of stay of pilgrims

S.No.	*Accommodation.*	*No. of pilgrims*	*Percentage*	*Remarks*
1.	Monasteries-Lumbini	44	22 %	
2.	Hotel & Lodges-Lumbini	90	45 %	
3.	Indian hotels	16	8 %	
4.	Bhairahawa Hotels	40	20 %	
5.	Relatives and Friends, House	10	5 %	

Source: Field Survey, 2012-13

Similarly 8% of them go Indiā across the border after their visit. 5% of the pilgrims stay in the houses of their relatives and friends at the time of their stay at Lumbinī. Other survey had also shown approximately result in 2005 (Ghimire, 2006:109). They generally visit archaeological garden, monastic zone, meditation-centers, bird-watching (*Saras*) and Nilgāi watching, dance, sing and enjoy themselves by undertaking various kinds of entertainments. By the nature of the accommodations these are classified into two categories as follows-

1. Hotels

According to the Hotel, Lodge, Restaurant, Bar and Guide Rules, 2038 and Internal Procedure Directory, 2064 criteria's of the tourists standard hotels have been effective. In the section 41 (1) of Procedure has incorporated simple tourist standard hotel should be equipped ,in minimum 10 rooms with proper ventilation, 25% should be attached bathroom and there should be one bathroom for each common rooms. The rooms should be well decorated to reflect Nepālese art and traditions. There should be facilitated of electricity, hot and cold water, telephone counter, reception counter, clean dinning, kitchen, senior staffs, heater, fan, first aid and fire fighting equipments. It includes hotels, boarding houses and inn. At the beginning there were no any rigid rules and regulations about it. Visitors used to stay at the private houses as a guest. There were no any systematic lodgings and foodings. In 1978 there were only 25 rooms in the vicinity of Lumbinî Garden only for temporary use (Tange, 1978:7). Standard Hotel Hokke was established with the patronize of Jāpān Hokke Club in 1990. It is providing standard service to the third country tourists, especially to the Japanese. It is located in the New Lumbinî village Sector, immediately north of Cultural Zone of master plan. Hotel Kāsāi (Former Mikasa Hotel) is also operating by the Japanese Kasai Group. It is also providing quality and reliable services for the foreigners. Pilgrimage House was also operated a few years ago. But it is not in operation at present. It will be operated after renovation in near future. Śri Laṅkan tourists are the highest number in course of visiting in Lumbinî. After management cheap, reliable and qualitative accommodation they will be motivated to visit more than once. Private hotels are established at Parsachoka, Mahilawar, Paderia and Tenuhawa, out skirts of the Lumbinî master plan. There are many hotels and guest houses in Lumbinî area. Tourist can choose one of them from the following list according to your budget and travel plan.

Table 7. 2

Hotels in Lumbinî

S.No.	Name	Type	Total Rooms	Room Types AC/Non-AC		Total Beds	Contact
		Star/ Non		AC Rooms	Non-AC Rooms		
1	Lumbinî Hotel Kasai	3 Star	30	30		60	Email:info@Lumbinihotelkasai.com Phone: 071-404036

S.No.	Name	Type Star/ Non	Total Room S	Room Types AC/Non-AC AC Room S	Non-AC Room S	Total 1 Beds	Contact
2	Lumbinî Hokke Hotel	Star Class	27	27		54	Email:nepalhokke@gmail.com Phone: 071-404056
3	Lumbinî Zambala Hotel	Deluxe	30	30		64	Email: Lumbinîzambalahotel@hotmail.com Phone: 071-580358
4	Mayadevi Guest House	Standard	20	6	14	32	Email: mayadeviLumbinî@gmail.com Phone: 071-580354
5	Hotel Buddha Palace	Standard	10		10	23	Email: hotelbuddhapalace@yahoo.com Phone: 071-580272
6	Peace Land Hotel	Deluxe	22	22		46	Email: info@hotel-peaceland.com Phone: 071-580286
7	Lumbinî Bambooo Resort	Deluxe	40	40		90	Email: infi@lbamboresort.com Phone: 071-580310
8	Manakamana Lodge	Lodge	7		7	28	Email: Phone:9804433448
9	Lumbinî Garden Lodge	Lodge	11		11	27	Email: Lumbinîgardenlodge@gmail.com Phone: 071-580146
10	Lumbinî Village Lodge	Lodge	12		12	20	Email: Phone: 071-580432
11	Sun Flower Travellers Lodge	Standard	11	11		26	Email : sunflower2099py@gmail.com P0hone:071-580004
12	Rahul Guest House	Lodge	6		6	36	Email: Phone: 071-580176
13	Lumbinî Guest House	Standard	26	5	21	88	Email: Lumbinîguesthouse@yahoo.com Phone: 071-580142
14	Royal Guest House	Lodge	8		8	20	Email: Phone:
15	Ashoka Guest House	Lodge	8		8	17	Email: Phone:071-580099
16	Shanti Guest House	Lodge	17	3	14	80	Email:santiguest66@yahoo.com Phone:071-580169
17	Lotus Resturant and lodge	Lodge	5		5	16	Email: Phone: 071-580373
18	Hotel Ananda inn	Deluxe	22			49	Email:info@hotelanandainn.com Phone: 071-580324
19	Buddha Bhomi Guest House	Standard	15		15	30	Email: buddhabhoomiguesthouse @gmail.com Phone: 071-580326
20	Lumbinî Garden New Crystal Hotel	Star Class	72			144	Email: lumcrystal@ntc.net.np Phone:071-580145
21	Siddhartha Guest House	Standard	20	5	15	40	Email: siddartha_004@yahoo.com Phone: 071-580238

S.No.	*Name*	*Type*	*Total Room S*	*Room Types AC/Non-AC*		*Total 1 Beds*	*Contact*
		Star/ Non		*AC Room S*	*Non-AC Room S*		
22	Gautam Buddha Lodge	Lodge	10		10	30	Email: Phone:
23	Buddha Maya Garden Hotel	Star Class	74	74		148	Email Phone:
24	Lumbinî Buddha Garden Resort	Deluxe	20		20	24	Email: Phone: 071-580220
25	Hotel Manasi	Lodge	8		8	12	Email: Phone:
26	Lumbinî Peace hotel	Lodge	10		10	40	Email:yadkadin@yahoo.com Phone: 071-580372
27	Hotel President	Lodge	10		10	40	Email: Phone: 017-580
28	Lumbinî Paradise	Lodge	12		12		
	TOTAL		**492**	**327**	**165**	**1061**	

Source: Hotel Association Lumbinî, 2013

Table 7.1 presents that 45 % of the total tourists of Lumbinî stay in lodge and hotels in the vicinity of the sacred complex. In the vicinity of LMP there are only 28 tourist standard hotels except small seasonable restaurants. Hotel Hokke has operating since 1995. Before the establishment of Kasai Hotel, Hokke had provided standard facilities to the third country tourists, especially Japanese. Hotel Kasai is 3 star hotel, operated by Japanese Kasai Group. Śri Laṅkan pilgrimage house is also finished. At the beginning it was called Hotel Mikasha. 1061 beds are available in 492 rooms. Among them 327 rooms are with AC facility. In the summer season these rooms are very comfortable. At Mahilawar, Paderia and Parasa village's residential accommodation are also providing services to the tourists. Home stay programmers are also launching in the vicinity of LMP. Star, deluxe and lodge accommodations are in options on the expenditure capacity of the tourists. The number of the hotels is increasing day today due to the attraction towards Lumbinî of the international tourists. About 1500 skilled and non-skilled man power has got the opportunity of employment. In the tourist high season more than 5000 people are providing various services to the tourists.

Table 7.3

Hotels of Siddharthanagar

S. No	Name	Proprietor	Room Nos	Grade	Bed Nos	Staff	Contract No.	Remarks
1	Hotel Sangria International	Bind Karle	10	C	35	15	071520020	
2	Hotel Magmata	Dipak Raj Ghimire	34	C	60	20	520312	
3	Pawan International	Ajaya Halwai	27	B**	40	30	523680	2 star
4	Hotel Aakasa and Restaurant	Dilipa Halwai	18	C	30	16	524372	
5	Hotel Jaya Bijaya	Sanjay Sharma	19	D	16	8	523029	
6	Hotel Nirvana	Shantalal Shrestha	40	A***	56	52	520837	3 star
7	Hotel Sangam and Catering	Raju & Krishna Karki	11	D	40	10	521286	
8	Hotel Himalayan Precious	Ananda Subedi	14	C	24	6	527765	
9	Hotel Rose	Madhava Paudel	8	D	12	2	520919	
10	Hotel Swagatam	Harka Gurung	10	D	40	5	526791	
11	Hotel Moon Light	Gyanishowari Shrestha	15	D	40	5	522808	
12	Hotel S.R. International	Ghanshyam Adhikari	11	C	20	15	523437	
13	Hotel Royal and Lodge	Laxman Bhandari	10	D	15	4	521845	
14	Hotel Joshi Manasarobar	Ajay Joshi	36	C	35	17	523686	
15	Hotel Plaza	Shree Chandra Gupta	8	D	8	4	522715	
16	Holiday Inn	Krishna Pandey	24	D	48	13	524986	
17	Hotel Naule	Suraj Singh Ale	15	D	20	5	527178	
18	Hotel Prakash and Prakash	Krishan Acharya	17	C	35	15	526934	
19	Hotel Central Point	Madhava Ghimire	10	D	16	16	527150	
20	Hotel Tannoo	Krishna Kshetri	30	C	20	20	524952	
21	Hotel Buddha	Giriprasad Ghimire	15		12	12		
22	Hotel Yeti Private Ltd.	Tilakraj Thapa	25	B	68	43	520551	
23	Hotel Ashoka International	Mainuddin Ahamada	28	C	60	18	525986	

S.No	Name	Proprietor	Room Nos	Grade	Bed Nos	Staff	Contract No.	Remarks
24	Hotel Peace Night	Mainuddin Ahamada	27	C	27	8	527582	
25	Hotel Gorkha Prince	-	35	C	35	7	522961	
26	Hotel Lord Buddha	Fakta bahadur Shah	15	C	60	20	521837	
27	Hotel Sea Princes	Ramkaji Gurung	15	C	35	6	520742	
28	Hotel Glassgow	Vishnu Gautam	20	C	14	8	521737	
29	Hotel Sambala	Vishnu Gautam	12	D	44	7	527473	
30	Hotel Mount Everest	Vishnu Gautam	17	C	40	9	520529	
31	Hotel Nansc Prakash	Chandra Shrestha	40	A***	60	50	524701	3 star
32	New Cottage Lodge	-	8	D	10	3	521961	
33	Hotel Buddha	-	15	D	12	3	521421	
--		--	--	--	--	--	--	
	Total		639		1087	472	--	

Source: Siddharthanagar Hotel Association, 2013

Siddhārthanagar is the main entry gate of Lumbinî. Either air transport or road transport foreign tourists can not go to Lumbinî complex without contact Siddhārthanagar. 33 hotels consists 639 rooms and 1087 beds are managed for the tourists here. 472 skilled and non-skilled man powers have got directly employment. Indirectly more than 5000 persons are engaged in the sectors of hotel, tour and travel, vegetable production, in furniture, clothing's and related others. Hotel Nansa is three star hotel, which is providing standard services to the foreign tourists. It has completed basic requirements as recorded in three stars. Hotel Pawan International, Hotel Nirvana, Hotel Yeti, Hotel Glassgow, Hotel Sambala, Hotel Everest, Hotel Lord Buddha and Hotel Mansarobar are providing standard services to the international as well as internal tourists.

Table 7.4

Hotels in Butwal

S.No	Name	Address No	Contract No	Room	Bed No	Remarks
1	Hotel Sindur	Butwal-8	071.5[illegible]0381	26	52	
2	Hotel New Era	Butwal-11	071.543833	20	40	
3	Hotel Santosa	Butwal-12	071.437190	11	22	
4	Hotel Royal	Butwal-8	071.549049	21	42	

S.No	Name	Address No	Contract No	Room	Bed No	Remarks
5	Hotel Park Plaza	Butwal-11	9847026175	18	36	
6	Guest House in BTI	Butwal-6	071.543588	14	28	
7	Hotel Kandra	Butwal-6	071.540175	25	50	
	Total			**135**	**270**	

Source- Hotel Association of Butwal

Butwal, about 45 km northeast of Lumbinî, is a commercial city of western Nepāl. Industrial Zone as well as standard enterprises are running here under the leadership of civil society. It is the centre of business tourism, nature tourism, pilgrimage tourism and adventure tourism. Many domestic as well as international tourist come through this route. During their visit tourist standard accommodations are provided to them. Natural beauty, cultural heritages and industrial activities are the locale attractions for the tourists. Table 7.4 shows only 7 tourist standard hotels in Butwal *bazaar*. 135 double rooms consisted 270 beds. About 300 persons are employed at these hotels. Besides these hotels there are more than 50 small restaurants and lodges for general visitors. In case of emergency other supplementary accommodations are also available here.

International Hotels

Almost all the international hotels are located at municipality as well as principal tourist centers in Rupandehi district including Lumbinî. These are classified on the basis of an internationally accepted systems and norms. Their criteria has incorporated in Hotel, Lodge, Bar and Tourism, Internal Action Procedure, 2064. According to the procedure numbers of AC and non-AC rooms, standard kitchen, dinning-rooms, reception, well ventilation and other facilities should be provided to the guests. These luxury and well facilitated hotels are categories into five ranking from 5 stars to 1 star on the basis of their facilities and services. These hotels provide luxury and comfortable experiences including accommodation. In Lumbinî Hotel Hokke, Kasai, New Crystal is providing these services to the high level tourists (Figs.23, 24 & 25). At Siddharthanagar Hotel Pawan International, Hotel Nirvana, Hotel Nans and Hotel Kasai are providing high quality services to the international tourists as well as internal visitors. These are providing well information counter, skillful receptionist, restaurant, and bar, entertainment in the form of various dances, songs, music, sports, games and other recreational sources on the interest of the guests. These hotels are managed by the qualified and experienced persons in the field of hotel. General Manager, Chief Administrator, is responsible for the over all management and operation through the various departments of the hotel. Conference, seminar, workshop and convention halls are available at these accommodations.

Commercial Hotels

The people visiting for commerce and business purpose, night stay at any hotel for some time is known commercial hotels. Such types of hotels are situated at the commercial cities, industrial areas and main exit points of transportation of goods. Belahiya being the main entry and exit point of the western Nepāl, hotels of Butwal, Sunauli, and Siddhārthanagar are servicing to the high level business men as well as foreign tourists. Hotels of Butwal, viz. New Era, Hotel Sindur, Hotel Royal, Hotel Parkplaza, Hotel Kandar and Pawan Hotel, Yeti Hotel, Sambala Hotel, Lord Buddha Hotel as well as Everst Hotels are providing proper services to the business men of the region. These are with restaurant, seminar hall, grill hall, functional accommodation as well as garage for vehicle travelers.

Resorts

Resort hotels are situated near the river side, lake side or in the middle of the Jungle in the area of Lumbinî. Bamboo Resort Lumbinī , Gold Dreamland resort Mani gram, Lumbinī Garden Resort are actively servicing to the internal as well ás foreign tourists. The man who likes away from his routine and busy working in search of peace, compassion, rest, recreation, refresh and relaxation, goes to the resort hotels for the time beings. Resorts provide natural atmosphere and non-polluted environment to the guest for their refreshment for their stay at the site. Swimming pool, boating, coffee shop, restaurant, games, shopping arcade and other recreational facilities are available at these resorts. These are categorized on the basis of climate topography, i.e., summer, winter, health, hill and all season resorts.

2. Supplementary Accommodation

Besides the standard hotels and restaurants there are hostels, guest rooms, vihar stay rooms, social halls, meditation halls and sewa halls in Lumbinî, Siddhartha agar and Brutal *bazaar*. These accommodations are providing voluntary services than commercial point of view.

Table 7.5

Supplementary Accommodation in Lumbinî Complex

S.No.	*Name of the Monastery*	*Country related*	*Established Year*	*Total Guest (Pilgimage) Rooms*	*Room Types (AC/Non-AC)* *AC rooms*	*Non-AC Rooms*	*Total Beds*
1	World Peace Pagoda	Jāpān	1993	4		4	20
2	The Royal Thai Monastery	Thāīland	1994				-
3	Cambodian Monastery	Cambodia	2006	8		8	100
4	Mahabodihi Society Temple	Indiā	1994	7		7	50
5	Dhamma Janani Meditation Centre	Nepāl	2001	54		54	100
6	Myānmār Golden Temple	Myānmār	1993	12	6	6	156
7	International Nun's Temple	Nepāl	1994	15		15	75
8	Sri Lankan Monastery	Sri Lankā	1996				-
9	Manang Sewa Samaj Stupa	Nepāl	2000	4		4	8
10	Karma Samtenling Monastery	Nepāl	2007	16		16	32
11	Dharmodaya Sabha Temple	Nepāl	1994				-
12	Drubgyud Choeling Monastery	Nepāl	1993	16	2	14	35
13	Panditarama Vipassana Meditation center	Myānmār	1999	20		20	20
14	Korean Mahabodhi Society Monastery	Korea	1995	82		82	492
15	Chinese Monastery	China	1996				-
16	Geden International Temple	Austria	2003	4		4	8
17	Vietnam Lumbinî Buddha Bhumi Vihar	Vietnam	1993	60	2	58	90
18	United Trungram Buddhist Temple	Nepāl	2006				-
19	Linhson Buddhist Monastery	France	1999			-	-
20	Tara Foundation (The Great Lotus Stupa)	Germany	1999	15	15		200
21	Sokyo Monastery	Jāpān	1992				-
22	France Buddhist Stupa (Association Lumbinî Shechen stupa)	France	2006				-
23	Urgen Dorje Chyiling Monastery	Singapore	2011				-
24	Tri Buddha Mahavihar	Nepāl	2011				-
25	Nepāl Bajrayana Vihar	Nepāl	2012				10
26	Dharma Swami Maharaj Vihar	Nepāl	1968	8		8	16
27	Rajkiya Buddha Vihar	Nepāl	1954				-
28	Tashi Rabten Ling Monastery	Nepāl	1999	24		24	48

Source: LDT, Informaation section, 2013

Almost all the accommodations of the monasteries are allotted to the pilgrims of the concerned nationality. Pilgrims take shelter and food at the monasteries and donate money on their interest. There is no fixed rate to pay them. Korean Monastery has built big guest houses. There are single as well as dormitory rooms. Capacity of guest houses is of 492 beds. Students, Nepālese visitors and poor tourists of Indiā and third countries can stay in cheap rate. Tara Foundation, Cambodian monastery and Gautami Nun's Association vihar are also providing proper services to the visitors. There are 1460 beds in total. Proposed cheap pilgrimage hotels and camping are not constructed by the authority. In this situation cheap shelter for Nepālese tourists as well as students is provided by Korean guest house. Gautami Nun,s building has also providing accommodation about 20 tourists. Mahabodhi Society monastery has seminar hall as well as guest cells for 100 persons. Myānmār guest houses have also provided more than 100 beds. Cheap pilgrims take rest in the hall at night. In the eastern zone Thai monastery is beautiful and enriched with art objects. Guest houses are also separately built. Thai pilgrims get chance to live there. The capacity of the rooms and hall is about for 55 persons. Cambodian monastery and its compartment are under construction. It is going to operate proper services more than 100 pilgrims as well as visitors. As proposed in Lumbinî Master plan a Vipassana meditation center has provided meditating packages to the National as well as international tourists. Only 9 units are mentioned in Master Plan (Tange, 1978:16). But more than 50 persons get chance to meditate here. It is systematically managed by the Management Committee. Chinese dharmasals are going in operation. About 200 pilgrims will get accommodation after completion. Single cells are also built for meditation.

In the promotion of tourism transportation, accommodation, attractions (natural as well as cultural heritages), security, proper information and communication are the basic elements. Among this accommodation should be provided on the interests of the tourists. Accommodation should be unique and comfortable than regular use. In this critical position, hotel industry is not so popularize in the area of Lumbinî. Hotel Hokke, Hotel Kasai, New Crystal and Peace land are providing proper services. In total there are 1061 beds in hotels and 1460 beds in supplementary accommodations. 2521 beds are always ready to serve the tourists. 1087 beds are made in tourist standard hotels at Siddharthanagar. Siddhartha Hotel Association has organized to manage and provide services to the tourists. Supplementary accommodation facilities are also providing by Nathamala-Giniyadevi Trust, Jayasawal Sewā Samāja, Thakāli Sewā Samāja, Madawāri Sewā Samāja, Magar Samāja, Tamu Samāja and Siddharthanagar Chamber of Commerce and Industry. These organizations can provide about 1000 beds in case of over flow of the tourists. About 2087 tourists can take rest at Siddharthanagar, which is only 22km from Lumbinî. Simple hotels and resorts can also serve about 500 visitors at Siddhārthanagar. 270 beds in tourist standard hotels at Butwal are also providing services. Besides these hotels simple hotel, bars, restaurants and supplementary accommodations are also available at Butwal and Manigram.

In the comparison of number of tourists and beds, high tourist season and low tourist season numbers should be compared with the hotel capacity. In case of 2012, total number of passport holder tourists were 1, 36,001 (Table No. 4.5). In low season, i.e. April, May, June and July months' tourists were 13628 and 122373 were in remaining eight months of high tourist season. Average monthly number in high tourist season was 15,297 and average daily number was 510. In average 3,407 in low tourist season and average daily number were 114. In November 2012, there were 21,740 pp holder tourists. Average daily number of tourists was 725 excluding Indian and Nepālese tourists. After adding 50% Indian and Nepālese tourists, total tourists will be about 1088 per day in tourist high season. All of them will not stay over night in Lumbinî. More than 2500 beds are ready in Lumbinî. About 2000 tourists can easily stay in Lumbinî complex. In this critical situation various programs should be launched in order to increase the number of tourists and quality.

CHAPTER EIGHT

TOURISM PROMOTION

Introduction

Tourism promotion is the basic component to meet the needs of the contemporary society. Its major sector is advertising to the national as well as international sectors. Advertising agencies, procedure, public relation and mass media play a vital role in the promotion. Various relation techniques, modes as well as printed sources are also supporting day today. In course of promotion Nepāl government has implied various acts, rule and regulations. Not only is this it also mentioned in the national plans. Creation of concept of satisfaction, coordination of all the publicity measures of the economic, cultural and tourist institutions, constantly analysis of the activities should be launched in proper time and situation (Bhatia, 2000:249). Press information kits are useful for supplying information about the country and its tourism resources to people and organizations out side the media. In the printed media information of road transport, air transport, and map of the destinations, climate, shopping facilities, hospital, accommodation, communication as well as tour and travel should be properly provided.

In course of advertisement Lumbinī Development Trust has published brochure, folder, shell-folder, sales letters, special offers and news letters on the various occasions (LDT, 2012). Trade travel fairs and exhibitions are also supporting to promote tourism in Lumbinī. Lumbinī, Taulihawa, Butwal and Siddharthanagar Trade and Commerce Chambers have also conducted agriculture, tourism and trade fairs since 2035 VS. Nepāl Visit year 1998, 2011 and Lumbinī visit year 2012 are also supporting to promote tourism in case of sustainability. In the context of Lumbinī LDMP has cleared the provision of tourism development infrastructures (Tange, 1978:12-15). Lumbinī, the birthplace of Lord Buddha, is the main attraction for all the peace loving people of all over the world. There are so many factors to effect in the promotion of tourism. But the limited elements, viz. role of the NGO, sock-economic condition, cultural concept, security, peach march and trade Expo are mentioned here.

The teachings of Buddha and Buddhism have been contributing to the development of socio-economic status, promotion of daily life styles, promotion of public awareness and humanity. The sacred places, associated with Lord Buddha, viz. Kapilvastu, Lumbinī, Bodhagaya and Kuśinagar have inspired to create peace, harmony and non-violence in twentieth century all over the world. Lumbinī, the birthplace of Buddha, has been contributing in up holding the social values, economic condition and cultural phenomenon through the interaction with domestic and foreign tourists; agencies or organizations who are involved to build monasteries, meditation-centers and other development works, monks and nuns coming from various countries. UNO, foreign and national agencies have taken keen interest to promote and develop the life styles of the local people and sacred complex. INGOs and NGOs have conducted many plan and programs in the periphery of Lumbinī, motivating by Buddhism and peace. Lumbinī is the main attraction of the devotees and donor parties to influence their plan and programs in this area.

Advertisement

Advertisement is a non-personal communication to purchasers or buyers of product or services. It can define as any activity made information to promote sales of marketable goods as well as services (Bhatia, 1997:213). Its main aim is to spread proper information among the consumers and their judgment in favor of the specific goods. Paid media is its main target in the process of advertisement. It is a paid public message to praise or inform the product and services. At the beginning public information was written on public walls. After the seventeenth century it began print primitive news papers. Photography, photoengraving and printing magazines and newspapers became popular to offer their products and services to mass consumers. Radio broadcasting and televisions are providing proper information of merchant's product and services. Lumbinī, being listed on world heritage property in 1997, is absolutely recognized as the birthplace of Lord Buddha. Due to its popularity all over the world more the seven hundred thousands tourists visit per year at this sacred complex. LDT, MoCTCA, UNESCO, NTB, Nepālese Embassies in related countries, INGOs, NGOs and individuals are playing a vital role to advertise the religious, archaeological as well as cultural significance of Lumbinī, birthplace of Buddha, all over the world.

Public relations in the field of tourism in Lumbinī have disseminated of information and created favorable image for the tourist products. Flims and slides, press releases, booklets, and brochures, news and features stories, photography, displays, exhibits, news letters, radio, television, house journals and research reports are creating positive image of Lumbinī as well as pilgrimage site all over the world. Non-governmental as well as governmental agencies have also contributing in the propagation of cultural and religious significance of Lumbinī and its vicinity. Local news papers, viz. Lumbinī Khabar, Siddhārtha Sandesa, Lumbinī Daily, Janasangharsa, Dainika patra, Sainā-mainā, Bhāvanā, Nayā Diśā etc; national news papers, viz. Gorkhāpatra, Kāntipur Daily, Samācharapatra and souvenirs of the NGOs and Government Offices have contributing to through light about the religious and pilgrimage significance of Lumbinī, Tilaurakot, Niglihawā, Gotihawā, Rāmagrāma and other Buddhist sites of the region. Lumbinī TV, Rupandehi TV, Buddha TV; national TVs, i.e. NTV, NTV 2, Kāntipur TV, Image TV, News 24 TV, Nepāl 1 TV etc are contributing to advertise the importance and tourist-products of Lumbinī region.

In order to spread the cultural value of Lumbinī as well as propagate the Lumbinī, birthplace of Lord Buddha, News 24 had organized 60 hours Lumbinī Expo in April 2013. That program had released the versions of the experts, Ambassadors and administrators in the area of Lumbinī. Hotel Associations, Tour and Travel Agencies, Chamber of Commerce and Industries of Kapilvastu, Lumbinī, Siddharthanagar, Parāsī, Butwal, Pālpā, Gulmi, Arghākhāchi and Chitawan are also playing a dynamic role in the promotion of tourism industry in Lumbinī and its neighbor's sites. Industrial, Agricultural and Tourist Fairs, organized at Lumbinī, Kapilvast, Parāsi, Siddharthanagar, Palpa and Butwal have played a vital role in the promotion of tourism industry. Books, booklets, directories, guide-books, journals, posters and maps are also published by the private sectors in course of publicity (Giri, 2003, 2008, 2010 & Bidari, 2003, 2004). The problem of publicity is further complicated by the discussion on the pros and cons of graphic and photographic posters. VDO, VCD and other electronic media are creating favorable situation in the motivation of visit in Lumbinī complex.

Facilitations

Facilitation means the act of assisting progress or helping more forward. It provides minimum entry and exit formalities for a temporary visitors. Facility of any sector makes enable tourists to enter, move and depart from the country with the maximum of ease and minimum of obstacles. It also provides secure maximum enjoyment of their rest. Basic information and other facilities are providing in Lumbinī and its vicinities. Major facilitation areas are passport, visa, money changer or exchange control, security check, tax system on tourists, health and hospital, customs rules and regulations and clearance of baggage, which are available at Siddharthanagar, Belahiyā, Butwal and Lumbinī complex.

International Union of Tourism Organization has made efforts in the field of facilitation of tour and travel formalities at least relaxed and standardization after Rome convention in 1963 (Bhatia, 1997:342). After the formation of WTO in 1975, facilitation issues were raised and efforts were made to make easy it from various barriers. In course of security and make easy excess controls and formalities can create conflict with the full exercise of the fundamental rights of the individuals. It should not be against the Article 13 of the Human right Declaration 1948, Manila Declaration tourist Bills of rights and Tourist code of WTO. On the basic of the contemporary needs facilitation committees should be formulated is various sectors as follows- Administration formalities, Custom formalities, Sanitary regulation and Currency regulation.

The First Buddhist Summit

The Buddhist Summit was held in Lumbinī during 30 November to 2 December, 1998. The main theme of the Summit was as "**Lumbinī the Fountain of World Peace**" (LDT, 2004:25). On that occasion Ananda

W.P.Guruge from Srī Lanka had presented a paper on the topic "**Buddhist Philosophy and World Peace**". He had emphasized that world peace is possible through the teachings of Lord Buddha. (Guruge, 1998:13-20). Hark Gurung from Nepāl had presented another valuable paper on the topic "**Developing Lumbinī As Pilgrimage Centre**". He had mentioned historical aspect, archaeological value, review of LMP, donors, contribution and present status of Lumbinī in his paper (Gurung, 1998:21-42). The speakers focused on planning for the development of Lumbinī, significance of Lumbinī as the holy shrine and peace center, promotion of academic activities in the holy complex of Lumbinī, Buddhism and its concern for social issues and on the state of the art of excavation and continuation of archaeological activities including research in an integrated manner (Vaidya and Khatry, 1998:75-84). Three days Summit had declared the commitments on the development of Lumbinī including Kapilvastu, Devadaha and Rāmagrāma; construction of international airport at Siddharthanagar, establishment of Buddhist University, to develop Lumbinī as the Fountain of World Peace and Holiest Pilgrimage Shrine (Ibid, 98-100).

It was also recommended that LDT should be autonomous body to work freely and unbiasily. On that occasion Yoshiaki Kitamura, UNESCO Representative to Nepāl, HE Lakshman Jayakody, Minister of Buddhasan and Leader of Srī Lankan delegation, HE Dago Tsering, Leader of the Bhutanese delegation, PK Baruya, representative of Bānglādesh, Dhruvanaryana Lal, VC of Purbanchal University, Mahashweta Maharathi, Rajgir Indiā, Jivraj Pokhrel, Architect Eng. Nepāl, Natasaran Seesalab, General Secretary WFB Bangkok, Henning Karcher, UNDP Representative to Nepāl and Nepālese experts had actively participated at the Summit (Ibid). During the summit period Buddhist organizations, scholars, monks, nuns and thousands of devotees were actively participated. That Summit had also released the proper information of Lumbinī, the birthplace of Buddha, as the symbol of Peace and Compassion, which had supported to propagate the name and fame of Lumbinī all over the world. It is a unique program in course of the promotion of tourism in Lumbinī, which became very interesting and fruitful this writer was eye witness on the occasion.

International Buddhist Conference

International Buddhist Conference held on February 1 -2, 2001 in Lumbinī had played a dynamic role in the promotion of tourism industry in Lumbinī area. The First Buddhist Summit 1998 had reconfirmed and enhanced the status of Lumbinī as the Fountain of World Peace as well as Sacred pilgrimage site to the peace loving people of all over the world (Khatry, 2002:Preface). The main theme of the Conference was "**Lumbinī in the New Millennium**". During that Conference two theme papers were presented by Mohan Man Sainju and Veṇ. Sugandha on the topics- "Lumbinī in the New Millennium: Role of the Youth", and " Lumbinī in the New Millennium: Youth in Buddhism" respectively. At the Conference fourteen points declarations had especially emphasized to complete of LMP in a time-bound manner, to formulate similar plans to other sites, i.e. Kapilvastu and Devadaha-Ramagram as well as participate to local communities in the development of Lumbinī.

Role of the youth and community in the millennium topics were actively discussed on that occasion. During that conference Dato Khoo Leong of Malayasis, Sritaptim Panitpan, WFB Standing Committee on Women Bankok; Tilake Attanayaka, President of World Buddhist Peace Foundation, Dago Sangye Wangchuk of Bhutan, Warayut Yoothongkam of Royal Thai Embassy, Prof. A.K.Narain of Indiā, Prof.Pal-Khim-Chun of Koreā and John D. Hughes of Australia had participated (LDT, 2004:27). That Conference had supported to release the cultural and pilgrimage importance of Lumbinī all over the world. Due to that Conference the number of national and international tourists had increased. Such international Conference, Summit, Seminar and Workshops play vital roles in the promotion of tourism industry.

The Second World Buddhist Summit, 2004

The Second World Buddhist was organized during November 30 to December 2, 2004 in Lumbinī. The theme of the Summit was "Lumbinī: A Symbol of Unity in Diversity-the Fountain of World Peace". During that Summit three theme papers were presented by Venerable Dr. Sugandha Mahasthavir, Sunao Miyabara and Kama Shakya on the topics Indispensability of Peace in the Present World, Lumbinī Development and International Co-operation and Developing Lumbinī as a World Peace City respectively. Its main aim was to promote Lumbinī as a symbol of international brotherhood, peace and prosperity as well as World Peace City. On that occasion the meaning of

Peace was defined as truth, beauty, love, amity, friendship, harmony, concord, tranquility, repose, quiescence, truce, pacification and neutrality. In other words it was categorized as a world without war, world justice and world order (Sugandha, 2004:3-4). On the paper of Ven. Sugandha Mahashavir rules of peaceful society, ten virtues, new path to achieve peace instruments used for peace had explained in proper way. (Ibid, 6-35).

During that Summit delegates Buddhist Summit had focused to fulfill the agendas passed at the first World in 1998. On the declaration of the Summit five precept zones to the sacred complex of Lumbinī and Peace education in formal process had mentioned. In declaration No.5 Kapilvastu, Devadaha and Rāmagrāma had proposed to be developed as tourist destination for domestic as well as international tourists. It was also decided that the holy site should be adequately publicity and develop as unique tourist destinations. (LDT, 2004:28). Environment development, tourism development and vision of world peace city were also major elements of that Summit. That Summit had also decided to conduct World Buddhist Summit in each four years in Lumbin (LDT, www). That Summit had played a vital role in the propagation of Lumbinī as a Peace City and Pilgrimage site all over the world.

Gautam Buddha International Peace Award

According to the decision of The First Buddhist Summit held in 1998, Nepāl Government has established a Peace Award in 2002. The main aim of the Award is to recognize the honor individuals or institutions from around the world, which has made significant contribution to keep world peace, non-violence, compassion and co-operation. Its selection criteria's are distinguished individuals or institutions who have contributed in the promotion of world peace, disarmament, non-violence, alleviation in human sufferings, promotion of human solidarity, peaceful resolution of conflicts through creative application of Buddhist philosophy, and the development of Lumbinī as a major global pilgrimage site (GBIPAW, 2011:3-4).

On the occasion of 2555 th Buddha Anniversary on May 17, 2011 Gautam Buddha International Peace Award was awarded to prize winners H.E. Dr.Tadatoshi Akiba, former Mayor of Hiroshima and H.E. Tomihisa Taue, mayor of Nagasaki of Jāpān by Dr. Ramavarana Yadav,

Right Honorable President. Honorable Vice President Paramananda Jha, Acharya Karma Sangho Sherpa, Vice President of LDT and other distinguished guests had also participated on that occasion. Management and Selection Committee was formed under the Chairmanship of Kul Chandra Gautam, Former Assistant Secretary-General of the UNO; including the members Bimal Prasad Koirala, Former Chief Secretary of Nepāl Government, Acharya Karma Sangbo Sherpa, Vice-Chairman of LDT, Urmila Garg, Renowned Nepāli Artist and Ani Choying Dolma, Renowned Buddhist Nun and Singer of Nepāl. Peace prayers and chanting were performed in the courtyard of Māyādevī Temple. 2555 oil lamps lighting, peace procession, food and gifts offering to the monks and nuns as well as cultural programs had performed during that period. Winners were awarded US 50 thousand dollar, gold medals and certificates by Dr. Yadav (LDT, 2069). That program was chaired by Honorable Minister of MoCTCA. The main aim of the program is to propagate the significance of Lumbinī as the birthplace of Lord Buddha all over the world. It is a unique and mass information process all over the world, which supports to increase the number of tourists directly and indirectly.

Goodwill Ambassadors Declaration

Nepāl Government and LDT had honored Khunying Sudarat Keyuraphan, the former Thai Minister and Ani Choing Dolma, the renowned Dharma Singer of Nepāl as the Good Will Ambassador on the occasion of Visit Lumbinī Year 2012 on the 6th March, 2012. The program was organized on the presence of Her Excellency Madam Sudarat's husband, Thai Member of Parliament Tawatchai Sutibongkot, Tom Kruesopon, a renowned Thai industrialist and Threetep Nopkhun, Charge d' Affairs, the Embassy of Kingdom of Thāīland to Nepāl, Ven. Maitri, nuns and monks Vice Chairman Acharya Karma Sangbo Sherpa, the Treasurer Om Prasad Aryal, Member Secretary Rajendra Thapa Magar and Project Chief Er Temba Sherpa in Lumbinī. On that occasion inaugurated the program by lighting a lamp and chanting Buddhist auspicious *mantras*. All the speakers had expressed their views that Good Will Ambassadors would have contributed in the promotion of Buddhism, Peace, tourism and all round development of Lumbinī. The Vice Chairman had provided images of the Buddhâ as a token of love from behalf of the LDT to the Good Will Ambassadors (LDT,2069:40).

Ani Choing Dolma had expressed her heartfelt gratitude to LDT and Government of Nepāl for honoring them as the Good Will Ambassador. She had committed that she would have worked for the promotion of Lumbinī all over the world in her approach. Khunying Sudarat had also thanked to Nepāl Government and Lumbinī Development Trust for the honor. The program was conducted by Hari D. Rai, the Information Chief.

A pilgrimage team of Thai devotees led by Khunying Sudarat Keyuraphan, Former Thai Minister performed Buddhism Sanctification Ceremony on 5th March, 2012. Thai Phoung Thai Buddhist Foundation and devotees had completed construction of foot trails and meditation platform in the vicinity of Māyādevī temple, the holy birthplace of Sākyamuni Buddha. The foundation had also established an Information Centre in the Sacred Garden. It is one of the unique programs to propagate the significance and sacred value of Lumbinī as a pilgrimage site.

Peace Marches

Lumbinī, being the centre of Peace and Compassion, many peace marches have organized from the point of Peace Flame of Lumbinī. Its main aim is to spread the value and significance of Buddha Teachings all over the world. Nipponzan Myohoji and other such institutes have also regularly organized such programs. In 2012 a six member team consisting Suraja Aryal, Iswarkumar Barawal, Ramkrishna Pudasaini, Ramahari Adhikari, Rajan and Prakash had launched their Peace March from Lumbinī complex. The team proposed to propagate nuclear less world, human right and gender equity about 60 countries within the period of five years. It is a positive aspect to promote tourism industry in Nepāl, especially in Lumbinī area.

Lumbinī-Sāgarmātha Youth Leader Peace March

Lumbinī, the birthplace of Buddha, and Sagarmatha, the highest peak all over the world, are the remarkable cultural and natural heritages of Nepāl, which are throwing light the name and fame of Nepāl. On the occasion of Lumbinī-Sagarmatha Peace March and regarding program of political leaders, viz. B.P. Koirala, P.L.Shrestha, Ganesh Man Singh, Madan Bhandari, Girija Prasad Koirala and Puspakamala Dahal (Prachanda) a ceremony was organized in Lumbinī by Lumbinī-

Sagaramatha Youth Leader Peace March Team on February 20, 2012. Honorable Prime Minister Dr. Baburam Bhattari, Chief Guest; Political leaders Puspakamal Dahal, Susila Koirala, Jhalanath Khanal, Vidhya Bhandari, Sahana Pradhan, Sujata Koirala and Sasanka Koirala had participated at the ceremony. Special cultural program had launched with the support of national artists, viz. Jivan Sharma, Shambhu Rai, Manoja Gajurel, B.B. Anuragi and Kamal Gaule. That program has supported to increase the number of tourists at the site.

Lumbinī Symposium

The Indian Council for Cultural Relations (ICCR), the Embassy of the Republic of India to Nepāl and LDT had jointly organized a Symposium on the topic "Cooperation on Promoting the Shared Buddhist Heritages between India and Nepāl" during January 15-17, 2013 in Lumbinī. The main theme of theSymposium was to link Buddhism to its earliest historic landscape, monuments and pilgrimage sites, Buddhist art, architecture, culture, philosophy and rituals, which are popular along the Himalayan foothills and the Genetic Plains. Ancient Buddhist sites, which are located in Nepāl and India, hold great importance for the peace and internationalal relations for hundreds of millions of people. Its target was to establish the dialogue process between the experts and authorities of the two countries in course of ensure the sustainable and effective development of the Buddhist sites across the borders.

On that occasion Prof. Dr. Triratna Manandhar, Vice Chancellor of Lumbinī Bauddha University, Khempo Chony Randol Lama, Prof.Dr.Nareshman Bajrachary,Ven. Prajaankar, C.D. Naik, Robin Coningham, Koshaprasad Acharya and Basanta Bidari had presented papers on the topics Buddism in Nepāl, Buddhism in Indiā and Early Buddhist Archaeology (Available papers). Good relations, mutual understandings, academic interactions about the Buddhist culture and archaeological sites; tourism development, mutual cooperation for development and conseving Buddhist sites were its main outcomes. It has played a vital role in the promotion of tourism industry between two countries.

Tourism Mart, 2013

Tourism, being an internationalal networking businesss, interaction and mutual understandings among the hosts and guests countries should be modify on the interest of the tourists and contemporary society. Sport, medicine, agriculture, culture etc tourisms are improving according to the needs and interests of og new generations in synchronous times. On that process Nepāl, Indiā and China have been conducting various interaction programs in the promotional area of tourism. In this situation Tourism Mart, 2013 was held in Lumbinī in January 2013 with the joint venture of Nepāl and Indian governments. The main aim of the Mart was to promote Buddhist pilgrimage at the Buddhist sites in India and Nepāl. That Mart was jointly inaugurated by Honorable Post Bahadur Bogati, Minister of MoCTCA Nepāl and His Excellency Jayanta Prasad Singh, Indian Ambassdor to Nepāl in Lumbinī. Indian and Nepālese officers, members of Chamber of Commerce and Industries; representatives of local agencies had participated on that occasion. It was a mile stone to network Buddhist sites of India and Nepāl in Buddhist Circuit. It is supporting in order to increase the numbers of Indian tourists in Lumbinī area.

Tourist Security

To secure the world heritage property as well as tourists of Lumbinī, Nepāl Government and LDT have managed security force in Lumbinī and its peripheral area. Nepāl Civil Police, Nepāl Armed Police, Military Force, Tourist Police and LDT Secuity Force have been providing proper security at the site. Among them Tourist Police Force is directly involved in order to secure of tourists and to promote tourism industry.

Tourist Police

Peace and security is one of the basic elements of tourism development. Without security no body go out from one's own residence for rest, recreation, relax and amusement. Due to this issue Nepāl government has organized a Tourist Police unit. It is a special unit of Nepāl Police, which was **established in Jan 26, 1979 under** the Ministry of Tourism and Civil Aviation. Its headquarter is located at Bhrikuti Mandap, Kathmandu, Tourist Service Center Building, and also have complaint counters at the Airport and Basantapur Durbar Square. Tourist Police motto is "Friendly, Fast and Right". As such, Tourist Police always contact close with travel agencies, hotel, airline, bus, and taxi to give away anything that information needed by tourists.

It is always attentive to deal with the problems of tourist and very sensitive in safety and security of the tourists. Its main aim is to offer safe and pleasant stay to all the visitors in Nepāl. The main function and responsibility of Tourist Police is to look after the welfare of tourist and to assure them a pleasant and a memorable stay in Nepāl. Its function is to advise and assist tourist in safety and security during traveling, trekking, rafting and hotel stay in any part of Nepāl. One of the units of this force is established at Belahiya, main entrance gate of the western Nepāl, especially to Lumbinī visit. Only four police persons are provided at Belahiya.

This unit opens 24 hours to provide security and peace to the tourists, who enter from this point. Nepāl Police Headquarters has been appointing police personnel who have a good command in English language to be posted as Tourist Police. Following the Visit Nepāl Year 1998, there was a rise in the number of tourists coming into the country, hence, the need and importance of an institution to guarantee security to them was largely felt. In this regard, organizations related to tourism sector initiated a positive step in setting up and developing the Tourist Police by offering substantial physical contribution which also nudged the government to take initiation in this line. Government of Nepāl, with the aim of developing a resourceful Tourist Police over the time, on the recommendation of the proposal presented by the Police Reforms Recommendation Taskforce, created additional thirty-one posts for tourist police that included six Sub-Inspectors, six Assistant Sub-Inspectors, seven head constables and twelve constables on 2062/7/22(Feb 2006). They have also given the added responsibility to overcome the various irregularities that exist in travel and trekking businesses. There is also an aim to set up sub-branches (beats) at various concerned sites. Tourist Police Reform Task Force has been formed by the Government to reform, develop and expand its services at other parts of the country.

The Reform Task Force has prepared both short and long term working plan, increasing the manpower according to the need of the time, expand resources and manage budget at eight Tourists Police post. Tourist Police post in Pokhara has 10 personnel; Likewise it will be expanded in 11 places Chitwan, Kanchanpur, Kakarvitta, Birgunj, Biratnagar, Kohalpur, Itahari and Janakpur with 193 employees to serve the tourists. At Rupandehi, Belahiya Siddharthanagar unit was established on vs. 2063.3.25 in the imitation of the local tourist stakeholders and government with specially focus to the visitor of

Lumbinī. Due to the major transit point of the western Nepāl, there happens so much events, but only a few comes in record as iceberg. Some of the registered cases at the Tourist Police Unit are mention in Table No. 8.1.

Table 8.1

Details of Registered Cases at Tourist Police Unit Belahiya, Siddharthanagar

S.No.	*Fiscal Years*	*Number of Cases*	*Special types of Cases*	*Remarks*
1	2065-66	27	missing bags, cheat, stolen, fraud	
2	2066-67	15	missing bags, cheat, stolen, fraud	
3	2067-68	15	missing bags, cheat, stolen, fraud	
4	2068-69	13	missing bags, cheat, stolen, fraud	
5	2069-70 (Magha)	07	missing bags, cheat, stolen, fraud	

Source- Tourist Police Office, Belahiya, 2013

Table 8.1 shows that the ratio of the cases is decreasing at later years than preceding years respectively. Twenty seven cases were registered in 2065-66. After that fifteen and thirteen cases are enrolled at the office. In case of any theft/loss/ other happens immediately contact to the Police Station or Tourist Police at Belahiya, Siddharthanagar. Drug-abuse, trafficking and sexual relation with children are strictly prohibited. The offenders will be punished according to the National law. There is no doubt that if the Tourist Police are given the necessary training within the country and in other friendly nations about the international standards of service and the prevailing tourism laws and also if they are established as a separate service entity with their own set of responsibilities and authorities, then the Tourist Police will be better equipped to discharge their duties towards the security of foreign tourists in Nepāl. Nepāl is a country blessed with the beauties of Nature that lure tourists in abundance from all over the world. Majestic snow-clad mountains, exotic flora and fauna, invaluable natural resources, archaeological and historical monuments, art and architecture motivate tourists. Rich Cultural Heritage is also another aspect, which motivates the people from different land. Tourist Police has played a very vital role in preventing harassment and misbehavior, control and discourage criminal activities against tourists. Since its inception, it has taken pains to provide security, facilities and render appropriate services at any place and situation. The Tourist Police at Belahiya have recently, expanded its services to register complaints and recommend for recommend for necessary action to help recover lost goods of the tourists and prepares a police report. To prevent harassment to tourists by the beggars, peddlers and cheats, tourists' sites are properly inspected. The activities of unlicensed hotels, travel agencies and rafting are regularly monitored to see that tourists are not exploited and cheated. Interaction program is conducted among the Taxi-drivers, and others and local guides to extend good and efficient services to the tourists.

Duties of the Tourist Police

Daily patrolling within the Tourist interested area in Lumbinī and other sites of Rupandehi. Quick action and investigation have taken seriously in any tourist complaints. They are ready to provide information on travel security, ensure hassle free trip by keeping hawkers, beggars and street children away from tourist. They assist tourist whenever need arises and create safety environment mainly in tourist areas. The team inspect (supervise) over hotel, travel, trekking & rafting agencies in case of other proven. Patroling, control unlicensed tourist guides, forward tourist related criminal cases for legal procedure to district police office, consulting with concerned embassy and provide tourism related information.

Information for Tourists

Tourists are requested to follow the rules and regulations of Nepāl Government to feel safe and pleasant journey in Lumbinī and other sites around Lumbinī. They are also informed about the problems and complaints, to take proper services of government registered travel/ trekking agencies only, to stay at government registered hotels/resorts/guest house/lodges only and to use only those porters who are authorized by travel agency or hotel. They are also made conscious about the exchange of foreign currency only at authorized agencies and make sure your wallet is in the inside jacket pocket or side pocket of the trousers.

Keeping in coordination with the Siddharthanagar Municipality, Belahiya Gau Samaja, Regional tourism Promotional Office Bhairahawa, Nepāl Tourism Board and Tourist associated organizations, this unit prepare brochure for the tourists. Necessary arrangement is made in the event of Nepāl Bandh (strikes) and vehicle strikes, which cause inconvenience for the tourist to visit Lumbinī,

Kapilvastu, Palpa, Pokhara, Kathmandu and Rāmagrāma. The unit assists the tourists to seek counseling with the concerned government authorities. Now Tourist Police has five personnel under the command of Assistant Sub-Inspector. The unit would be strengthened and stability and harmonious environment would be fully utilized to increase country's image as friendly destination tourists. According to the Unit In-chare, Assistant sub-Inspector Gitaram Bhusal, non-qualified tourist guides, broker system, lack of direct tourist bus from Sunauli to Lumbinī, illegal of IC note of Rs. 500 and 1000 and main problems at this entry point.

Locations including Lumbinī, Kapilvastu, Rāmagrāma, Devadaha, Palpa, Pokhara and other related sited should be clearly written in English, Srilankan, Thai and other essential languages and indicated at the maps and hoarding boards in proper directions. Travel and Tour Agencies are also not punctual to obey their professional obligations. Their agents are cheating to the guests, who visited to the Holy and Peace land Lumbinī. An event had happened at this Unit that South African tourist named SHAUN SWILLING ZAF of 48, passport no. 421538418 suddenly felt ill in case of unconscious in January 3, 2009 at Belahiya. At that time Tourist Police took care of and admitted at the Universal Medical College. After the diagnosis of the Dr it was exposed that he was patient of sugar and lay on land due to low of sugar. Before coming his friend from Indiä, Traffic Police took care at the hospital with out any special facility. Thus, the Unit should be upgraded involving minimum ten persons with vehicle, telephone and Lumbinī tourist Police Unit should be separate Unit only for that area.

Administration and Organization

Administration is a mechanism to govern the connected agencies, corporated bodies and individuals in proper sectors. An organization is a combination of groups of individuals whose aims and objectives are similar to each other. In the field of tourism tour and travel agencies; tourism associations, groups, official and semi-oficial bodies are involved in tourism industries. These are catogorized into official and private voluntary organizations. National, regional and local government offices in Lumbinī area are actively working in the field of tourism. Under the umbrella of MoCTCA, LDT has been playing a dynamic role in the promotion of tourism in Lumbinī. LDMP, LDT Act 2042, LDT Rules 2058 (Including revisions); and Tourism Act, 2035,

Tourism Rules 2046 and Tourism Action Plan, 2064 have also indicated the responsibilities of the various posts (LDT, 2067:84-87, 2068:98-100 &2069:38-43). Nepālese Embassies in various friendly countries have also been contributing to provide proper information to the concerned areas of Lumbinī as the sacred birthplace of Lord Buddha.

Lumbinī Regional Tourism Promotional Office Bhairahawa, NTB Belahiya Office, LDT Information and Hospitality Section, DDC Rupandehi Tourism Committee, Sustainable Tourism Development Committees of Lumbinī Adarsa VDC, Tenuhawa VDC, Madhuwani VDC, Ama VDC, Khudabagar VDC, Bhagawanpur VDC, Ekala VDC are also working at their target area. Due to the lack of proper budget these Committees are not activily functioning at proper sitesactive. LRPTP has product tourist informative brochures, pamplets and booklets in Nepāli, Hindi and English medium. LRPTP has published a book on the topic "*Lumbinī Ksetra Sano Chinari* " (A Brief Introduction of Lumbinī) in 2011. Administrative mechanism of tourism from top to bottom is not so effective as the needs of the contemporary society.

Lumbinī Day and Buddha Jayanti

LDT always celebrates Buddha *Jayanti* and Lumbinī Day on the occasion of birth date of Gautam Buddha *Vaisakha sukla Purnima* (April-May). The Trust formulates various committees to do proper duties on that occasion. Essay competition among the school students, debate, quiz competition, Peace March, rally and cleaning programs are conduct (LDT, 2067:34). On that schedule, 2555 th Buddha Anniversary was celebrated at Kapilvastu, Devadaha, Rāmagrāma and Lumbinī with the participant of local agencies and communities. Peace prayer, chanting, candles lighting, Māyādevī scholarship distribution and blood-donation programs are performed on that occasion. During the period of Buddha *Jayanti* national as well as internationalal tourists and day visitors also participate.

Role of Non-governmental Organizations

Ancient Lumbinīgrama buried under the earth before the exploration of General Khadga Shamsher in the last decade of the nineteenth century. Yadav, Lodha, Muslim, Kewat, Harijan, Brahaman, Kurmi, Mallha, Paswan , Teli, Tharu, Dhobi, Kumal etc. castes reside around the sacred complex of Lumbinī (CBS, 2002:82-94). Some of them had emigrated from Indiā and migrated from the hills of Nepāl. Tharu is known as an aboriginal caste of this Terai region. Führer has purposed that Tharus were the ancestor of the Śākyas of Kapilvastu, belonged to Buddha. This study depends on the life style and changes of the local people around the Master Plan of Lumbinī project especially Ama, Bhagawanpur, Ekala, Khudabagar, Lumbinīadarsa and Madhuwani VDCs. priest, monks, nuns and other people who reside in project area are also observed to know their changes and modernization including physical development of the complex. Several kinds of changes have slowly crept into the traditional beliefs customs, food and drinks, dress and ornaments, position of family members, literacy rate, vocational training, organization of functional groups, increasing of income sources and cultural activities due to the verbal communication and project works of the guests, who come to visit Lumbinī. Elements of modernization is clearly reflected in the management and maintenance of the life-style of the people, monks , nuns, hoteliers, shop-keepers and worker who reside in Lambing area.

Before the formation of Lumbinī Development Committee, local people were not conscious to change and modernize their life-styles due to lack of verbal communication of pilgrims and donated-property in the project area. After launching various programmes and project-works at Lumbinī, they got chance to employ as well as project-activities in their villages. The effect of modernization has been felt not only in the nuclear part of Lumbinī but also in the life-style of the people of the villages located on the outskirts of Lumbinī complex. Master plan, attractions of UNO donor agencies, schooling , networks of roads, metallic road from Siddhārthanagar, plane-service, fast means of communications, i.e. telephone, television, e-mail, internet and various activities, conducted by NGOs are the main contributing factors to this change and modernization. These modern facilities have played a vital role in the acceleration of complete life-style and soci-cultural activities of Lumbinī.

Due to the keen interest of donor agencies, NGO, INGO and governmental authorities have been launching various development activities through the channel of Rupāndehi DDC and separately in their interest. District Health strengthening program (DFID), Nepāl Safe Motherhood program (DFID), TRPAP, UNDP, SNV, Livelihood community forest program (DFID), Rural urban partnership program, PPPP, RK , IBS, PVDP, Cross Flow, FINIDA, BP with poor and LDT programs have been launching in this area. Their main target is to and outskirts of Lumbinī. The elements of changes and modernization are reflecting on social, economic and cultural aspects of the people.

Social activities have been running under the aegis of Rupandehi DDC, which are initiated by the donor agencies. Their life-style, food and drink, dress and ornament, social behaviors as well as traditions, viz. *bala vivaha, anamela vivaha,* dowry system and *parda pratha* have also under gone changes and modernization due to these social activities. Here only a few people are seen dressed their traditional objects. The youths of Lumbinī area visit monastery zone for employment. They generally interact the pilgrims and the people who come to enjoy the fair and festivals, especially Buddha Ajanta, by organizing dramas, dances and music programmes and other kinds of activities. In this process TRPAP has formed a group of *Biraha Geeta,* traditional song of indigenous people, and sing on special request of the visitors in charge. Management capacity enhancement training, group management, book keeping, strategic plans etc are few examples of the training. Involvement of more women in the decision making level is the main focus of TRPAP. At present household women have been able to come out of their houses and participate in the different training program such as women empowerment.

Eco-social Sector

Centre of Rural Development and Self-help, Collective Development and Multi-purpose Co-operative, Pragatishil Women Development Co-operative, Indreni Rural Development Centre, TRPAP, FINIDA etc have launched various programmes to promote the economic status of the people. These programs have been supported to the objectives of poverty alleviation underlined in the Ninth and Tenth Five year plans of HMG. The self-reliant concept is needed in order to match with there source base of the poor communities, VDCs and DDCs, especially in the remote area. In order to focus further on the weaker section communities, the programs have made a special provision of support fund for poor.

TRPAP, FINIDA, RK, IBS, Cross Flow, Bisweswar with Poor etc programs have played a significant role for sustainable development and income generation. Almost the plans and programs have concentrated to the sacred complex of Lumbinī, associated with Buddha and Buddhism. FINIDA and BP with poor programs had conducted rainwater using and household latrine schemes to be deprived and disadvantaged community together with the collaboration of DDC. Such collaboration among the same agencies has added a new dimension in addressing the needs of the poorer communities in rural area.

In course of the promotion the tourism Bhagawanpur, Lumbinī Adarsa, Madhuwani, Tenuhawa and Akala VDCs were trained in vegetable farming and account respectively under the aegis of Rupendehi DDC. Seven persons of Tenuhawa were trained in bee-keeping sector. Bee-keeping is a suitable and cash-oriented industry in this area. 25 members were also skilled in modern concept for live-farming sector (Giri, 2008:191-93).

TRPAP has been given different types of skill development training to the people of Lumbinī area to enhance their skills and help them generate income for their living. The various training includes hotel management, fish farming, rickshaw pulling, banana farming, vegetable farming, making statues of clay, making *dhakkis* and basic hospitality. These training programs have motivated about the importance of their skills and increasing sense towards the values of cultural heritage. Such scenarios of capacity enhancement developing training activities are conducting. First of all leadership development and net working was conducted to mobilize the man power and motivate to the local people. MCET, mushroom cultivation, account-keeping, small hotel and lodge management, local guide, artistic handicraft, ICS making and tourism sector were launched. 37.25% female have involved in these training, which is function-oriented training.

Almost the Hindu and Muslim people reside in the outskirts of Lumbinī complex. Buddhists are also coming from various sites to reside in the monasteries and in their own houses. The atmosphere of Lumbinī area is favorable to create unity in diversity due to the tolerance of various sects, groups and communities. On the occasions of fair and festivals, local clubs and groups generally entertain the pilgrims by organizing traditional dance, music and drama. Dance and music are organized in Buddhist tradition based on *Jataka* stories. The mother tongue of the natives is Bhojapuri. Now-a-days they use Nepāli, Hindi, English and Bhojapuri language due to the verbal communication among domestic and international visitors. The youths who work in the hotels, restaurant and monasteries speak Japanese, Chinese, Korean, Tibetan and Tamil languages in proper situation.

Realizing the necessity and importance of the cultural elements, an organization named"Lumbinī Cultural Buddha *Biraha Geet Sadak Natak"* is established for the conservation, promotion and to show in proper situation.

The monks and nuns of the Theravada and Mahāyan monasteries are coming from the related countries. Their life-style, food and drinks, habits and social behaviors have also under gone changes. Old priest of Māyādevī temple is also changing his life-style in Buddhist rules and regulations, who was Hindu at the beginning. Mixed-Buddhist culture and traditions have been practiced in this complex. Physical progress has brought a tremendous change and modernization. In the process of modernization, several kinds of changes have crept into social, economic, cultural life of the people of Lumbinī. The changes are not only in the life-style but also in its physical development, food, drinks, dress, ornaments and aesthetic traditions. Almost the elements of changes and modernizations have depended in the process of promotion of tourism.

All the basic requirements should be managed in order to promote tourism. Besides the modes of transport, accommodation, entertainment and local attractions, other promotional activities should be provided to the tourists on their basic needs and interests. Local FMs, radios, TVs, papers and national media have playing a vital role in the promotion of tourism industry in Lumbinni area. Tourism information centre, money exchangers, market information and service centres are always providing services. In course of international understanding and mutual friendship First and Second World Buddhist Summits had organized in 1998 and 2004 respectively in Lumbinī complex. International Buddhist Conference had also conducted in 2001. On that occasions international scholars as well as government officials had come, which had propagated the cultural significance of Lumbinī all over the world. Gautam Buddha Peace Award has also declared to provide the peace loving individuals and institutions, contributors against the violence and especial contributors for the development of Lumbinī. Lumbinī Visit, Tourist Mart, Peace Marches, Security, transparent administration, Lumbinī Day and Buddha Jayanti; NGO, s and Civil Societies' activities are supporting to increase the number of the tourists day by day.

CHAPTER NINE

CONCLUSION

The researcher has made an attempt in this research work to throw light on the geography, history, Buddhist heritages, and scenario of tourist's movement, pilgrims and pilgrimage, modes of transport, tourist accommodation and tourism promotion of Lumbinī. In course of this present study primary data and field survey have been used. Lumbinī is located about 22 km from Siddhārthanagar; headquarter of Rupandehi district in the western Terai region of Nepāl. It is on the foot of Churiā range, which is formed of the molasses deposit of the Siwālika group. This area is composed of gravels and sands of the late Pleistocene to Holocene age. The river systems of Telār, Dano, Harahawa, Koṭhī and Tinau have formed this area. During the Buddhist period this area, with hot and humid weather was covered with indigenous trees. At present, Lumbinī Development Trust (Committee) has planted hedge plantation, which is converted into a dense forest. Telār and Harahawā are the main rivers in the periphery of Lumbinī complex. Lumbinī was the ancient pilgrimage route from north to south, east to west, north to west and north to east. Lumbinī has been occupied from the Mauryan period up to modern times; we find remains of the human activities during all these periods. Archaeological geophysical survey in 2012-13 has indicated its antiquity about 11th century BC. But it will be clear after laboratory test.

During the reign of the Śākyas and Koliyas a lot of art activities started in the field of pottery, terracotta human and animal figurines, coins and architectural fragments. In the third century BC Aśoka installed monolithic stone pillar inscribed in Brāhmi script. The pillar inscription of Lumbinī is the concrete evidence of the historical importance. Lumbinī is an important pilgrimage sites not only too the Buddhists, but also other human beings. It is playing a vital role in integrating the societies of this part of the world into one cognate order. The religious merits support and lead one to attain *Nirvana* in the end. Aśoka, Chinese visitors i.e., Shui-Chi-Chu, Fa-hien, Hiuen-Tsiang and Ripu Malla had visited in Lumbinī in ancient and medieval periods in course of their pilgrimage. After exploration and excavation by Khadga Shamsher, A. Führer, P.C. Mukherj and Keshar Samsher J.B.R., many renowned persons had visited in Lumbinī. In 1967 U-Thant, the then General Secretary of the UNO had visited Lumbinī. Late King Mahendra Bir Bikram Shah had shown keen interest to promote Lumbinī as a sacred complex for all the human beings. Chinese pilgrims Fa-Hien, Hiuen-Tsiang and Shui-Ching-Chu had also mentioned the pilgrimage tradition and cultural details of Lumbinī. Their details throw light on the anthropological modes of the synchronous times. Khasa, Malla and Sen Dynasties had ruled here in the medieval period. After the unification of this area by Gorkha a conflict arose between the Company Government of Indiā and Nepāl due to the possession of land of Butwal area, including Lumbinī. This area was given to Nepāl in course of Sugauli Treaty between East Indiā Company and Nepāl.

To promote Lumbinī as the internationalal pilgrimage site, an International Lumbinī Development Committee was formed in 1970 under the chairman of Nepāl. The Committee has the representatives of 15 nations under the leadership of UNO. The Master Plan of Lumbinī was prepared by the renowned Japanese architect Prof. Kenzo Tange and Urtect in 1978. With a total area of 25 sq mile is used in Master Plan. New Lumbinī Village, Monastic Zone and Sacred Garden areas cover one sq. mile area in each complex from north to south respectively. Asian Highway is also proposed from the north of New Lumbinī Village. Foundation of school building, standard tourist Hotel Hokke, Hotel Kasai; middle class accommodation Śri Lańkan pilgrimage house and Śānti Stupa have been completed at this area.

Lumbinī, the birthplace of Buddha, is the major focus point for the national as well as internationalal tourists. Its main attraction is Buddhist pilgrimage site. Like Mecca-Madina and Jerusalem it is the peace and compassion for all human beings. Here are some attractions to the visitors. Not only the Buddhists, but also all the peace loving people all over the world come here in order to pilgrimage and research. Aśokan pillar, Māyādevi temple, Sacred tank, ruins of ancient stūpas and vihars are at the Sacred Garden. Theravada and Mahayana monastic zone, immediately south of Friendship Bridge of Harahawā River, have been rapidly developed into Buddhist World. Thāiland, Mahabodhi Society Calcuttā, Myānmār, Śri Laṅkā and International Num's Association have built monasteries in their national styles and tradition in the eastern portion. Chinā, Koreā, Vietnām, Jāpān, Bhutān, Mongoliā, Germany and Nepālese nations and institutes have been operating. Eternal Peace Flame is burning as the symbol of World Peace immediately south of central canal. International Research Institute and Lumbinī Museum have been operating at cultural complex.

Art is an effective medium as expressing the soul of human civilization. It reflects the socio-culture, economic and religious modes and thoughts of a community. The sacred complex of Lumbinī yielded terracotta human and animal figurines, stone sculptures, coins, seals and sealing's, beads, bangles and pottery from sixth century BC up to the Gupta-Pala periods. Finding of a "Conglomerate Stone" in excavation of the complex has also provided a definite evidence to fix the exact birth-place of Lord Buddha. Panel of Buddha and Yasodhara in Royal bed, *Dharmacakra*, Avalokiteśwar of terracotta, Nativity sculpture of Buddha and stone fragments are unique pieces of art of this complex. Sunga tradition in terracotta figurines were made in the mould techniques. A bronze figure of Padampani Avalokiteśwar, image of Gaṇeśa and a figure of the devotee throw light on the metal work and the tradition of Sena-Pala art tradition in the complex of Lumbinī. Different types of pottery from Lumbinī help us in understanding the cultural components of the various periods of human occupations. Religious architecture of Buddhism, viz. monolithic stone pillar, railing, stūpas, vihars and temple of Māyādevi from the Mauryan to Gupta periods are the major attractions to the archaeologists, researchers, pilgrims and historians. Inscribed Aśokan pillar is the real evidence to identify the birth-place of Buddha.

The ancient temple of Māyādevi was based on nagar style. Restoried-Māyādevi temple is based on stūpa model on its superstructure. Remains of ancient temple are covered in the sanctum of the shrine. Ring-well had been constructed of precisely hewn slabs of bricks in the courtyard of the vihar complex. According to Master Plan concerned nations as well as institutes have constructed stūpa, vihar, monasteries and guest-houses on the basis of their national architectural traditions and techniques. Wall-paintings of the shrines are belonged to the life-styles, teaching and events of Gautam Buddha. Fresco paintings of Royal vihar of Nepāl (now collapsed), Mustang-vihar and Lotus Stūpa of Tara Foundation are remarkable heritages to the tourists.

Scenario of the visitors indicates the status of tourism industry in Lumbinī as mentioned in Master Plan. During the period of 2003 to 2012, it was very critical after the seize fire of the Maoist movement. In 2003 the ratio of the tourists was drastically increased in +50.4%. During the ten years period 44.40% had increased in 2007. But it was not satisfactory in 2008, which was only 3.80% increasement. In 2009 it was increased in 4.34% only. In 2010 it was improved in +13.61% than preceding year. Increasement ratio was 30.49% in 2011, which was declared **"Nepāl Visit Year 2011"** by the Nepāl government. In 2012, **Lumbinī Visit Year** was declared by the authority. National as well as internationalal medias were used for its advertisement, but the ratio of the tourists was increased only 8.39% in 2012, which was not target meet. It was only regular ratio of visit. In course of field study it shows that third country tourists had come due to the motivation of Indian and other country tour guides and package policy of the Indian tour and travel agencies. Nepāl Tourism Board office of Belahiya and Nepāl Government Regional Tourism Office have not played any vital role to motivate and to provide proper services to the tourists. Government offices, tour and travel agencies and local communities must be active and reinforce to improve good relation and understanding in foreign countries in order to increase the number of the tourists in this area.

In modern trend mass tourism, cultural tourism, pilgrimage tourism and nature tourism are very useful in the promotion of the local people as well as to generate national income as the holy site for the Buddhist. Due to the violence and unlawful activities in Nepāl, foreign tourists did not visit so many during the conflict period. Śri Laṅkā, South Koreā, Jāpān, China, Taiwan and Thāiland are potential for

Lumbinī visit. In the comparison of the land entry from Sunauli-Belahaya and Lumbinī, the changes ratio is not so difference. In 2006, the entry ratio of the tourists by land at Belahiya and Lumbinī was 21.34% and 24.63% respectively. In 2007 increasement ratio of Belahiya was 44.40% and the ratio of Lumbinī was 43.26%, which is rationalism at both sites. In 2009 the number of the tourists at Belahiya entrance decreased in 4.34% than last year. In Lumbinī complex it was only 0.45% progress than previous year. In 2011, 30.49% increased in Belahiya and 34.29% in Lumbinī complex. Its increasement ratio was 8.39% and 6.03% at Belahiya and Lumbinī in 2012 respectively. In course of declaration "Lumbinī Visit Year 2012" it was not fruitful and satisfied. The number of the tourists at Belahiya and Lumbinī reveals that Belahiya is the main land entry point for Lumbinī. The number of the tourists at Belahiya indicates the actual ratio of the tourists in Lumbinī Both sites are related to promote tourism in Lumbinī and its periphery. About 10% of the visitors of Lumbinī use air route for their visit.

According to Master Plan stūpas, vihars, monasteries and rest-houses have been constructed by the various nations and institutes to promote pilgrims and pilgrimage tradition of Lumbinī. A large number of people since the ancient period have continued to come here from Chinā, Indiā and other western countries. The pilgrims from Jāpān, South-Koreā, Thāiland, Taīwan, China, Indiā, British, Frānce etc usually come here on the important days of festivals to offer their prayer and respect to Lord Buddha. In course of field study, the ratio of the pilgrims had categorized on the basis of profession, literacy, age-group, number of a team, modes of stay, number of national and international pilgrims. The study reveals that 25 % peasant, 20 % student and 12 % of higher professionals visit Lumbinī. Businessmen as well as monks and nuns also visit from various countries. Bhairahawa being a main entrance gate of western Nepāl, businessmen who come at Bhairahawa they reach in Lumbinī at their free time. About 22% of the business persons were presence in course of this field work. Monk and nuns had visited 8 % during this period. Co-operatives as well as rural development agencies had also taken to the farmers in Lumbinī.

Due to the border side Indian guests come frequently in all seasons and can go back easily in a day. Some of them from far i.e. Mahārastra, Gujarāta and Punjāb spent three or more days in Lumbinī and

Kapilvastu. Various performances had been conducted with full preparation, devotion of mind and sense of obligation. Daily and special performances had been conducted in the premises of the shrines. Daily performances of the vihar, monastery and stūpas have been conducting by the concerned authorities in the morning and evening, twice a day. Theravada, Mahayana and Vajrayāna chant their traditional *sutras* and *mantras* on the occasion of daily worship in the shrines. Theravada follow up Pali verses in hard and fast. They do not like to change original *sutras*, i.e. triple gem, five, eight and ten precepts. Mahāyana and Vajrayāna play musical instruments in course of their prayer. Buddhist songs are charming and interesting to create peace and harmony in the mind of the devotees. Thāi, Indiā, Myānmār, Srilankā and Nuns Association of Nepāl follow up Theravada rules and monasteries in the western complex, viz. Chinā, Koreā, Vietnam, Germany etc follow up Mahayana tradition. Mustang Vihar and Japānese Nipponzan Myohoji belong to Vajrayāni traditions.

They follow up tantrika rule and regulations. These activities are also motivating factors to the foreigners. Nepālese as well as Indian Tour and Travel Agencies have informed to 15 % tourists. Buddhist religious books, written in Nepāl and Indiā, have also supported to spread the significance of Lumbinī in Buddhist as well non-Buddhist countries. In course of visit to Lumbinī 51 % of the total tourists go back in a day. They pass only 24 hours and use their baggage for food. Only they take rest at the cheapest accommodations. Their activities can not effect in the economic aspect of this area as project in Lumbinī Master Plan. 18 % of them pass two and three days in the process of their visit. 5 % and 4 % among them respectively pass four and five days in Lumbinī complex far their journey of Lumbinī. 4 % visits more than five days, who are Thai, Śri Laṅkan, Myānmār and Korean.

The fairs and festivals are an integral part of the culture, tradition, rite and rituals of the Buddhist as well as Hindu society. In course of conducting religious activities people feel the entertainment by praying, singing, dancing and meeting with the people and feasting. Due to the mixed settlement of Hindu, Buddhist and Muslim people in the periphery of Lumbinī Buddha Jayanti, *Barsāvassa, Dashain, Deepavali, Chhata, Maghi, Sivaratri, Basanta Panchami, Holi purnima, Rama navami* and *Chaitra purnima* have been celebrating by the local people.

Buddha Jayanti, *Barsavassa* and Peace March are directly associated with Buddha and Buddhism in Lumbinī. *Barsavassa* starts from *Shravana purnima* to *Kartika purnima* about three month to live at a site to the monks and nuns. LDT and other local agencies celebrate Buddha Jayanti in three day at Vaiśākha sukla purnima. On this occasion, the main functions are cleaning the sacred site and worshiping the shrines. Inter school oratory competition and inter campus essay writing competition on the topic belonging to Lumbinī have also organized on this occasion. At the last day of this occasion the Chief Guest provide prizes, scholarship and certificates to the winner in various competitions. Other special fair and festivals are celebrated by the local people on the basis of their spiritual feelings.

Transport as well as accommodation are also the back bone of tourism industry. Motor car took the place of private car and coach for both short and medium range journeys. East-west High way was started in 2019 VS to connect all the parts of Nepāl. North-south roads were also constructed in Siddhartha High way from Bhairahawa to Pokhara has played a vital role to promote tourism industry in the region. It joins East-west Highway at Butwal. Bhairahawa to Lumbinī road was also proposed in Lumbinī Master Plan to approach domestic as well as international tourists. By the support of UNESO, UNDP and Nepāl Government it was completed in 1985. Kapilavastu to Lumbinī, Nawalparasi to Lumbinī, Highway at the point of Rudrapur to Lumbinī and other internal roads are also support to approach domestic as well as international tourists in Lumbinī. Kakrahawā (Indiā) to Lumbinī, Chakarchaudā to Lumbinī, Sorajagadha to Lumbinī and Sunauli to Lumbinī roads are connected.

Indian and third country tourists enter from these routes, public bus, private cars, taxi are providing proper facilities to the tourists. About 35 buses are allotted from Bhairahawā to Lumbinī and 5 from Kathmandu to Lumbinī per day. Direct and high speech coaches are launching at night as well as on day from Kathmandu to Lumbinī. Bbuses are regularly running from Bhairahawa to Lumbinī. Bhairahawa to Lumbinī bus service provides transport to the tourists from India, Butwal, Tansen, Pokhara and from other sites. Mobility is one of the major causes of the development of the motor transport from Bhairahawa to Lumbinī. Speed also economizes on time, which supports to travel to distant places with limited amount of time. At the construction of wide motorways from Bhairahawa to Lumbinī domestic tourists as well as foreigners are also increasing to relax their holidays. But the bridges are not extanded. Industrial bipass road is needed to keep peace and silence on the way of Lumbinī .

Regular plane service is available from Kathmandu to Gautam Buddha Airport, Siddharthanagar. About 30 minute's public bus reach in Lumbinī from Airport. Taxi services are also available here. Taxi fare is NC Rs. 12 00/- from Airport to Lumbinī except internal visit charge. If engaged for 8 hours it will be about 3,000/- only. Day visitors go back with in 4-5 hours. They are not tourists. In this study they are not counted. The number of vehicles is fixed on the basic of the flow of the tourists. Decision is made by the Yātāyāta Vyavasthā Samittees, viz. Paśchimāñchal and Siddhārtha Yātāyāta Samittee. Six lane international business road from Belahiya to Butwal is also supporting to promote tourism.

A traveler who leaves his house required accommodation at the destination and during journey which can not complete in a single day. For this he needs over night accommodation. Tourists like peace, clean and well facilitated accommodation in course of their journey. It is one of the attractions in order to motivate to them. Forty five percent of the total tourists of Lumbinī stay in lodge and hotels in the vicinity of the sacred complex. In the vicinity of LMP there are only 28 tourist standard hotels except small seasonable restaurants. Hotel Kasai is 3 star hotels, operated by Japanese Kasai Group. At the beginning it was called Hotel Mikasha. Hotel Hokke has operating since 1995. Before the establishment of Hotel Kasai, Hotel Hokke had provided standard facilities to the third country tourists, especially Japanese. There are 1061 beds in 492 rooms in Lumbinī complex. There are 327 rooms with AC facility. In the summer season these rooms are very comfortable. At Mahilawar, Paderia and Parasa village,s residential accommodation are also providing services to the tourists. Home stay programs are also launching in the vicinity of LMP. Star, deluxe and lodge accommodations are in options on the expenditure capacity of the tourists. The number of the hotels is increasing day by day due to the attraction towards Lumbinī of the international tourists. About 1500 skilled and non-skilled man power has got the opportunity of employment. In the tourist high season more than 5000 people are providing various services in this sector.

Siddharthanagar is the main entry gate of Lumbinī. Either air transport or road transport foreign tourists can not go to Lumbinī complex without connection of Siddharthanagar. There are 33 hotels consists 639 rooms and 1087 beds for the tourists. About 472 skilled and non-skilled manpower have got direct employment. Indirectly more than 5000 persons are engaged in the sectors of hotel, tour and travel, vegetable production, in furniture, clothings and related other professions. Hotel Nansa is three star hotel, which is providing standard services to the foreign tourists. It has completed basic requirements as recorded in three stars. Hotel Pawan International, Hotel Nirvana, Hotel Yeti, Hotel Glassgow, Hotel Sambala, Hotel Everest, Hotel Lord Buddha and Hotel Mansarobar are also providing standard services to the international as well as internal tourists.

In the promotion of tourism in Lumbinī non-government agencies are more active than government offices. In the case of tourism industry and poverty alleviation through it, TRPAP, Cross-Flow, IBS, DDC etc governmental and non-governmental organizations have also played a vital role to promote and to alleviate poverty in this region. Several kinds of changes have slowly crept into the traditional beliefs, customs, food and drinks, dress and ornaments, position of family members, literacy rate, vocational training, organization of functional groups, increasing the source of income and cultural activities due to the verbal communication and project works of the guests. Elements of modernization are reflected in the management and maintenance of the life style of the local people, monks, nuns, shop-keepers and labourers who reside in Lumbinī area. These are the indicators of changes and modernization of the life style of the people of the Lumbinī region.

The structure of the sacred performances is operative at all Buddhist shrines and hence all the places of Buddhist pilgrimage have the unity of beliefs and practices. But the places of pilgrimage may be differentiated from one another also on the basis of the sacred performances peculiar to them. There are varieties of rituals of Buddhist sects as well as specialists. Besides the specialists i.e. monks and nuns who direct the rituals there are also some persons who assist at the time of performance. The florists, the musicians, the barbers, gardeners, guards and guides are the examples of ritual associates. The intrinsic relationship between sacred and secular is truly reflected in Lumbinī cultural complex- in its settlement pattern, sacred performances and the professions involved in the sacred complex. Man's final desire of enjoying beauty his sense of aesthetics is amply fulfilled in his sacred performances. All ritual performances are made with a perfect sense of aesthetics held with deep devotion. Sacred Complex is an industry. A lot of population is dependent upon the pilgrim industry. Several thousands of people are employed in sacred total occupations of various kinds. It is hard to make a distinction between sacred and secular so far as the style of earning, the attitude towards earning and the professional ethics are concerned. It is also by this mechanism that Buddhist civilization has been integrating through the ages of the geographical and cultural diversities of Nepāl.

It will further help to prepare plans for the conservation of important historical and archaeological monuments and the works of arts which are decaying in the absence of proper care. The tourism industry is expected to respond to the challenges of times and help the country to forge ahead on the path of national development. Cultural tourism plays a major part in increasing national as well as international good well and understanding. Various activities conducted in Lumbinī and its neighbors villages have been changed and modernized the life style and standard of the local people. A ring road should be constructed all around the Buddhist sites connecting Lumbinī. This will facilitate the pilgrimage tour and travel of Buddhist sites by bus or train. Local museum must be enriched of art concerned to Buddha and Buddhism especially of Lumbinī. All the development programs of Lumbinī should be conducted on the basis of mutual understanding between LDT and concerned party, who are interested to invest and develop of Lumbinī.

Monks, nuns, priests, musicians, guards, gardeners and barbers are directly and indirectly involved in daily performances of the shrines. Being the potential site of tourism Lumbinī is not developed due to lack of network of communication, transportation and other infrastructure needed for healthy-tourism. Therefore, some problems and recommendations have been pointed out for the promotion of healthy tourism in Lumbinī and its peripheral area. Qualitative smokeless vehicles-viz. auto-rickshaw, rickshaw, bi-cycle, mini-bus and bus should be provided as preferred means of visiting sites at reasonable rate at this complex. Gautam Buddha Airport of Siddharthanagar should be upgraded in International Airport to increase the flow of tourists in Lumbinī. According to LDMP high, middle, pilgrimage as well as camping accommodations must be managed in Lumbinī area. Private hotel, restaurant and bars should be managed under the umbrella of hotel association of Lumbinī for quality and reliability. Rules and regulations of Nepāl Government must be actively followed in course of providing service to the tourists. Tourists should be informed all of the sites, viz. monasteries, meditation-centers, LIRI, museum, New Lumbinī Village etc, who visit properly at Māyādevī temple.

Lumbinī Festival should be organized on the occasion of Buddha Jayanti in each year. Art reflects the accurate and authentic evidences of the past life ways of the people. Museum plays a vital role to collect, exhibition, conservation and preservation of the art remains. In this situation, concerned coins, architectural-fragments, sculptures, paintings, photography, replicas of Buddha etc should be collected and properly displayed in Lumbinī Museum in the promotion of cultural tourism. Natural heritages, i.e., various birds like *saras*, garden, blue-cow, Telar river, Harahawa river, farming etc must be used for tourism.

Modes of road transport and air transport must be easily available to the tourists. Internal net work of transport must be well managed. All the Buddhist sites of the region viz Tilaurakot, Gotihawa, Niglihawa, Kudan, Arorakot, Sisahania, Devadaha, Ramagrama etc and other sites like, Siddhababa, Butwal Ramapithecus in great Lumbinī area etc must be connected by the Buddhist circuit. It will support to change the life style of the local people and international understanding. Drinking water is directly provided from the boring-system. It is not purified with the use of proper chemicals and problem of *arsenic*. Purified water should be supplied using reservoir system after chemical treatment. Toilet facility should be provided near the temple, monastery and vihar to the visitors without charge. Mobile toilet and some huts of toilets on the side of the central canal are not managed in systematic ways. Available sources should be used in proper ways. Otherwise open toilet-tradition will create great problem of pollution. Tourist-guides should be capable to interpret native languages of the guests, especially Thāīland, South Koreā, Japanese, Chinese and Cambodian languages. Such training institutes should be conducted at local level and local people should be participated at these programs.

Local cultural activities like *Birāha* music and dance should be organized. Tharu culture and their life style should be preserved of Lumbinī area. Hotel and local community groups should be made aware for their cultural activities. Awakening programs should be carried out organizing meeting, seminar workshop and symposium to make conscious of their sacred monuments, sacred rituals, sacred functionaries, religious processions and festivals. Local people should be motivated that these are the potential sources for the growth of tourism in the region. Governmental and non-governmental organizations should also organize tourist awareness training programs in the neighbor villages of Lumbinī complex including and extending the programs of TRPAP. The tradition of local art and crafts should be encouraged, i.e. basket and mat weaving, moulding the images of Buddha and local products should be supplied for sale in the market. It will encourage involving at the tourist activities to the local people.

A tourism information centre, especially for the motivation to Lumbinī, should be operated at Butwal, Bhairahawā Lumbinī-road (Buddha-choka), Kāthmandu, Nārāyanagadha and other proper sites in Nepāl and foreign countries. TRPAP had promoted only two Tourist information centers at Belahiya and LDT complex, which must be up-graded in proper way in proper situation. Having been so popular Buddhist pilgrimage site cheap and reliable informative tourist materials, viz. folders, guide books, posters, pamphlets, booklets, cassette, maps, VCD, tape recorder and photographs are not available in proper sites. These materials should be made available to the tourists having interest in knowing in details about Lumbinī. The authority should be careful for stopping the begging monks and beggars, controlling noise, cleaning the garbage and litters. Industries should not be established about 15 km east, north, south and west from the sacred complex of Lumbinī. About 3 km on right and left side of Siddharthanagar to Taulihawa road there should be strictly prohibited to establish polluted factories. It should be developed as a **Peace Land** of the world. The demarcations of Siemreap's five protected zones of Angkor are useful to prepare plan for Lumbinī. ZEMP recommendations more precisely will be designed for environmental protection of this complex. The protection categories and demarcations may be-Zone1: Monumental Sites, Zone 2: Protected Archaeological Reserves, Zone 3: Protected Cultural Landscapes, Zone 4: Sites of Archaeological, Anthropological or Historic Interest and Zone 5: Socio-cultural and economic as proposed by KWAAK E.S.P.R.I, Korean International Cooperative Agency. Authority should be active to implement proper plans indicated by UNESCO in proper time. It will be basic requirement for endemic and sustainable tourism of Lumbinī.

LDT, CFNT, IBS, PPPP, DDC, VDCs and other such agencies have carried out integrated programs for the development of Lumbinī and its out skirts for long times. Their action plan and programs are duplication lack of proper co-ordination among them. As a whole co-ordination committee should be constituted among the governmental and non-governmental organizations not only for tourism, but also social changes of Lumbinī area. Various requirements should be available to increase the number of tourists as well as to increase their length of stay. National and international mass media, viz. TV, VCD, Radio, Internet and E-mail facilities should be used to advertise of this Sacred Complex. Local groups and communities should be aware to mobilize local resources to promote all the pre-requisites for attraction of the area in the international markets. LDT, local VDCs, DDC and STDC must be active to use natural and cultural heritages of Lumbinī complex. Master Plan of KWAAK should be studied in details and taken response of the stalk holders.

In the comparision of number of tourists and beds, high tourist season and low tourist season numbers should be compared with the hotel capacity. The ratio of 2012 was choosen in this study. In low season, i.e. April, May, June and July months' tourists were 13628 and 122373 were in remaing eight months of high tourist season. Average monthly number in high tourist season was 15,297 and average daily number was 510. In average 3,407 in low tourist season and average daily number was 114. In November 2012, there were 21,740 pp holder tourists. Average daily number of tourists was 725 excluding Indian and Nepālese tourists. After adding 50% Indian and Nepālese tourists, total tourists will be about 1088 per day in tourist high season. All of them will not stay over night in Lumbinī. More than 2500 beds in tourist standard are made in Lumbinī. About 2000 tourists can easily stay in Lumbinī complex. In this critical situation various programs should be launched in order to increase the number of tourists and quality.

All the proposed components of the Master Plan must be completed in time. If proposed budget is not available Plan should be revised in Nepālese context. After completion of these basic elements of this area, tourism industry will be sustainable and endemic for the regional development of Lumbinī. It will be the major resource of the government as well as private sectors. concerned NGO, INGO, GO and members of civil society must be careful to co-ordinate various plans and programs in course of implementation. We must not forget that "***Peace, Compassion and Friendship***" are its main instruments for implementation.

BIBLIOGRAPHY

English Books

Ananda, M.M. (1976). *Tourism and hotel business in Indiā;* New Delhi: Prentice Hall of Indiā.

Anderson, N.(1961). *Work and leisure;* London: Routeledge and Kegan Paul.

Archer, B.H.(1973). *The impact of domestic tourism;* Cardiff: University of Wales Press.

Arvill, R. (1967). *Man and environment;* London: Penguin.

Atzori, Angela, et.al., (Ed.).(2006). *Lumbinī : present status and future challenges;* Kathmandu:UNESCO.

Bernecker, Paul. (1961). *Method and media of tourist publicity;* Vienna: Austrian Tourist Office.

Bhatia, A.K. (1978). *Tourism in Indiā- history and development;* New Delhi: Sterling Publishers Private Limiated.

.... (1997). *Internatiinal tourism- fundamentals and practices;* New Delhi: Sterling Publisher Pvt.Ltd.

.... (1998). *Tourism management and marketing;* New Delhi: Sterling Publishers Private Limiated.

.... (2000). *Tourism development principles and practices;* New Delhi: Sterling Publishers Private Limited.

Bhatta, D.P. (2006). *Ecotourism in Nepāl;* Kathmandu: Anju Bhatta

Bidari, B. (2002). *Lumbinī : A haven of sacred refuge;* Lumbinī : The Author.

Brownell, G.G. (1975. *Travel agent management;* Brimingham: Southern University Press.

Brunner, E.(1945). *Holiday making and holiday trades;* London: Oxford University Press.

Burkart, A.J.(1981). Tourism: past, present and future; London: English Language Book.

Burton, T.L. (Ed.). (1970). *Recreation, research and planning;* London: Allen and Unwin.

Central Bureau of Statistics. (2012). *Population of Nepāl;* VDC, Municipalities wise -caste/ethnicity/mother tongue and religion.

Christopher, J. (1983). *The business of tourism;* England: Macdonal Evans.

Clayne, R. J. (1977). *Leisure and recreation- introduction and over view;* Philadelphia: Lea and Febiger.

Committee for the Development of Lumbinī .(1970). *Lumbinī : the birth place of Buddha* ; New york : International Committee.

Cunningham, A.(1990). *The ancient geography of Indiā;* Reprinted, Delhi: Low Price Publishers.

Cuepper, C. (1996). "Lumbinī international research institute", *Souviner;* Lumbinī; Liri:

.... (2012). "The library collection of the Lumbinī International Institute", *Lumbinī darpana;* Lumbinī : LDT. vol. III.

Davis, H.D. (1968). *Potentials for tourism of developing countries;* London: Finance and Development.

District Development Committee (2062). *Participatory district tourism development and management plan, 2062-67;* Rupandehi: DDC.

Deeg, M. (2003). *The places where Siddhartha trod: Lumbinī and Kapilvastu;* Lumbinī : Lumbinī International Research Institute.

Deo, S.B. (1968). *Archaeological investigation in the Nepālese Terai, 1964;* Kathmandu: Department of Archaeology, H.M.G.

DEVA. (2004). *Lumbinī visitors' survey;* Submitted report to TRPAP, Kathmandu.

DDC. (2062). *Participatory district tourism development and management plan, 2062-67;* Rupandehi:

Douglas, P. (1987). *Tourism today;* New York: Longman.

Falk, H.(1998). *The discovery of Lumbinī;* Lumbinī : LIRI.

Finland Government and HMG Nepāl (2003). *Rural water supply and sanitation support programme;* Annual Report, Fiscal Year 2002-2003

Führer, A.(1972). *Antiquities of the Buddha's birthplace in the Nepālese Terai;* Reprinted, Delhi: Indological Book House.

GBIPAS. (2011). *Gautam Buddha international peace award;* Lumbinī : LDT and MoFACAPAC.

Gearing, C.E. (1976). *Planning for tourism development;* New York: Praeger Publishers.

Giles, H.A. (Trans.) (1981). *The travel of Fa – hsian (399-414 A.D.) or the records of Buddhist kingdoms ;* Reprinted, America : Green Word Press Publisher West Point C.

Giri, G. (2002). *Cultural touristic sites of Lumbinī zone;* Siddharthangar: Lumbinī Youth Rural Development Form.

.... (2003). *Art and architecture remains in the western Terai region of Nepāl;* New Delhi: Adroit Publisher.

.... (2008). *Lumbinī : the Buddhist world;* Lumbinī : Lumbinī Academy

Hashimoto, S. and others (Ed.) (1973). *Geography of the Nepāl Himālayas;* Tokyo: Saikan Publishing.

Hunziker, W.(1951). *Social tourism: it's nature and problems;* Geneva: Alliance Internationale de Turisme.

International Buddhist Society (2004). *Lumbinī;* Special Issue of Second World Buddhist Summit; Year 10, No.12.

Jha, M. (1971). *The Sacred complex in Janakpur ;* Allhabad : United Publishers.

Jina, P.S. (1994). *Tourism in Ladakh;* New Delhi: Indus Publishing Company.

John, M.B. (1973). *Tourism and development;* London: Cambridge university Press.

Kunwar, R.R. (1997). *Tourism and Development- Science and Industry Interface;* Kathmandu: Laxmi Kunwar.

.... (2002). *Himalayan heritages;* Kathmandu: Laxmi Kunwar.

.... (2002). *Anthropology of tourism: a case study of Saura:* Delhi: Adroit Publishers.

Lickorish, L.J. and Kershaw, A.G. (1974). *The travel trade;* London: Practical Press.

Lumbinī Development Committee, (1975). Lumbinī d*evelopment project aide memoir;* Kathmandu : LDC.

Maccannel, D. (1976). *The tourist: a new theory of leisure class;* London: Mac Million.

Medlik, S. (1972). *Economic development of tourism;* Surrey: University of Surrey.

.... (1972). *Profile of the hotel and catering industry;* London: Heinemann.

.... (1980). *The business of hotels;* London: Heinemann.

MoCTAC (2011). *Nepāl tourism statistics;* Kathmandu: Government of Nepāl.

LDT. (2004). *Introducing Lumbinī the fountain of World Peace;* Lumbinī : Second World Buddhist Summit

Mitra, D. (1972). *Excavation at Tilaurākoṭ, Kodan and exploration in the Nepālese Terai;* Kathmandu: Department of Archaeology.

Mishra, T.N. (1996). "The archaeological activities in Lumbinī 1984-1985" *Ancient Nepāl;* No. 139.

.... (n.d). *The location of Kapilvastu and archaeological excavation;* Kathmandu: Lumbinī Development Committee.

Mukherji, P.C. (1969). *Antiquities of Kapilvastu Terai of Nepāl;* Reprinted, Delhi: Indological Book House.

National Museum of Nepāl, (1998). *Buddhist collection of the national museum of Nepāl;* Kathmandu; Department of Archaeology.

Nepāl Tourism Board (2008). *Tourism product of Nepāl;* Kathmandu: NTB.

Okada, EF. (1969). *The Lumbinī garden area Rupandehi district Nepāl : A Socio-economic Survey,* Kathmandu: Nepāl Goverment and Unoted Nations.

Pandey, R.N. (2000). *Sacred complex of Ruru ksetra;* Delhi: Adroit Publisher.

.... (2008). *Nepāl through the ages;* New Delhi: Adroit Publishers.

Petech, L. (1950). *Northern Indiā according to the Shui-Ching-Chu;* Rome: Institute Italiano Peril Medio Ed. Estremo Oriento.

Pradhan, B.L. (1979). *Lumbinī Kapilvastu Devadaha* ; Kathmandu : Tribhuwan University, CNAS.

Pradhan, K. M. (1997). *Planning tourism in Nepāl;* New Delhi: Vikas Publishing House.

Pudney, J. (1953). *The Thomos Cook story;* London: Michael Joseph.

Rae, W.F. (1891). *The business of travel;* London: Thomos Cook and Son.

Rhys Davids, T.W. (1993). *Buddhist Indiā;* Reprinted, Delhi: Motilal Banarashidass Publisher Pvt. Ltd.

Rijal, B.K. (1996). *100 years of archaeological research in Lumbinī , Kapilvastu and Devadaha;* Kathmandu : S.K. International Publishing House.

Robinson, H.A., *Geography of tourism;* London: MacDonald and Evans.

Rockhill, W.W. (1972). *Life of Buddha;* Reprinted, Varāṇasii: Orientalia Indiā.

Rupandehi DDC (2005). *Decentrilized local goverance support programmes;* NEP-04/002, (Unpublished noted Report of DDC).

Satyal, Y.R. (2000). *Essentials of tourism;* Delhi: Adroit Publishers.

.... (2000). *Tourism in Nepāl- a profile;* Delhi: Adroit Publishers.

.... (2002). *Pilgrimage tourism in Nepāl;* Delhi: Adroit Publishers.

Sessa, A. (1970). *Tourism in developing countries;* Paris: Reprinted from manual on the convention, UNESCO.

Seth, P.N. and Seth, S. (1993). *An introduction to travel and tourism;* New Delhi: Sterling Publishers Pvt. Ltd.

Seth, P.N. (1997). *Successful tourism management;* New Delhi: Sterling Publishers Pvt. Ltd.

Sharma, C.K. (1977). *River systems of Nepāl;* Kathmandu: Sangeeta Sharma.

Sharma, R.C. (1995). *Buddhist art;* New Delhi: Wiley Eastern Limited.

Shrestha, H.P. (2000). *Tourism in Nepāl marketing and challanges;* New Delhi: Nirala Publication.

Tange, K. (1978). *Master plan for the development of Lumbinī phase II final report;* Kathmandu: Lumbinī Development Committee.

Uesaka, S. (1997). *Achaeological survey record of Māyādevi temple;* Lumbinī: Japanese Buddhist Federation Unpublished Seminar Paper.

UNESCO, (2006). *Lumbinī : Present status and future challenges;* Kathmandu: UNESCO office.

.... (2012). *Environmental impact assessment of industrial development around Lumbinī , the birthplace of the Lord Buddda, world heritage property;* Kthmandu: UNESCO office.

.... (2013.a). *Photo book on Lumbinī , the birthplace of Lord Buddha;* Kathmandu: UNESCO office.

.... (2013.b). *Lumbinī , the birthplace of Lord Buddha in Nepāl,* (completing the Kenzo Tange Master Plan); Kathmandu: UNESCO office, (United Nations. (2001). *Tourism satallite account recommended methodology framework;* New York.

Vaidy, T.R. and Khatry, P.K. (1998). *Proceedings of the world Buddhist summit;* Lumbinī : LDT.

Vidyarthi, L.P. (1961). *The sacred compex in Hindu Gaya;* Bombay

Asian publishing House.

.... (1979). *The sacred complex of Kashi;* Delhi: Concept Publishing Company.

Vijayatunga, (1960). *Lumbinī to Kusinagar;* Srilanka: Saman Press.

Vimalananda, M. (2043). *Homage to Triple Gems;* Lumbinī ; The author.

Warren, H.C. (1986). *The life of the Buddha ;* Reprinted, Delhi : Eastern Book Linkers.

Nepāli Books

गिरी, गितु (2067), लुम्बिनीको इतिहास, लुम्बिनीः लुम्बिनी अन्तराष्ट्रीय अनुसंधान संस्था

महर्जन, वसन्त, (2062), लुम्बिनीः ऐतिहासिक तथा पुरातात्विक अध्ययन्; काठमाठौः बसामी डटकम।

Hindi Books

Upadhaya, B.S. (2018). Buddha kā*lina bhāratīya bhugol;* Prayag: Hindi Sahitya Sammelan,

English Journals

Baral, H. (2012). "Lumbinī : a paradise for bird lovers", *Lumbinī Darpana;* Lumbinī : LDT.

Bhattarai, S. (2013). "The activities under by physical and planning (engineering) department in 2069", *Lumbinī darpana;* (vol. iv), Lumbinī : LDT.

Bhattarai, S. (2013). "Buddhist architecture and its connection", *Lumbinī darpana;* (vol. iv), Lumbinī : LDT.

Butler, T.L., (Ed), (1974). *The social implication of tourism development;* Tourism Research, 2:2.

Cohen, E. (1972). "Towards a sociology of international tourism", *Social Research;* 39 (1), pp. 164, 182.

Coningham, RAE et al, (2011). "A cultural and environmental monitoring of the UNESCO world heritage site of

Lumbinī", *Ancient Nepāl;* No.176, pp 1-8.

Coningham, RAE et al, (2011). "A Pilot geophysical and auger core evaluation with in the UNESCO World Heritage Site of Lumbinī", *Ancient Nepāl;* No.176, pp.9-24.

Cuellar, J.P.(2067). "Message from the UNO Secretary General", *Lumbinī Darpana;* Lumbinī : LDT.

Cuepers, C. (2006). "Lumbinī : present status of the site in religious terms", *Lumbinī : present status and future challenges;* Kathmandu: UNESCO.

Ghimire, H.L. (2006). " Lumbinī : A tourist overview ", *Present status and future challenges;* Kathmandu: UNESCO Kathmandu offfice

.... (2013). "Lumbinī pilgrimage", *Lumbinī darpana;* Lumbinī : LDT.

Giri, G. (2011). " Role of TRPAP in Lumbinī ", *Lumbinī darpana;* vol. 2

.... (2011). "Tourism development in Lumbinī ", *Lumbinī festival special issue;* Siddharthanagar: Nepāl Rastria Udhoga Vyapar Sangathan.

.... (2013). " Tourism in Lumbinī ", *Lumbinī darpana;* vol. 4.

Guruge, A. WP. (1998). "Buddhist philosophy and world peace" Ed.Vaidy, T.R. and Khatry, P.K. (1998). *Proceedings of the world Buddhist summit;* Lumbinī : LDT.

Gurung, H. (1998). "Developing Lumbinī as pilgrimage centre", Ed.Vaidy, T.R. and Khatry, P.K., *Proceedings of the world Buddhist summit;* Lumbinī : LDT.

LDT. (2004). *LDT Newsletter*: (vol.I), No.1 & 2.

LDT. (2010). *Lumbinī darpana;* (vol. I), Lumbinī : LDT.

LDT. (2011). *Lumbinī darpana;* (vol. II), Lumbinī : LDT.

LDT. (2012). *Lumbinī darpana;* (vol. III), Lumbinī : LDT.

LDT. (2013) *Lumbinī darpana,* (vol.IV), Lumbinī : LDT.

LDT Information Section (2010). "Recording and analysis of visitors data", *Lumbinī darpana,* No.1

Lumbinī Institues. (2004). "Recommmendations for the future development of Lumbinī", *Lumbinī;* IBS, Year 10, NO 12.

Kurt W. (2067). "Message from the UNO Secretary General", *Lumbinī Darpana*; Lumbinī : LDT.

NTB. (2004). *NTB Newsletter*; vol.5, Issue 36&39.

Pandey, R.N. (1985). "Archaeological remains of Lumbinī", *Contributions to Nepālese studies*, Kathmandu: CNAs, T.U. vol. 12, No.3.

Rai, H. (2012). "Lumbinī Visit year 2012 for world peace and prosperty", *Lumbinī darpana*; Lumbinī : LDT.

Sangachhe, S.B. (2067). LDMP and it,s philosophical aspects", *Lumbinī darpana*; Lumbinī : LDT.

Singer, M. (1958). *Traditional Indiā: structure and change;* Journal of American Folklore, Vol. 78, No. 281

Shah, A. (2069). "Sustainable economic development", Special Issue Nepāl Rastra bank; Kathamndu. English section pp.1-3.

Shakya, M.B. (2067). "Lumbinī as the holy pilgrimage site of the Buddhists", *Lumbinī darpana*; Lumbinī : LDT.

Shrestha, KM. (2010). "Lumbinī : the fountain of peace and the holiest pilgrim centre of peace loving people of the world", *Ancient Nepāl*; (No.175) Kathmandu: DOA.

Shrestha, KM. (2011). "Buddhism for peace", *Ancient Nepāl*; (No.178), Kathmandu: DOA.

Suwal, R.(2011). "Script for nature walk in Lumbinī ", *Lumbinī darpana*; Lumbinī : LDT.

TRPAP. (2061). *Village tourism newspaper*; Rupandehi: Year 2, No2.

U-Thant (2067). "Message from the United Nations Organization Secretary General 1970", *Lumbinī darpana*; Lumbinī : LDT.

Yoshida, M. and Arita, K. (1982). "On the Siwaliks observed along some routes in the central Nepāl" *Journal of Nepāl geological society*, Vol. 2 Special Issue.

Nepāli Journals

कडेल, चेतनाथ, (2064). "ग्रामीण पर्यटकीय क्षेत्र का विद्यालयहरूमा पर्यटन तथा

वातावरणीय शिक्षाः केही व्यवहारिक अनुभवहरू", हाम्रो सम्पदा; काठमाडौः श्यामकुमार बस्नेत (वर्ष 7, अंक 1)

खडका, कृष्ण बहादुर, (2013), "कपिलवस्तु तिलौराकोट किल्ला पर्खाल उत्खनन् तथा संरक्षण, 2011–12", लुम्बिनी दर्पण, (अंक 4), लुम्बिनीः लु.वि.कोष।

गिरी, गितु, (2069), "लुम्बिनीमा पर्यटन", क्याम्पस जर्नल, सिद्धार्थनगरः त्रि.वि.भैरहवा क्याम्पस।

गिरी, गितु, (2069), "लुम्बिनीमा प्रकृति पर्यटन", क्षितिज, सिद्धार्थनगरः त्रि.वि. भैरहवा क्याम्पस।

नेपाल, शंकरप्रसाद, (2068), "पर्यटन उद्योगः सन्दर्भ नेपाल पर्यटन वर्ष 2011", क्याम्पस जर्नल, सिद्धार्थनगरः त्रि.वि.भैरहवा।

पाण्डे, ध्रुवनारायण, (2013), "आ.ब. 2069–70 को लुम्बिनी संग्रहालयको प्रगति विवरण", लुम्बिनी दर्पण, (अंक 4), लुम्बिनीः लु.वि.कोष।

प्रजापति, रत्न, (2069), कृषि लगानी बहुआयामिक प्रभाव"; सन्ताउन्नौ विशेषाङ, काठमाडौः नेपाल राष्ट्र बैंक, (नेपाली खण्ड, पृ. 90)।

भट्टराई, नवराज, (2069), ग्रामीण विकास र गरिबी निवारणको मुख्य अस्त्र"; सन्ताउन्नौ विशेषाङ, काठमाडौः नेपाल राष्ट्र बैंक, (नेपाली खण्ड), पृ. 60–65)।

शाक्य, कर्ण, (2069), "पर्यटन र लुम्बिनी", *Lumbinī Darpana*; Lumbinī : LDT.

Unpublished Reports

Khatry, P.K.& Vaidya,T.R. (2002). *Master plan of Lumbinī and its implimentation;* (unpublished paper presented on workshop conducted by Lumbinī Development Review Project), 28-29 December, Kathmandu: submitted its proceeding to UNDP Local Office, Nepāl.

Nepāl Rastra Bank, (2013), *Half-yearly report of economic activites;* Siddharthanagar: unpublished report, NRB.

Appendix - A

Questionnaire

LUMBINĪ TOURISM DEVELOPMENT

Nepālese Visitors

S. No. Code No. Date:

1. Name: .... Address: .... Age: ....

   Sex: .... Caste: .... Sect: ....

   Education: .... Profession: ....

   How many times came to visit here: ....

   Participant Number with him / her: ....

2. Visited / to visit Sites (Tick Mark √)

   Name of the sacred Centre Purpose Frequency Remarks

   Tick

   i) Māyādevi temple complex
   ii) Nepāl Vipasna Center
   iii) International Bhikkhuni Sangh
   iv) Myānmār Temple
   v) Śri Laṅkān Monastery
   vi) Mahabodhi Monastery
   vii) Thāi Monastery
   viii) Panditarama
   ix) Manang Sewa Samaj Monastery
   x) Chinese Temple

xi) Korean Temple

xii) Austrian Vihar

xiii) Viettnam Vihar

xiv) Seto Gumba

xv) Tara Foundation Duesseldrof, Germany

xvi) Lumbinī Museum

xvii) Lumbinī International Research Institute

xviii) Nipponzan Myohoji (World Peace Stūpa)

xix) Natural Scenes i.e.saras, nilgai, bird watching.

xx) Any other place/heritage

3. What are the major problems to visit at the sacred complex?

i) ....

ii) ....

iii) ....

iv) ....

v) ....

vi) ....

4. How the tourism support to alleviate poverty in this area?

5. What should be done to promote tourism? Write 1,2,3,4 & 5 in priority basis.

- Transportation
- Accommodation (Hotel and Restaurant)
- Information Technology
- Proper Guidence
- Security Management

Note: If more please note on the back

Appendix - B

Questionnaire

LUMBINĪ TOURISM DEVELOPMENT

Schedule for Studing Foreign Pilgrims/ Tourists

(Passport Holders only)

S. No. **Code No.** **Date:**

1. Name of the pilgrim ....

   Age : .... Sex ....

   Religion:Hindu / Buddhist\ ....

   Other.............................. Caste:...

   Ethnic group: ....

   (In case of monks / nuns.................... sect)

   Country:......................... Profession: ....

   Education: ....

   Mother Tongue:.............. Other language: ....

   Local Address: ....

2. Pilgrimage to Lumbinī Ksetra

   i) Main purpose of

   ....

   ....

   ii) No. of his/her visit to this temple / shrine ....

   iii) Duration of stay in Lumbinī Ksetra ....

   iv) Stayed at

a) Hotel / Lodge:

b) Dharmashala / Vihar

c) Friends / Relatives

v) Visiting:

a) Alongs

b) With family members

c) With friends / Relatives

d) Participant Numbers:

vi) Description of any special event, observation or happening by the informant (pilgrim) in Lumbinī Ksetra. Give details precisely.

3. Places / sacred centres, Vihar, Monastery, Stūpa etc. visited or to be visited. Tick ($\sqrt{}$) your visit sites-

i) Māyādevi temple complex (Sacred garden)

ii) Nepāl Vipasna Center

iii) International Viskchhuni Sangh

iv) Myānmār Temple

v) Śri Laṅkān Monastery

vi) Mahabodhi Monastery

vii) Thāi Monastery

viii) Panditarama

ix) Manang Sewa Samaj Monastery

x) Chinese Temple

xi) Korean Temple

xii) Tara Foundation Duesseldrof, Germany

xiii) Lumbinī Museum

xiv) Lumbinī International Research Institute

xv) Nipponzan Myohoji (world peace Stūpa)

xvi) Natural Scenes i.e.saras, nilgai, bird watching.

xvii) Any other place

4. Saced Performance (if any during your visit of Lumbinī Ksetra)

i) Simple darshan

ii) Any ritual

a) Name:

b) Place:

c) Assistance of Priest, monk, nun or specialist, if any:

d) Frequency of performance:

5. Other Buddhist pilgrims sites visited by the informants in Nepāl / Indiā / Else where

i) ....

ii) ....

iii) ....

iv) ....

6. Motivated by:

7. Knowledge about Lumbinī, Buddhism and Tourism:

8. Problems to visit

i) ....

ii) ....

iii) ....

iv) ....

v) ....

9. Suggestions to Promote Tourism in Lumbinī Area

i) ....

ii) ....

iii) ....

iv) ....

v) ....

Note: If more please note on the back side)

Appendix - C

Questionnaire

LUMBINĪ TOURISM DEVELOPMENT

Schedule for Studing Foreign Pilgrims/ Tourists

(Indians only)

S. No. **Code No.** **Date:**

1. Name of the pilgrim ....

   Age : .... Sex ....

   Religion:Hindu / Buddhist\ ....

   Other............................... Caste:..

   Ethnic group: ....

   (In case of monks / nuns...................... sect)

   Country:.......................... Profession: ....

   Education: ....

   Mother Tongue:.............. Other language: ....

   Local Address: ....

2. Pilgrimage to Lumbinī Ksetra

   i) Main purpose of

   ....

   ....

   ii) No. of his/her visit to this temple / shrine ......

   iii) Duration of stay in Lumbinī ksetra ....

iv) Stayed at

a) Hotel / Lodge:

b) Dharmashala / Vihar

c) Friends/Relatives : ....

v) Visiting:

a) Alongs

b) With family members

c) With friends / Relatives

d) Participant Numbers:

vi) Description of any special event, observation or happening by the informant (pilgrim) in Lumbinī Ksetra. Give details precisely.

3. Places/sacred centres, vihar, monastery, stūpa etc. visited or to be visited. Tick (√) your visit sites-

i) Māyādevi temple complex (Sacred garden)

ii) Nepāl Vipasna Center

iii) International Viskchhuni Sangh

iv) Myānmār Temple

v) Śri Laṅkān Monastery

vi) Mahabodhi Monastery

vii) Thāi Monastery

viii) Panditarama

ix) Manang Sewa Samaj Monastery

x) Chinese Temple

xi) Korean Temple

xii) Tara Foundation Duesseldrof, Germany

xiii) Lumbinī Museum

xiv) Lumbinī International Research Institute

xv) Nipponzan Myohoji (world peace Stūpa)

xvi) Natural Scenes i.e.saras, nilgai, bird watching .

xvii) Any other place

4. Saced Performance (if any during your visit of Lumbinī Ksetra)
    i) Simple darshan
    ii) Any ritual
        a) Name:
        b) Place:
        c) Assistance of Priest, monk, nun or specialist, if any:
        d) Frequency of performance:
5. Other Buddhist pilgrims sites visited by the informants in Nepāl / Indiā / Else where
    i) ....
    ii) ....
    iii) ....
    iv) ....
6. Motivated by:
7. Knowledge about Lumbinī, Buddhism and Tourism:
8. Problems to visit
    i) ....
    ii) ....
    iii) ....
    iv) ....
    v) ....
9. Suggestions to Promote Tourism in Lumbinī Area
    i) ....
    ii) ....
    iii) ....
    iv) ....
    v) ....

Note: If more please note on the back side)

Appendix - D

Questionnaire

LUMBINĪ TOURISM DEVELOPMENT

Hotels

S. No. Code No. Date:

1. a) Name of the Hotel: ....

   b) Location: ....

   c) Standard: star-......./ Non-star ....

   d) Contract Phone No: .... Mobile No..............

   e) Established on: ....

2. Facilities:

   a) Room Numbers-..

      i) Single-...... ....

      ii) Double-..

      iii) Dormitority-..

   b) Facilities -Tick (√) if available

      i) TV..

      ii) Telephone..

      iii) Attached Bath & Toilet rooms..................................

      iv) Recreational Facilities- *Dohari,* Dancing bar or other..

3. Last Year visitor Number:..

4. What kind of change do you notice with the increasement of number of tourists visiting in Lumbinī ?

   Please rank in order of important by assigning 1 for the most important..

   .... More dirty

   .... Increasing deforestation

   .... Price rise

   ..... Local people more selfish

   ..... Opportunity creation

   ..... Production increase

   ..... Market extend

   ...... Crime increase

   ...... Others (Please specify)

5. Do the unmanaged waste influence to visit tourist ?
6. What type of toilet facility you have ?

   .... cistern flush toilet

   .... pour " "

   ... Latrine

   .... None, use of neighbours

   .... None, use out door

   .... Others

7. Do you a speti tank ? Yes.....No.......
8. Do you have over flow ? Yes.......No......
9. Do you have drain facility ? Yes.....No....
10. How much solid waste do you generate each day ?
11. Where do you dispose your waste ?
12. Do you think there is a need for improvement in garbage pick up and control of waste ?
13. If yes, how much are you prepare to pay per month for this service ?

    Rs. per month

14. Major Problems in your sector:

i) ....

ii) ....

iii) ....

iv) ....

v) ....

vi) ....

15.. Suggestions to promote tourism:

i) ....

ii) ....

iii) ....

iv) ....

v) ....

Note: If more please note on the back side)

Appendix - F

Questionnaire

LUMBINĪ TOURISM DEVELOPMENT

Questionnaire for the Proper Person and 0ffices belonged to Lumbinī Area.

S. No. **Code No.** **Date:**

1. Office Name: .... Telephone No. ....
2. Respondent's Name:
3. Programmes:
4. Future plans for tourism promote:

SL.No.	Plans	Target Group	Target Number	Remarks

5. Suggestions to promote the life style of the local people:

Note: If more please note on the back side)

GLOSSARY

anamela vivāha..... *difference the age more than twenty years between bridge and bridge-groom.*

āshrama..... approximately 100 years life of the Hindus is divided in to four *āshramas* in order to perform the duties on the basis of ages, i.e. *Brahmacharya, Grihasta, Vanaprastha* and *Sanyāsa.*

Aśoka tree..... Saraca indico-

bala vivāha..... *marriage under the age of 16 and 18 of the boys and girls respectively.*

barsāvāss..... *resting of the monks and nuns during the rainy season.*

Basanta Panchami..... Māghaśukla panchami, Saraswativpūjā.

bhumi-sparsa-mudrā..... land touching posture.

bighā..... land measurement unit.

Biraha Geeta..... *traditional songs of the native land of Lord Buddha.*

Chaitra purnimā..... full moon day of Chaitra month.

Chāra kose jhāsī..... about thirteen kms. deep forest.

Chaubīsī..... twenty-four principalities during the early medieval period in middle hilly region.

Chhata..... festival to worship the Sun on the occasion of Kartikasukla sixth day in terai region.

chhatrāvali..... parole at the top of the stupa.

***Chittalata* grove**..... beautiful garden of inner heart.

Churiā pahād..... small hills between Terai and high hills.

crew members..... foreign air or ship crews decked or in lay over and who use the accommodation establishment of the country visited.

crews..... who are not residents of the country visited and stay in the country for the day.

cruise passangers..... Normally included in excurionists. Seperate classification of their visitors is neverthness recommended.

dāijo..... dowry system.

dakshinā..... donation.

Dal bergia Sissa..... Sisau.

darśana..... *to pay devotional feelings.*

Dasai..... national festival of the Hindus, which celebrate during September- October. .

day visitors..... visitors who come and leave at the same day.

Deepāvalī..... Tihar festival celebrate during the October-November.

dhakkis..... *types of baskets use on the occasion worship, marriage, farming-fasting etc.*

dhamma..... religion.

Dharmachakra..... symbol of Buddha,s teachings spread.

dharma-chakra-pravartana-mudrā..... in the position of Buddha,s teachings spread.

dhoti..... *loin cloth.*

dhyāna-mudrā..... meditation posture.

excursions..... visitors who do not spend one or more night in the country visited and return by their ship/bus or other vehicles with out economic activities.

galā..... neck

Gandakī ksetra..... the area between Rāptī and Gaṇḍakī Rivers.

grāma..... village.

hāra..... necklace.

harmikā..... four-sided middle portion of the stupa and upper part from dome.

Holi purnimā..... full moon day of Phagun month.

Jayanti..... birthday.

juńgle..... forest.

kankar..... thinner layers of small grits.

katyavalambita..... hands resting on the waist.

nauclea cordifalia..... Kolan.

kumbha**.....** vessel.

kundalas**.....** ear rings.

kundas**.....** wells, tanks.

Lumbinīvana**.....** *Lumbinī forest.*

Māghī**.....** festival, especially of the Tharu community celebrate in the months of January.

Mahābhārat pahāda**.....** lower hills between Terai and upper hills.

Mahavansa**.....** a Buddhist sacred text.

maṇdala**.....** box chambers of the structure in Mayadevi temple.

Mangifera indica**.....** mango tree.

mantras**.....** *sacred stanza to recite.*

Nāga pujā**.....** worship of snake.

Nidāna kathā**.....** stories about Buddha and Buddhism.

Om mani padme hum**.....** Buddhist mantra.

pākhī**.....** a kind od blanket.

pakkā **.....** metalize using kiln-burnt bricks.

pardā prathā**.....** *tradition not to show the face.*

Parinirvāna**.....** event of death of Buddha.

Paśchimāñchala**.....** western region of nepal.

phala**.....** result.

Phūlabāri**.....** garden.

pinus longifolia**.....** chir.

Ficus religiosa**.....** pipal tree.

Ficus lacor**.....** plaksha tree.

prabhāmandala**.....** circular halo.

Pradimokṣa vana**.....** sacred forest during the Buddhist period.

Priyadarsi**.....** title of Aśoka.

pujā**.....** worship.

purpose of visit..... Main purpose of visit as defined by the Rome Conference (1963).

Puskariṇi **or** ***Siddharth kupa*****.....** sacred tank of Lumbinī , where Mayadavi had bathed before and after the birth of Buddha.

Rājamārga**.....** high way road.

Rāma navami**.....** festival celebrate on the occasion of the birth day of Ram, Epic hero.

Raṅga mahala**.....** recreational house of the Sena dynasty.

ratnakuṇḍala or mukta-phala kuṇḍala**.....** wears a solid earlobe

representative of consulates..... When they travel from their country of origin to the duty station vs. vice-versa (including house hold servents and dependants accompanying or joining them).

ROHACHI-SESSION**.....** A weak fasting festival of Nipponzan Myohoji.

Shorea robusta..... sal.

Salmalia malaboica..... simal.

Samāja..... society.

Saṅgha..... organization.

silā-vigada-bhicha..... Marker stone kept at the spot of birth place of Buddha.

Sivaratri..... birth day festival of Siva.

sthānaka..... standing pose.

supplementary accommodation..... Vihar, guest houses, stupa and community halls for the shelter to the tourists except hotels, restaurants and resorts.

Tathagata..... *Bodhisattava, in the path of Buddha.*

tirthas..... holy place.

tirtha-yätra..... *spiritual feelings and visit to the holy places.*

transit passangers..... who do not leave the transit area of the airport or the port. In certain countries, transit may involve a stay of one day or more. In this case, they should be included in the visitors statistics.

upavita..... *sacred thread.*

URTEC..... a partner company with Kenzo Tange.

Uttara path..... *northern part.*

visitors..... Who spent at least one night in the country visited.

vyākhyana-mudrā..... explaining posture.

Yãtãyãta..... transportation.

INDEX

ILLUSTRATIONS

1. Aerial View of LMP

2. Mayadevi Temple

3. Asoka Pillar

4. Structural Remains in Mayadevi Temple

5. Archaeological Garden

6. Puskarini Tank

7. Circular Levee

8. Central Canal

9. Boating in Central Canal

10. Western Monastic Zone

11. Myānmār Vihar Complex

12. International Gautami Bhikkhuni Saṅgha

13. Śri Laṅk Monastery

14. Monastery of Mahabodhi Society Indiā

15. Thāi Monastery

16. Stūpa of Mananga Sewa Samāja

17. Geden International Austria vihar

18. Viettnam Monastery

19. orean Monastery

20. LIRI & Lumbinī Museum Complex

21. Lumbinī Peace March

22. Lotus Stūpa of Tara Foundation

23. Hotel Hokke

24. Hotel asai

25. Śri Laṅk Pilgrimage House.

26. Crane and Blue Cows in Lumbinī

27. Peace Stupa Aerial View

28. Peace Stupa

29. Devotees in Prayer in Mayadevi Temple complex

30.Devotees in Māyādevi Temple area.

31. Chinese Monastery

32. Worshipping at Mayadevi Temple

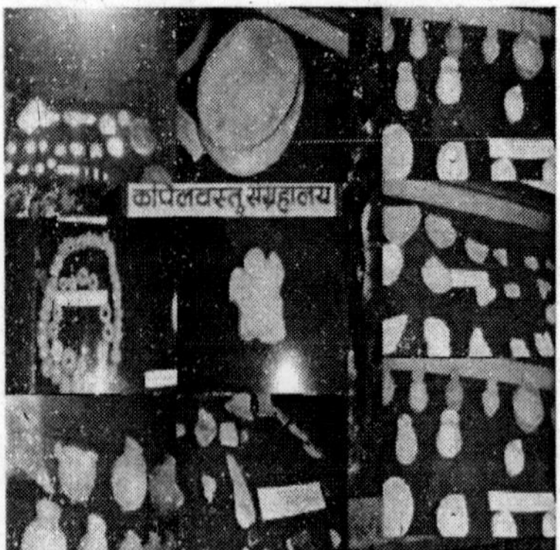

33. Display of apilavastu Museum

34. Puja performing at Mayadevi Temple

35. Visit Lumbinī 2012

36. LumbiniVisit 2012

37.Lumbinī Visit 2012 Good well Ambassdors s Welcome

38. Tourist Mart 2013

39. Buddha Jayanti Cultural Program

40. Chhata Puja

41. Devotees in Lumbinī Complex

42.Lumbinī Gate

43. Butwal International Expo. 2012

44. Sunauli-Belhiya Welcome Gate